Singapore

"All you've got to do is decide to go
and the hardest part is over.

So go!"

TONY WHEELER, COFOUNDER – LONELY PLANET

THIS EDITION WRITTEN AND RESEARCHED BY

Shawn Low, Daniel McCrohan

Contents

(left) **Baba House (p57)**

(above) **Deepavali festival (p23)**

(right) *Kueh pie ti*, a Nonya speciality (p91)

Welcome to Singapore

Singapore is the perennial stopover no more. The city is jostling to be Asia's, even the world's, best city.

Bright Lights, Small City

Singapore is small in size but huge in ambition. In recent years it has lifted its global profile by means of numerous shots of adrenalin to its tourism industry. Integrated resorts bring in tourists and big money (mostly thanks to casinos), the arts and music scenes are overloaded with international acts, and the Formula One night race is now well established. It's hard to keep track of the changes sometimes. Singapore's great strides in the last few years have been mapped onto its skyline, a breathtaking hybrid of low-slung British colonial buildings and towering skyscrapers.

Shop Till You Drop

Electronics, fashion, video games, raw cloth, spices, Chinese medicine – the list of things you can buy in Singapore is as long as it is varied. Shopping is almost a spiritual pursuit in Singapore and the heart of it all can be found at Orchard Rd, a veritable canyon of concrete, glass and steel. Singaporeans love their malls, spending vast amounts of leisure time bathing in icy air-conditioning while shopping, eating and movie-going. Prices are no longer dirt cheap, but the extraordinary variety and the decadence of the setting make shopping in Singapore memorable.

Fried Rice Paradise

Singaporeans are food crazy; along with shopping, eating ranks as Singapore's national pastime. Food is both a widespread passion and a unifier across ethnic divides, with a profusion of establishments offering Chinese, Indian, Indonesian and Nonya (a hybrid of Chinese and Malay culinary traditions) specialities. Although the city's hawker centres and food courts are justifiably its greatest claim to fame, eating in Singapore is not just about rubbing sweaty shoulders with locals. While much of its best food might originate over a humble wok, cooking in Singapore is elevated to an art form at many haute cuisine restaurants.

Garden State, Diverse Spaces

Most people come to Singapore for the legendary eating and shopping, but the city's numerous lush and exotic gardens are a surprising bonus. Urban planning is important to the government, and there are large swaths of green spaces that break up Singapore's concrete landscape. There's the innovative (a rooftop garden on top of the Marina Barrage) to the serene (the MacRitchie Reservoir has a stunning treetop walk) and the natural (Sungei Buloh is a stopover point for thousands of migratory birds).

Why I Love Singapore

By Shawn Low, Author

Singapore is my second home (I grew up here) and each time I visit, there's always something new to see. It's a city that's constantly being tinkered with, and it's not all just about malls. There are new gardens, museums, art galleries, cool bars and a gazillion restaurants.

I love that Singapore never sleeps. I've lost count of the number of times I've rocked up with my brother to the local coffeeshop for cheap beer at three o'clock in the morning. And the food, oh the food. In Singapore, home isn't where the heart is...it's where the stomach leads.

For more about our authors, see p224.

Above: Singapore cuisine

Singapore's
Top 10

Hawker Food (p168)

1 Singapore's hawker food is the stuff of legend, and celebrity chefs from Anthony Bourdain to the late *New York Times* writer Johnny Apple have raved about the dazzling array of cheap and delicious dishes available. There's really no better way to get into the Singapore psyche than through its cuisine, so roll up your sleeves and get ready to sweat it out over steaming plates of yummy local favourites. KITCHEN OF A CHANGI VILLAGE HAWKER CENTRE RESTAURANT (P93)

✗ *Food*

Singapore Zoo and Night Safari (p99)

2 Let's put it out there: this is possibly the world's best zoo. The open-air enclosures allow for both freedom for the animals to roam and unobstructed visitor views. The Singapore Zoo is one of the few places outside of Borneo or Sumatra where you can stand under trees with orang-utans a few feet above your head, or where mouse deer and lemurs scamper across your path. As evening closes in, the Night Safari next door uses open-concept enclosures to get visitors up close and personal with nocturnal creatures such as leopards, free-ranging deer and Malayan tigers.

⊙ *Northern & Central Singapore*

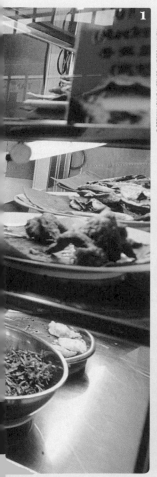

HEATH HOLDEN / LONELY PLANET IMAGES ©

Pulau Ubin *(p121)*

3 Singapore's very own rustic island getaway offers a glimpse at the *kampong* (village) life that was a big part of Singapore as recently as the 1960s. By hopping aboard a chugging bumboat from Changi, visitors can experience Pulau Ubin's old-growth mangrove swamps, then cycle past tin-roof shacks or rampage along a cross-country mountain bike trail and end the day with a seafood meal. If the great outdoors is not your bag, you can take a cooking class instead. If island life gets to you, you can always stay a night or three at the local resort.

⊙ *Sentosa & Other Islands*

Little India *(p65)*

4 The most atmospheric of Singapore's historic quarters is as close it gets to Singapore of the old chaotic days. Experience it with the masses on the weekends when it gets packed to the gills with Indian workers wanting a slice of home. The five-foot ways of the shophouses spill over with aromatic spices and colourful products. The trendy set are drawn to cool little bars and if you have insomnia, simply head to Mustafa Centre for shopping: buy an iPad at 3am before heading for a *teh tarik* and a *roti prata*. SRI SRINIVASA PERUMAL TEMPLE (P67)

⊙ *Little India & Kampong Glam*

MJ / ALAMY ©

Baba House *(p57)*

5 This (free!) living museum is one of the best-preserved Peranakan heritage homes found in Singapore, and offers a glimpse into the Chinese-Malay hybrid culture of Singapore's Baba-Nonya minority. The stunningly restored Chinese mansion – complete with period furnishing – recreates a wonderful window into the life of a wealthy Peranakan family c 1928. Fact-filled and entertaining 90-minute guided tours run twice a week and need to be booked in advance.

◉ *Chinatown & the CBD*

Botanic Gardens *(p104)*

6 Singapore's Botanic Gardens make a welcome escape from the bustle of city life. At the tail end of Orchard Rd, this sprawling oasis is a great place to take a picnic and people-watch. Or stroll through the orchid gardens, looking out for Vanda Miss Joaquim, Singapore's national flower. The Singapore Symphony Orchestra gives free monthly performances at the pavilion.

👁 *Holland Village, Dempsey Hill & the Botanic Gardens*

Orchard Road *(p77)*

7 With every brand imaginable and over 20 malls packed into this 2.5km strip, you can shop till you drop, pick yourself up, and continue shopping some more. It's retail therapy at its decadent best. When you've stashed your purchases back at the hotel, duck out to Emerald Hill for its Peranakan architecture and happy-hour bar specials. ION ORCHARD MALL (P83)

🛍 *Orchard Road*

6

FELIX HUG / LONELY PLANET IMAGES ©

Bukit Timah Nature Reserve *(p98)*

8 Hiking in sunny, humid Singapore? Why not? After all, the country's British forefathers, Sir Stamford Raffles and William Farquhar, were great naturalists. And Singapore has a surprising number of green pockets. A must-do is to hike the trails at Bukit Timah Nature Reserve. A cacophony of insects, roving monkeys and lush canopy hark back to a time when Singapore was mostly wilderness. Also check out the Southern Ridges (p112), a 9km stretch of trails across shaded parks, hills and the stunning leaf-like suspended walkways of the Alexandra Link.

⊙ *Northern & Central Singapore*

Sentosa Island *(p117)*

9 The world-class resort island of Sentosa may look gaudy from the outside, but the opening of Resorts World means Singapore's playground now has something for everyone. Parents can let their kids go nuts at Universal Studios, then in the evenings live the high-roller life at the casino. Or you can lose the shirt off your back in a different way: by kicking back on the beach, cocktail in hand.

⭐ *Sentosa & Other Islands*

FELIX HUG / LONELY PLANET IMAGES ©

KEVIN CLOGSTOUN / LONELY PLANET IMAGES ©

River Cruises *(p51)*

10 The Quays were once the beating heart of trade in Singapore. These days, the hectic *godowns* (warehouses) and polluted waterways have been transformed into buzzing restaurant and entertainment districts. Jumping on a dressed-up bumboat and chugging along the Singapore River out into Marina Bay offers unparalleled views of Singapore's iconic cityscape – Marina Bay Sands opposite the Merlion, which is standing guard at the river mouth.

👁 *Colonial District, Marina Bay & the Quays*

What's New

Marina Bay

The Marina Bay area, when it's actually finished in mid- to late 2012, will fit in with the Singapore government's vision of building a vibrant cityscape. The entire area comprises the Marina Barrage, the gate at the mouth of a freshwater reservoir, and links up to Singapore's next botanic gardens, Gardens by the Bay. Of course, capping it all is the now-iconic Marina Bay Sands integrated resort. And right across are the soaring skyscrapers of the CBD. (p53)

Baba House

This immaculately restored Peranakan house is a living museum that looks like it did in its heyday in 1928. Ninety-minute tours give you the low-down on Straits Chinese family life. (p57)

Gardens & Green Spaces

Park connectors (shared cycling and footpaths) link up various parks and housing estates together in a unified 'green' chain. In particular, the Southern Ridges and Kranji are new and standout places.

Art at Tanjong Pagar

Unused warehouse space. Check. Art galleries. Check. Part of the Tanjong Pagar Distripark, next to the port area, has been converted into some high-profile, very cool art galleries showcasing modern local, regional and international art. (p64)

Boutique Chic

Fantastic new boutique hotels such as Wanderlust eschew boring shades of 'hotel' brown and opt for quirky colour schemes and chic furnishing. (p147)

Sentosa

After several makeovers over the past 15 years, it seems as though Sentosa has found its groove with the tacky (some say fun) Resorts World, top-notch activities and accommodation, and beachside bars. (p117)

What? More Malls?

Mall-laden Orchard Rd just got, well, even more mall laden. ION Orchard, Somerset Central and 313 Somerset set the shopping and eating bar even higher (both literally and figuratively). (p83)

Celebrity Chef Restaurants

It's not just Michelin-star chefs setting up shop here; local culinary stars have also upped their standards (and prices).

Duxton Hill

The once-seedy Duxton Hill area was filled with loud and brash KTV pubs. Today, cool bookstores sit next to hip bars and restaurants. Some pubs still cling on, but it's only a matter of time... (p55)

Indian Heritage Centre

Under construction at time of writing, this $12 million state-of-the-art centre will showcase Indian culture in an ultramodern, shimmering building in the style of Bejing's Water Cube. ETA 2013. (p67)

For more recommendations and reviews, see **lonelyplanet.com/singapore**

Need to Know

Currency
Singapore dollar ($)

Languages
English (primary), Mandarin, Bahasa Malay, Tamil

Visas
Generally not required for stays of up to 90 days. Issued upon entry.

Money
ATMs and moneychangers widely available. Credit cards accepted in most shops and restaurants.

Mobile Phones
Local SIM cards can be used in unlocked GSM phones. Purchase from convenience stores.

Time
GMT/UTC plus eight hours

Tourist Information
Singapore Visitors@Orchard Information Centre (Map p212; ☑1800 736 2000; cnr Orchard & Cairnhill Rds; ⊙9.30am-10.30pm; ⓂSomerset) Brochures, maps, information about Singapore, helpful staff.

Your Daily Budget

Budget less than $150
➡ Dorm bed $16–40
➡ Hawker centres and food courts for meals
➡ Supermarkets for picnics

Midrange $100–350
➡ Double room in average hotel $100–250
➡ Two-course dinner with wine $50
➡ Drinks at a nice bar $15–20 per drink

Top-end over $350
➡ Four- and five-star double room $250–500
➡ *Dégustation* in top restaurant $250 or more
➡ Theatre ticket $150

Advance Planning

Two months before: Book tickets if you plan on watching short-run, West End–style shows or big-ticket events such as the Formula One race. Reserve a table at hot top-end restaurants.

One month before: Book bed if you are planning on staying at a dorm over the weekend.

One week before: Look for last-minute deals on Singapore accommodation and check for any events or festivals.

Websites
➡ **Lonely Planet** (www.lonelyplanet.com/singapore) Destination information, hotel bookings, traveller forum and more.

➡ **Visit Singapore** (www.visitsingapore.com) Official tourism board website.

➡ **Singapore.SG** (www.sg.com) Another official site to Singapore with general information.

➡ **Sistic** (www.sistic.com.sg) One-stop shop for tickets to all sorts of concerts and shows in Singapore. Useful events calendar too.

WHEN TO GO

Singapore is tropical and humid year-round. School holidays fall in June and July, the hottest time, so try and avoid travelling in these months if you can.

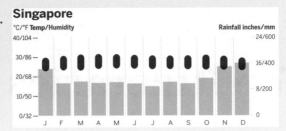

Singapore

°C/°F Temp/Humidity   Rainfall inches/mm

Arriving in Singapore

Changi Airport MRT train, public and shuttle bus to town. 6am to midnight, $1.80 to $9. Taxi ride $18 to $35, 50% more between midnight and 6am, plus airport surcharges.

For much more on **arrival**, see p178.

Getting Around

Get an EZ-Link card. This is a credit-card-sized electronic travel card that you can use on MRT trains and local buses. Just tap on and off at the sensors. You can buy one, and top up your card's credit, at all MRT stations.

➡ **MRT** Local subway. Most convenient way to get around. 6am till midnight.

➡ **Bus** Goes everywhere the trains do and more. Great for views. 6am till midnight, some night buses from the city.

➡ **Taxis** Fairly cheap if you're used to NYC or London prices. Flag one on the street or at taxi stands. Good luck getting one on rainy days. Don't be surprised by hefty surcharges during peak hours and from midnight to 6am.

For much more on **getting around**, see p180.

Sleeping

Singapore has some of the most pricey beds in Southeast Asia. You'll need to book in advance (and pay more) on weekends or during international events such as the Formula One night race. Booking online, staying weekdays and during low seasons (February to May and August to October) will save money.

Hostels are cheap, though standards aren't stellar. You'd be hard pressed to find a private room with an attached bathroom. **Boutique hotels** offer good midrange options, but expect rooms to be on the petite side. There are plenty of **hotels** to suit budgets from midrange to oil-sheik-wealthy.

Useful Websites

➡ **Lonely Planet** (http://hotels.lonelyplanet.com) Book rooms on Lonely Planet's website.

➡ **Hotels Online** (www.hotels.online.com.sg) A long-running hotel-booking website.

➡ **Wego** (www.wego.com/Singapore_Hotels) Popular deals site.

For much more on **sleeping**, see p140.

HOW LONG TO STAY FOR?

Singapore is stopover central for long-haul flights and most people stay a day or two. That may be enough to scratch the surface, but if you want to get beyond Singapore slings at the Raffles Hotel, spend at least four days here. This way, you'll get to see all the top sights, eat at some of the best hawker places, be surprised by the nature reserves and have time to get some shopping done.

Top Itineraries

Day One

Colonial District, Marina Bay & the Quays (p40)

 A stroll around this area offers visitors a glimpse at the colonial influence left on the city. Get museumed out at the **Singapore Art Museum**, the **National Museum**, the **Asian Civilisations Museum**, or the **Peranakan Museum**. Take your pick – they're all worth your time.

> **Lunch** Maxwell Rd Hawker Centre (p60).

Chinatown & the CBD (p55)

While the whole area has a tourist-trap feel about it, the **Sri Mariamman Temple**, **Buddha Tooth Relic Temple** and **Thian Hock Keng Temple** are worth checking out. Wander around the revitalised **Ann Siang Hill** and **Duxton Hill** areas – loads of cool bars, restaurants and coffeeshops are kicking out the seedy KTV bars.

> **Dinner** Splash out at popular Peranakan restaurant Blue Ginger (p58).

Northern & Central Singapore (p96)

Come late evening, make a date with nocturnal animals at the **Night Safari**. Kids and adults alike enjoy getting up close and personal with the animals via the train-car ride.

Day Two

West & Southwest Singapore (p109)

 The **Southern Ridges** walk is one of the best routes in Singapore. Do the (mostly) shaded 4km route from **Kent Ridge Park**, through **HortPark** across to **Telok Blangah Park**, going along the stunning **Henderson Waves** walkway before finishing at **Mt Faber**, from where you can take a cable car down the hill. Bring lots of water and start early to beat the heat.

> **Lunch** Eat at one of the *nasi padang* places in Kampong Glam (p72)

Little India & Kampong Glam (p65)

The golden-domed **Mohammad Sultan** mosque in Kampong Glam is the centrepiece of Singapore's Malay district. Radiating out around it are an eclectic mix of restaurants, shophouses, bars and the former **Sultan's Palace**.

> **Dinner** Tapas and drinks at Zsofi p69), after biryani at Bismillah Biryani (p69)

Little India & Kampong Glam (p65)

 A stroll through frenetic Little India will erase every preconceived notion of Singapore as a squeaky-clean metropolis. Come weekends and nights, the place gets packed and chaotic. Stalls spill goods across the five-foot ways and the scent of spices permeates everything. And if you can't sleep, **Mustafa Shopping Centre** is open 24 hours – the place stocks EVERYTHING.

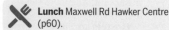

Day Three

Holland Village, Dempsey Hill & the Botanic Gardens (p102)

 A morning stroll through the idyllic **Botanic Gardens** at the end of Orchard Rd will calm your nerves in preparation for the afternoon shopping scrum. The **Orchid Garden** has an amazing array of species and the Singapore Symphony Orchestra performs for free some weekends.

> ✗ **Lunch** For a casual, al-fresco feed, grab a wood-fired pizza at Casa Verde (p106)

Orchard Road (p77)

 You're on a mission when you come to Orchard Rd. It's shop till you drop here. With over 20 malls to choose from, your credit card might fail before your feet. Retail overload at its very best. When you're done, head to **Emerald Hill** for happy-hour pints.

> ✗ **Dinner** Order the *crab bee hoon* at Sin Huat Eating House (p90).

Eastern Singapore (p85)

☾ Keeping with the theme of excess, **Geylang** is a seedy red-light district juxtaposed against temples, mosques, and some of the best food in Singapore. Pick a local coffeeshop, order a cheap Tiger beer and watch the world go by.

Day Four

Sentosa & Other Islands (p116)

 Head to Changi where you can catch a bumboat to **Pulau Ubin**. This is Singapore, 1960s style. Rent a bicycle and go around the island to check out tin-shacked houses and walk along the mangrove boardwalk. There's even a mountain-bike park with trails for varying skill levels.

> ✗ **Lunch** Pick a seafood restaurant around the Pulau Ubin pier (p118).

Sentosa & Other Islands (p116)

 After lunch, continue your exploration of sleepy **Pulau Ubin** with a visit to the **Wei Tuo Fa Gong Temple**. When you get off the bumboat in Singapore, wander around the shops at **Changi Village**. This might very well be Singapore's sleepiest neighbourhood!

> ✗ **Dinner** Enjoy local hawker fare at the Changi Village Hawker Centre (p93).

Colonial District, Marina Bay & the Quays (p40)

☾ Take a stroll along the Singapore River. Start at Boat Quay: look out for the grand **Fullerton Hotel** and grab a pint or two before heading down towards **Clarke Quay**. It's party central here, with clubs and bars galore. If you'd rather sit by the riverside for a drink, continue on to **Robertson Quay**.

If You Like...

Museums & Galleries

Peranakan Museum The Straits Chinese culture is exactingly detailed through video displays and top-quality artefacts. (p43)

National Museum of Singapore Set in a beautifully restored colonial building, Singapore's national museum pays homage to its history...and its food. (p43)

Asian Civilisations Museum Packed to the gills with a wide variety of exhibits from across Asia, this museum is one of Singapore's best and most varied. (p43)

Singapore Art Museum & 8Q SAM An excellent showcase of Asian contemporary art. The 8Q wing across the road is more experimental. (p43)

NUS Museums This clutch of three modestly sized galleries tucked away in the local university is proof that good things come in small packages. (p111)

Hawker Food

Lau Pa Sat Can't decide what to eat? This massive steel structure has everything. At night, you can sit at wooden tables to scarf down your satay. (p60)

Maxwell Rd Hawker Centre Arguably Singapore's most famous hawker centre and one of the most centrally located. The fish porridge and chicken rice are favourites. (p60)

Marine Parade Food Centre Old-school, local favourite. Sample

Clarke Quay (p48)

Singapore hawker food's greatest hits. Just look for the longest queue and join it. (p92)

Golden Mile Food Centre It may not look like much, but the *tulang* (bone-marrow soup), *char kway teow* (fried flat-rice noodles) and *ah balling* (glutinous rice ball dessert) are all famed. (p73)

East Coast Lagoon Food Village By the seaside, this open-air hawker centre is perennially packed. Great for beer and satay. (p92)

Clubbing

Zouk Twenty years of age and going strong, Zouk is Singapore's oldest and best-known club. It's actually three interconnected themed clubs to suit most musical tastes. (p48)

St James Power Station St James might not have the historical pedigree of Zouk, but it makes up for it with sheer size and variety. (p115)

Butter Factory If you want to party with a younger set, Butter Factory is the place to do it. (p50)

Clarke Quay Love it or hate it, Clarke Quay has plenty of places for shaking it. Head to Attica, Pump Room, Zirca or anywhere with a queue snaking out. (p48)

Parks & Gardens

Southern Ridges It doesn't matter where you start, you could walk from as far away as

Kent Ridge, Mt Faber or come via HortPark, but make sure to get across the Southern Ridges. (p112)

MacRitchie Reservoir Get ready for a steam clean while you hike the trail towards the treetop walk, a 250m-long suspension bridge. (p99)

Sungei Buloh Wetland Reserve For bird nerds. This 87-hectare wetland is home to over 140 species of migratory birds, plus it has mangrove boardwalks... and mosquitoes. (p113)

Singapore Botanic Gardens For those less inclined to sweat it out on a trail, the Botanic Gardens offer a chance for an amble through manicured greenery. (p104)

Kranji Farms Get out of town! For a most un-Singapore experience, get to Kranji. It's hard to imagine farms in urban Singapore, but Kranji is home to agriculture and livestock farms worth visiting. There's even a spa resort for those who really want to kick back. (p114)

East Coast Park This stretch of beach and parkland along the coastline is where families pitch tents, have barbecues, cycle, rollerblade and do watersports. (p88)

Temples, Mosques & Churches

Sultan Mosque The hub that holds the Kampong Glam area together, the golden-domed Sultan Mosque is a working mosque that can host 5000 worshippers. (p68)

For more top Singapore spots, see
➡ Eating (p26)
➡ Drinking & Nightlife (p29)
➡ Entertainment (p32)
➡ Shopping (p34)

St Andrew's Cathedral Occupying a nice chunk of city real estate, and one of Singapore's oldest and most impressive churches, built in 1862. (p43)

Sri Mariamman Temple Take snaps of the *gopuram* (tower), and wander round the back for great views of the temple set against the CBD cityscape. (p57)

Thian Hock Keng Temple Visit Singapore's most famous Chinese temple, decorated with stone lions and elaborately carved gold-painted wooden beams. (p57)

Island Getaways

Pulau Ubin Jump on a bumboat from Changi. Hire a bike and go for a meander round this charmingly sedate retro island. (p121)

Sentosa Some may think it's tacky, garish and over the top, but Sentosa is Singapore's Vegas/beach resort/Disneyland, and great for families. (p117)

St John's & Kusu Islands Join worshippers on a pilgrimage to Kusu Island, and don't forget to pack your bathers for a dip at St John's. (p122)

PLAN YOUR TRIP IF YOU LIKE...

Month by Month

January

New Year's Eve equals parties and overpriced drinks. But Thaipusam is a unique festival well worth seeing.

✯✯ Thaipusam

This is one of the most dramatic Hindu festivals, in which devotees honour Lord Subramaniam with acts of amazing masochism. In Singapore, Hindus march in a procession from the Sri Srinivasa Perumal Temple (p67) on Serangoon Rd to the Chettiar Hindu Temple on Tank Rd carrying *kavadis* (heavy metal frames decorated with peacock feathers, fruit and flowers). The *kavadis* are hung from followers' bodies with metal hooks and spikes that are driven into their flesh. Other devotees pierce their cheeks and tongues with *vel* (metal skewers), or walk on sandals of nails. Ouch.

February

Chinese New Year is a big deal in a country where the majority of the people are Chinese. The holiday coincides with a two-day holiday and much colourful festivity.

✯✯ Chinese New Year

Dragon dances and pedestrian parades mark the start of the New Year. Families hold open house, unmarried relatives (especially children) receive *ang pow* (gifts of money in red packets), businesses clear their debts and everybody says 'Gung hei faat choi' (I hope that you gain lots of money). Chinatown is lit up, especially Eu Tong Sen St and New Bridge Rd, and the 'Hongbao Special' along the Singapore River and Marina Bay features *pasar malam* (night market) stalls, variety shows and fireworks.

✯✯ Chingay

Singapore's biggest street parade, Chingay (www.chingay.org.sg), occurs on the 22nd day after Chinese New Year. It's a flamboyant multicultural event held around the Colonial District, with flag bearers, lion dancers, floats and other cultural performers. Buy tickets in advance for a seat in the viewing galleries, or battle the crowds for a place at the roadside barriers.

March

The northeast monsoon peters out and the mercury starts rising.

✯✯ Mosaic Music Festival

Roll up, roll up! An annual 10-day feast of world music, jazz and indie music at the Esplanade, Mosaic (www.mosaicmusicfestival.com) features acts local and international, renowned and obscure. There are also free concerts held in the Esplanade's smaller venues.

✯✯ Singapore Fashion Festival

Not quite Paris, but probably as close as you'll get in Southeast Asia, the Singapore Fashion Festival (www.singaporefashionfestival.com.sg) features a fortnight of shows from local designers as well as prominent international names.

April

One of the busiest months, events-wise, with everything from religion to food to music.

★ Qing Ming Festival

On All Souls' Day, the Chinese traditionally visit the tombs of their ancestors to clean and repair them and make offerings. Singapore's largest temple complex, Kong Meng San Phor Kark See Monastery (www.kmspks.org), is the place to be on consecutive weekends throughout the month, when relatives descend on columbaria en masse.

★ Timbre Rock and Roots Festival

Bob Dylan kicked off the inaugural two-day festival (www.rockandroots.sg) in 2011. John Legend headlined the following day. Expect future festivals to also rock.

★ Singapore International Film Festival

Independent and art-house movies are pretty thin on the ground in Hollywood-obsessed Singapore, so this showcase of world cinema (www.filmfest.org.sg) is a rare chance to see cinematic talent from some of the planet's other countries.

May

It's the quiet month leading towards the peak of the 'summer' heat and **the busy school holidays. This is a good time to visit Singapore.**

★ Vesak Day

Buddha's birth, enlightenment and death are celebrated by various events, including the release of caged birds to symbolise the setting free of captive souls. Temples such as Sakaya Muni Buddha Gaya Temple (p67) in Little India throng with worshippers, but the centre of the activity is the Buddha Tooth Relic Temple (p57) on South Bridge Rd.

June

School holidays coupled with sales galore means that people will be out in full force. It's one of the hottest months on the calendar, so get ready to sweat it out.

★ Great Singapore Sale

The Great Singapore Sale (www.greatsingaporesale.com) runs from the end of May to the beginning of July. Orchard Rd and all big malls are decked out with banners, and retailers around the island cut prices (and wheel out the stuff they couldn't sell earlier in the year). Some bargains to be had if you can stomach the crowds. Go early!

★ Dragon Boat Festival

Commemorating the death of a Chinese saint who drowned himself as a protest against government corruption, this festival is celebrated with boat races at Bedok Reservoir. Check the website (www.sdba.org.sg) for other races and practices held throughout the year.

★ Singapore Arts Festival

Organised by the National Arts Council, this is Singapore's premier arts festival (www.singaporeartsfest.com), with a world-class program of art, dance, drama and music.

July

The dry months continue, and so do the school holidays.

✕ Singapore Food Festival

A month-long celebration of all things edible and Singaporean (www.singaporefoodfestival.com). Well-known restaurants lay on events, and there are cooking classes, food-themed tours for visitors and plenty of opportunities to sample classic Malay, Chinese and Indian dishes. Action also happens at Clarke Quay.

August

National Day, Singapore's best-known event (at least for the locals), is held every August. Even the unpatriotic love it because it's a public holiday.

★ Singapore National Day

Held on 9 August (though dress rehearsals on the two prior weekends are almost as popular), the huge frenzy that is Singapore National Day (www.ndp.org.sg) takes the whole year to prepare and sees military parades, extravagant civilian processions, air-force fly-bys, furious flag-waving and a concluding fireworks display. Tickets are snapped up well in advance.

★ Hungry Ghost Festival

Marks the day when the souls of the dead are released to walk the earth for feasting and entertainment. The Chinese place offerings of food on the street and light fires. Chinese operas and other events are laid on to keep these restless spirits happy.

September

While the Formula One night race is the hottest ticket on the annual calendar, it does mean that local hotels jack up prices. And beds are still hard to find, especially in the Colonial District where the action happens.

☆ Formula One Grand Prix

The F1's first ever night race (www.f1singapore.com) was held in 2008 on the scenic street circuit around Marina Bay. This is one of the most unique of the circuits and its popularity means it's here to stay.

★ Mooncake Festival

Celebrated on the full moon of the eighth lunar month, and also known as the Lantern Festival. Chinatown is decked out with lanterns. Mooncakes are made with bean paste, lotus seeds and sometimes a duck egg, though an endless variety of flavours are now available to suit modern tastes.

(Top) Street opera, Hungry Ghost Festival
(Bottom) Deepavali festival at Sri Mariamman Temple (p57)

✱✦ Navarathri

The Hindu festival of 'Nine Nights' is dedicated to the wives of Siva, Vishnu and Brahma. Young girls are dressed as the goddess Kali; this is a good opportunity to see traditional Indian dancing and singing. The Chettiar Hindu Temple, Sri Mariamman Temple (p57) and Sri Srinivasa Perumal Temple (p67) are the main areas of activity.

October

This is the dry month bookended by the southwest monsoon and the northeast monsoon, so leave the umbrella at home.

✱✦ Deepavali

Rama's victory over the demon king Ravana is celebrated during the 'Festival of Lights', with tiny oil lamps outside Hindu homes and lights all over Hindu temples. Little India is ablaze with lights for a month, culminating in a huge street party on the eve of the holiday.

✱✦ Pilgrimage to Kusu Island

Tua Pek Kong, the god of prosperity, is honoured by Taoists in Singapore, who make a pilgrimage to the shrine on Kusu Island in the ninth month of the Chinese lunar calendar, sometime between late September and November. At weekends the island almost sinks under the weight of pilgrims.

✱✦ Hari Raya Puasa

Also known as Hari Raya Aidilfitri, this festival celebrates the end of the Ramadan fasting month (it can also occur in September). Head to Kampong Glam for nightly feasts during Ramadan.

November

As always, Singapore's cultural calendar is packed with religious events, and November has two of them.

✱✦ Hari Raya Haji

An event celebrating the conclusion of the pilgrimage to Mecca. Animals are ritually slaughtered in the mosques, after which the Koran dictates a portion of the meat must be handed out to the poor. The event will take place in November in the years 2012–14.

✱✦ Thimithi

At this eye-opener of a firewalking ceremony, Hindu devotees prove their faith by walking across glowing coals at the Sri Mariamman Temple.

December

A sense of festivity (and monsoon rains) permeates the air as the year winds down. The rainy season means that you'll need an umbrella to avoid getting drenched, though the weather is mercifully cool.

☆ Zoukout

Zoukout (www.zoukout.com) is possibly Singapore's biggest and best outdoor dance party. A who's who of international DJs play to a 25,000-strong crowd on Siloso Beach, Sentosa. Have the Red Bull on standby as the party starts at 8pm and wraps up at 8am the next morning.

✱✦ Christmas

Singapore has enthusiastically embraced the commercial aspects of Christmas. But no matter how cynical you are, the light display that stretches for a kilometre or more down Orchard Rd, starting in late November, is breathtaking.

With Kids

Singapore is one of the easiest countries in Asia to travel in – it's safe and clean, with efficient public transport. Kids are welcome everywhere, and there are facilities and amenities catering to children of all ages. Oh, and don't be surprised if locals fawn over your little one(s)!

Animals Galore

Singapore Zoo & Night Safari

With penguins, polar bears, orang-utans and cheeky proboscis monkeys, the zoo and night safari have plenty of animals to put a smile on the face of even the most finicky of children. There are also animal shows for those who like their entertainment served up to them.

Island Fun

Sentosa Island

Expect a whole day of fun in the sun at Sentosa. Older kids will get a kick out of the rides at Universal Studios. The young ones can frolic on the beach or get aquatic at Underwater World.

Pulau Ubin

Getting there is half the fun: you take a bus to the extreme eastern tip of Singapore and switch to a rickety bumboat for a short jaunt to Pulau Ubin. The island itself is idyllic, and the best thing to do would be to rent a bicycle and set off in any direction you please.

Kid-Friendly Museums

National Museum of Singapore

Audio-visual displays, artefacts and child-friendly signs make this museum a good place for slightly older children (six and up). The food section has 'see' and 'smell' displays of Asian fruits, herbs and spices.

Singapore Art Museum

There's a gallery dedicated to children and the museum also periodically organises kids' activities.

Singapore Science Centre

Fun exhibits showcase various physics and chemistry concepts. The electrifying Tesla coil is hair-raisingly popular. The Omni-max theatre rounds off the experience (the darkened theatre is a great time for parents to take a quick power-nap too!).

Rainy-Day Fun

Orchard Road

Where do you go when it's pouring down with rain (as it often does in Singapore)? Mall-laden Orchard Rd, of course. Keep dry via underground mall walkways. There are cinemas, IMAX screens, kids' indoor play areas, and of course Toys 'R' Us.

Tours

The embarrassingly fun Duck Tours (p51) transports visitors on a brightly coloured amphibious former military vehicle. The tour is loud and over the top, especially when the vehicle drives off-road into Marina Bay! Or board one of the boat tours that ply the Quays out to Marina Bay and back.

Trishaws were once a popular mode of transport in Singapore. These days, you'll mostly find them operating out of a trishaw rank (p182). Jump into the bicycle sidecar and go for a ride around the central areas of Singapore.

Like a Local

From taking a train out into the 'heartlands' to knowing where to go for cheap beer, you don't have to look too hard for an authentic local experience.

Cheap Beer

Coffeeshops

When Singaporean says 'coffeeshop', they aren't referring to a place for cappuccinos, but rather a food court. Peppered throughout the island are these large collections of food stalls under one roof. Many run late into the night, and some are open 24 hours. While the ambience isn't flashy, you'll get a large bottle of Tiger for $6, alfresco seating and decent food. Each MRT station has a neighbouring coffeeshop. You won't go wrong if you head to Geylang – there's always somewhere to plonk yourself for beer and food.

Happy Hour

Travellers bemoan the expensive drinks in Singapore, and while it's true, you can have cheap drinks if you know where and when to go. Most bars do 'happy hour' deals that start anywhere from noon to 9pm. Deals range from 'one-for-one' (two for the price of one) drinks to $10 cocktails and pints.

Local Obsessions

Foot Reflexology

This Chinese form of relaxation involves lying in a chair and letting the masseur knead and press all the pressure points on your feet. In theory, the different bits of your foot are connected to vital organs, and getting the circulation going is good for you. In reality, it can be bloody painful. People's Park Complex (p64) is a popular place to visit. Most malls have a foot reflexology place. Or cross Orchard Rd from Somerset MRT towards Centrepoint and continue east to the Cuppage Centre next door. There are several foot reflexology places open way into the night.

Bubble Tea

Sweetened milk tea is mixed with tiny boiled tapioca balls (aka pearls). The resulting concoction is quite the treat in hot, sticky Singapore. Gong Cha at Scape (p83) is a good place to get a taste of this Taiwanese import. Go for the ice milk tea with pearls.

The Heartlands

Orchard Rd and the CBD area are great for the tourist, but the locals hoof it in their own neigbourhoods. Pick any MRT station to stop at and you'll usually emerge in a local mall. Wander away from the mall and you'll see local life in a big way: wet markets, local coffeeshops, tailors, barbers, Chinese medical halls and the like. Lively neighbourhoods are Tampines, Jurong, Bishan, Toa Payoh and Ang Mo Kio.

24-Hour Shopping

Bored at 2am? Jump into a taxi and head to the Mustafa Centre (p75) in Little India. This popular complex sells everything. Cameras, diamonds, Bollywood DVDs, underwear, toys, spices, food and more.

Challenger Superstore at Funan DigitaLife (p54), the IT Mall, is also open round the clock.

Kueh pie ti, a Nonya speciality (p91)

Eating

Food is truly one of Singapore's greatest claims to fame. Its diverse range of dishes and cuisines has impressed and filled the stomachs of many a famous chef. So, forget the calories and splash on a 10-course dégustation menu, or sit down with the locals over a steaming platter of chilli crab. If there's one piece of advice we can offer, it's to follow your stomach.

Hawker Centres & Kopitiams

You'll find the history of Singapore spread out before you in edible form at a hawker centre (large complex filled with food stalls) or local coffeeshop, also called *kopitiam* ('tiam' is Hokkien for 'shop'). There are dishes from China, Malaysia, Indonesia, India; food is the one great leveller among Singaporeans. It doesn't matter who you are, when you get to a hawker centre you'll have to slum it with everyone else –share a table,

queue for food and sweat it out (hey, the next guy's mopping his brow too).

Not Sure What to Eat? Just Queue

Singaporeans are quite happy to spend half an hour in line to get a dish that's new, popular, or famous. According to local wisdom, if you want the best food, join the longest queue. Stalls go in and out of favour very quickly, but if you want to witness or join in with this phenomenon, you can find sure-fire mammoth queues for black-pepper crab at Eng Seng Coffeeshop (p91) in Joo Chiat or *satay bee hoon* (peanut sauce–flavoured noodles) at East Coast Lagoon Food Village (p92). See the menu decoder (p187) for help with what's what.

Haute Cuisine & Celebrity Chefs

'A fool and his money are soon parted.' That adage should be firmly in mind when you decide where to splash out for a top-class meal. The integrated resorts have lured big names to Singapore, and Michelin-star chefs Tetsuya Wakuda, Guy Savoy, Joël Robuchon and others have set up in Singapore. But are the restaurants any good? Reviews are mixed and, as always, Singapore restaurants struggle with getting quality service staff. Before you part with your cash, do some research: in this guide and locally published food guides.

Everything Else

There are *dégustation* menus and there's cheap-as-chips hawker fare. Then there's everything in between. In Singapore, you'll easily find restaurants for all tastes in the midrange bracket. Pop into any shopping mall and you'll find everything you could hanker for. Japanese, Thai, burgers, coffee, dumplings…it's all there. These places are air-conditioned and comfortable.

Serious About Eating? Equip Yourself

Start with KF Seetoh's superb *Makansutra*, the bible of hawker centre food. For high-end restaurants, pick up *Singapore Tatler* magazine's *Best Restaurants* guide or the *Miele Guide*. The reviews in *Time Out* and *I-S Magazine* are a good source of news.

Singapore's cottage industry of food bloggers risk clogging their arteries in order to outdo each other:

www.ieatishootipost.com Savvy foodie Leslie Tay has made a business of his food blog.

www.bibikgourmand.blogspot.com Evelyn Chen has reviews galore.

www.ladyironchef.com Psst, Lady Ironchef is actually a bloke, but it doesn't make a difference.

www.makansutra.com KF Seetoh's blog.

www.hungrygowhere.com Loaded with lots of user-generated reviews.

NEED TO KNOW

Price Range

Bear in mind that most restaurant prices will have 17% added to them at the end: a 10% service charge plus 7% for GST. You'll see this indicated by ++ on menus. In our listings, we've used the following price codes to represent the all-inclusive price of a single dish or a main course.

$	less than $10
$$	$10 to $30
$$$	over $30

Opening Hours

➡ Hawker centres, food courts, coffeeshops: 7am to 10pm, sometimes 11pm and even 24 hours.

➡ Midrange restaurants: 11am to 11pm.

➡ Top-end restaurants: noon to 2.30pm and 6pm to 11pm.

Reservations

➡ Book a table for expensive and 'hot' restaurants.

➡ Book a table for midrange restaurants for Friday to Sunday nights.

Tipping

Tipping is unnecessary in Singapore, as most restaurants impose a 10% service charge – and nobody ever tips in hawker centres. Some restaurants don't impose the service charge. In such cases, tip at your discretion.

PLAN YOUR TRIP EATING

Cooking Courses

Cookery Magic (✆6348 9667; www.cookerymagic.com; classes $65-130) Ruqxana conducts standout Asian-cooking classes in her own home. She also conducts classes on an ecofarm and on Pulau Ubin (in an old *kampong* home).

Shermay's Cooking School (Map p216; ✆6479 8442; www.shermay.com; 03-64 Block 43, Jalan Merah Saga, Chip Bee Gardens, Holland Village; classes from $90; ☐7, 61, 77) Singaporean, Thai, Peranakan, chocolate and guest chefs are Shermay's specialities! Hands-on classes cost more.

Coriander Leaf (✆6732 3354; www.corianderleaf.com; 02-03, 3A Merchant Court, Clarke Quay; classes from $120) This Asian fusion restaurant also runs regular classes in Italian, French, Thai and Vietnamese.

Lonely Planet's Top Choices

Maxwell Rd Hawker Centre (p60) Singapore's best hawker centre is also its most popular.

Iggy's (p79) This mainstayer has remained top of the haute cuisine scene.

Sin Huat Eating House (p90) People come from around the island to sample the best crab *bee hoon* (noodles) in town.

Best by Budget

$
Bismillah Biryani (p69)

Gandhi Restaurant (p69)

Tekka Centre (p75)

Gluttons Bay (p46)

East Coast Lagoon Food Village (p92)

$$
DB Bistro Moderne (p45)

Kilo (p45)

Cocotte (p72)

Guan Hoe Soon (p91)

Nan Hwa Chong Fish-Head Steamboat Corner (p72)

Din Tai Fung (p80)

$$$
L'Atelier de Joël Robuchon (p119)

Au Jardin (p105)

L'Angelus (p58)

Best by Cuisine

Chinese & Peranakan
Dim Joy (p58)

Tonny Restaurant (p91)

Wah Lok (p47)

Blue Ginger (p58)

Guan Hoe Soon (p91)

Indian
Gandhi Restaurant (p69)

Samy's Curry Restaurant (p105)

Bismillah Biryani (p69)

Sankranti (p69)

Malay & Indonesian
Cumi Bali (p58)

Tepak Sireh (p72)

Zam Zam (p72)

Western
DB Bistro Moderne (p45)

Saveur (p90)

Cocotte (p72)

Fusion
Kilo (p45)

Food For Thought (p45)

Japanese
Central Mall Food Outlets (p47)

Maeda (p91)

Best Hawker Centres & Food Courts

Lau Pa Sat (p60)

East Coast Lagoon Food Village (p92)

Food Republic, Wisma Atria (p80)

Takashimaya Food Village (p80)

Gluttons Bay (p46)

Best for Crab

Eng Seng Coffeeshop (p91)

No Signboard Seafood (p90)

Roland Restaurant (p92)

Bars near the Quays (p48)

🍷 Drinking & Nightlife

Whip out your dancing shoes and line your stomach – Singapore has plenty to offer in the partying and drinking stakes. There are loads of bars and clubs to keep you going until the birds are twittering, seven nights a week. And if you're hung over, the burgeoning coffee scene will supply enough caffeine to wake the dead.

Bars

Recipe for the burgeoning Singapore bar scene: mix equal parts rooftop bars, microbreweries, Irish pubs, quirky bars and local watering holes. The Colonial District is dotted with rooftop bars offering unparalled city views. Next door, Clarke Quay is home to the popular Brewerkz (p48)...no prizes for guessing what they have on tap. Further out, you'll find everything from microbreweries to bespoke cocktails in the expat enclaves of Holland Village and Dempsey Hill. If you need a sundowner after a long day of shopping at Orchard Rd, duck along Emerald Hill Rd (p82) – there's a whole raft of bars here. For something more mellow and bohemian, visit Kampong Glam, where you can smoke sheesha in between brews. With so much choice, you'll truly be enjoying 'happy' hour.

NEED TO KNOW

Prices

Regular bars add 17% to your bill: 10% for service charge, 7% for GST. You'll see this indicated by ++ on drink lists.

Opening Hours

➡ Bars: 3pm till late.

➡ Clubs: 6pm till late.

➡ Cafes: 10am to 6pm.

Entry Fees

➡ Unless you know someone at the door or get signed in by a member, at the hottest clubs you'll have to join the queue.

➡ You can avoid the cover charge for some bars and clubs if you go early.

Clubbing

With a party on most nights, you'll never lack for a good time. Dance clubs proliferate Clarke Quay (p48), and St James Power Station (p115) houses Firefly, a trendy Canto/Mandopop club, Movida, a live Latin club and several other themed clubs. Home Club (p50) is packed with the latest and greatest DJs spinning to a house full of trendy hipsters. Rooftop bars such as Ku Dé Tah (p49) bring in international guest DJs on select nights.

Zoukout is a dance party held every December on Sentosa's beach. It's organised by Zouk (p48), Singapore's oldest and best-known club.

Singapore's Best Coffee

Something is brewing in Singapore: artisanal coffee made with ethically sourced, locally roasted beans. If you can't put up with the sweetened local brew or the milky soup from Starbucks, here are places you have to check out. Look beyond espresso coffee and ask for coffee brewed with Japanese siphons, French press or pourovers. Highlights of the scene include the following:

➡ **Plain** (p63) Cool, minimalist decor.

➡ **Loysel's Toy** (p45) Well-made lattes at the base of an industrial building.

➡ **Soho Coffee** (p51) Central location; also does tasty burgers.

➡ **Oriole Cafe & Bar** (p81) They roast their own beans at this cafe-restaurant.

Say What? How Much?!

Singapore is probably the most expensive place in Southeast Asia for drinking and nightlife. A beer at most city bars will set you back between $10 and $18, and it's not uncommon for cocktails to ring in at $20 upwards. In addition, most dance clubs have entrance fees of $20 or more (though these will usually include a drink).

If you're looking to save on libations, hit the bars early to take advantage of the happy hours; these typically stretch from around 5pm to 8pm, sometimes starting earlier and finishing later. At these times you'll generally get discounted drinks, two drinks for the price of one and cheaper 'housepours'. On Wednesday or Thursday nights, some bars offer cheaper (sometimes free) drinks to women (a common practice in Singapore and not intended to be sleazy). Those who don't mind plastic tables and fluorescent lights can hang out with the locals at hawker centres and coffeeshops, drinking $6 bottles of Tiger. Of course, if you're really tight, you can always drink $5 beers in your hostel.

GLBT Singapore

While homosexuality is technically illegal and lesbianism not even acknowledged, the GLBT (gay, lesbian, bisexual and transgender) scene in Singapore exists nonetheless. Every August, the gay community rallies around the pride celebration, **Indignation** (www.plu.sg/indignation). You can find resources on GLBT bars and clubs at www.pluguide.com, www.fridae.asia and www.utopia-asia.com.

Lonely Planet's Top Choices

Zouk (p48) Singapore's oldest club still rocks the house.

1 Altitude (p49) Best view from a bar ever? Yes.

Emerald Hill Bars (p82) You'll be spoilt for choice here.

Brewerkz (p48) Tasty microbrews with a riverside setting.

Best for Dancing

St James Power Station (p115)

Butter Factory (p50)

Zirca Mega Club (p50)

Home Club (p50)

Best for Drinks with Views

Lantern (p49)

Level 33 (p49)

New Asia Bar (p50)

Ku Dé Tah (p49)

Best for Beers

Tiger Brewery (p113)

Paulaner Brauhaus (p50)

Brussels Sprouts Belgian Beer & Mussels (p49)

Red Dot Brewhouse (p107)

Best for Chilling Out

eM by the River (p50)

2am: Dessert Bar (p106)

Tippling Club (p107)

Loof (p49)

Zsofi Tapas Bar (p73)

☆ Entertainment

There's never a dull moment in Singapore. There are live gigs and local theatre year-round, while at certain times of the year Singapore explodes into a flurry of car racing, arts festivals and international music gigs. What's more, there's plenty of opportunities for pampering and thrill seeking.

Theatre

The Singapore Arts Festival (www.singapore artsfest.com) is held every June. Quality drama, music, art and dance are featured. The associated Singapore Fringe Festival (www.singaporefringe.com) has plenty of street performances. Esplanade – Theatres on the Bay (p52) is one of the brightest spots in Singapore's vibrant theatre and dance scene. Visiting Broadway musicals are put on at the Marina Bay Sands theatres (p52), and local theatre groups such as Wild Rice and the Singapore Repertory Theatre regularly put up local plays as well as the occasional adaptation. Shakespeare in the Park, anyone?

Live Music

Sure, a lot of average Pinoy cover bands grace hotel bars, but an enthusiastic local music scene also thrives (to a point). The outdoor atrium at the Esplanade has the regular free performances and the Singapore Symphony Orchestra plays, for free, at the Botanic Gardens monthly.

If local music isn't your thing, international acts and Cantonese and Mandarin pop/rock acts visit with startling regularity. Timbre also organises the Rock and Roots festival in May each year. If all else fails to entertain, there are plenty of raucous Thai discos you could always visit...

Film

Take an affluent society, chuck it on a tiny island beaten down by the sweltering sun for 12 months a year and blammo, you've got the perfect recipe for a country full of movie buffs. Singaporeans love to watch movies, and at around $10 per ticket, it's great value. Multiplex cinemas abound, and most are clustered around the city area, on or near Orchard Rd. Singapore's cinemas are notoriously chilly places, so wear something warm.

Sports & Thrills of all Sorts

Each September, the Formula One night race comes to town, along with its crazy circus of performers (Linkin Park and Shakira have previously provided entertainment). If you want to be on the active side of the sporting fence, Singapore has plenty of outdoor activities for those undaunted by climate. Somewhere in the region of a quarter of the island is taken up by parks, many of which are joined by a series of underground park connectors and overhead bridges. This means that you can walk, cycle or skate through much of the city without fighting traffic.

Spas & Massage

Spas, massage and paid-for relaxation are big business in Singapore. Midrange to high-end spas can be found in most malls and five-star hotels. **Spa Esprit** (www.spa-esprit.com) is a popular beauty empire.

Another place worth a visit is the People's Park Complex (p64), which boasts several floors of stalls offering reflexology, shiatsu and even places where you can soak your feet in a pool of dead-skin-eating fish. Rates vary from around $25 for a foot massage to more than $200 for a full-day package.

Lonely Planet's Top Choices

Universal Studios (p117) Gold-standard thrill rides for kids and adults.

Home Club (p50) Comedy 'masala nights' offer stand-up laughs aplenty.

TAB (p83) A rotating calendar of music acts keeps punters entertained.

Timbre@Substation (p51) Order a beer and rock out to tunes by local bands.

Best for Theatre

Singapore Repertory Theatre (p52)

Theatreworks (p52)

Necessary Stage (p94)

Best for Local Bands

TAB (p83)

Timbre@Substation (p51)

Crazy Elephant (p51)

BluJaz Café (p74)

Home Club (p50)

Best for Film

Parco Bugis Junction (Map p208)

Suntec City (p54)

Marina Square complex (p54)

Cathay (Map p212)

Cathay Cineleisure Orchard (Map p212)

Plaza Singapura (p84)

Shaw House (Map p212)

Best for Pampering

Willowstream Spa (p52)

Spa Botanica (p120)

People's Park Complex (p64)

Best for Hikes

Southern Ridges (p112)

MacRitchie Reservoir (p99)

Bukit Timah Nature Reserve (p98)

Best for Kicks

Ultimate Drive (p52)

SKI360° (p94)

Exotic Tattoo (p84)

G-Max Reverse Bungy (p52)

Universal Studios rollercoasters (p117)

Best for Bike Rentals

East Coast Park (p88)

Pasir Ris Park (p89)

PLAN YOUR TRIP ENTERTAINMENT

NEED TO KNOW

Prices

➜ $20 to $50 will get you a ticket to a local theatre production.

➜ It's often free to watch local bands at local nightspots; some places have a small cover charge.

➜ International music acts are expensive and tickets often average $100 to $300.

➜ Big-budget musical tickets cost $65 to $200.

➜ Expect to pay through the nose during Formula One season in September – hotel prices often triple. Decent grandstand tickets to the F1 start at $298, but if you're on a budget you can get walkabout tickets from $38.

Tickets

Tickets and an events calendar can be found on the Sistic website, www.sistic.com.sg.

Shopping

While it's not the shopping haven it once was (Hong Kong and Bangkok have stolen Singapore's thunder), there are clusters of cool local fashion designers and enough international high-street brands to sate the shopping needs of most visitors. IT nerds can also rejoice at the low prices and wide range of cameras and gear...available at any time of the day!

Shopping Strips

Everybody's heard of Orchard Rd, Singapore's shopping mecca. Once lined with plantations of the natural kind, it now seems to grow new malls every few years. You'll find most of what you want here; in particular, all the fashion brands.

If you're buying electronics or computer equipment, Funan DigitaLife Mall (p54), Sim Lim Square (p75) and the Mustafa Centre (p75) are all good places to visit. You have to shop around and be prepared to bargain at Sim Lim Square. For second-hand camera gear, wander around Peninsula Plaza (p54) and Peninsula Shopping Centre (p54). You can haggle slightly here.

If you're after art or antiques, it pays to know your original piece from your cheap copy. For Asian antiques, the best places to head are Chinatown (p63), Dempsey Rd (p108) or Tanglin Shopping Centre (p83). There's also a collection of contemporary art galleries at the Ministry of Information, Culture and the Arts building (MICA; p52).

For fabrics and textiles, head to Little India (p75) and the Arab Quarter (p75).

IN SEARCH OF FASHION, NOT JUST SHOPPING *NIKI BRUCE*

If you're looking for something different, skip the usual high-street brands and check out some original, Singapore fashion.

RAOUL is a 'masstige' (combination of mass and prestige) brand for men and women that's developing a following for its minimalist style and is one of the few Singaporean brands that tends towards European cuts, meaning you're more likely to find 'larger' sizes. RAOUL accessories are particularly good; the structured leather bags look like Celine, but at a quarter of the price.

If you prefer a more feminine look, check out alldressedup for its combination of soft draping and structured tailoring. Known for its unique use of prints and colour, this is the go-to brand for workwear and accessories like chunky necklaces and clutch bags.

Among the up-and-coming Singapore designers, names making waves include max.tan, a cross between Comme des Garçons and Givenchy's Ricardo Tisci, and young&restless, with its unstructured draping and voluminous tailoring. Other young designers to check out include Depression, a monochrome mix of unisex jersey pieces and neat tailoring; AL&ALICIA, soft 'boyfriend' jackets, shorts and cute dresses; Reckless Ericka, Japanese inspired men's and women's wear; and WYKIDD, smart casual menswear with hand-worked detailing. For a good overview of new labels check out multi-label boutiques Blackmarket and Front Row or visit Parco Next Next in Millenia Walk (p54). *Female* and *Her World* are local magazines that regularly feature the best of local and international design.

Niki Bruce is the editor of herworldPLUS.com, a Singapore fashion & lifestyle website.

Lonely Planet's Top Choices

Orchard Rd (p83) You'll find *everything* in Singapore's retail mecca.

Haji Lane (p69) The latest indie chic housed in restored shophouses.

Little India (p75) Five-foot ways redolent of spices and dripping with atmosphere.

Dempsey Rd (p108) A quiet and cool enclave of upmarket delis and furniture shops.

Best for Gadgets

Funan DigitalLife Mall (p54)

Mustafa Centre (p75)

Sim Lim Square (p75)

Best for Cameras

Peninsula Plaza (p54)

Peninsula Shopping Centre (p54)

Sim Lim Square (p75)

Best Malls

ION Orchard (p83)

Ngee Ann City (p83)

VivoCity (p115)

313 Somerset (p83)

Raffles City (p53)

NEED TO KNOW

Opening Hours

➡ Retail stores: 11am to 9pm or 10pm.

➡ Mustafa Centre and Challenger at Funan DigitalLife Mall: 24 hours.

Bargaining & Returns

Prices are usually fixed in all shops, except at markets and in some shops in touristy areas. It pays to know the prices of gear back home in case you get over-quoted at independent stores. If you do have to haggle, stay good-humoured and don't get petty (erm, that's the price of a 70¢ can of Coke) – this causes everyone to lose face. Shops in Singapore don't accept returns. Exchanges are accepted if the item has its original tags and packaging.

Taxes & Refunds

Visitors leaving from the airport can get a refund of the 7% GST on their purchases, under the following conditions:

➡ Minimum spend of $100 at one retailer on the same day for no more than three purchases.

➡ You have a copy of the GST refund form from the shop (they aren't available at customs).

➡ Present the refund form, items and receipts to customs at the airport. They stamp the form, then you can claim the refund, which is processed here.

➡ Smaller stores may not participate in the GST refund scheme.

Explore Singapore

BOLEH DIGUNA
UNTUK MENJAHIT
"BAJU KURUNG &
KEBAYA"

DRESS MATERIAL

SINGAPORE'S
TOP SIGHTS

Neighbourhoods at a Glance

① Colonial District, Marina Bay & the Quays (p40)

The former administrative enclave of the British is home to a swath of colonial architecture, museums and the track for the Formula One night race. High rollers try their luck at Marina Bay. Bisecting it all, the Singapore River also connects the three quays – home to restaurants, clubs and bars.

② Chinatown & the CBD (p55)

After the government shunted out the residents, Singapore's Chinatown became a pale shadow of its former self. Today it's filled with stores that hawk trinkets, but several temples and the heritage centre make the trip there worthwhile. The CBD forms the stunning backdrop for the everchanging skyline: rooftop bars jostle with old-school tem-

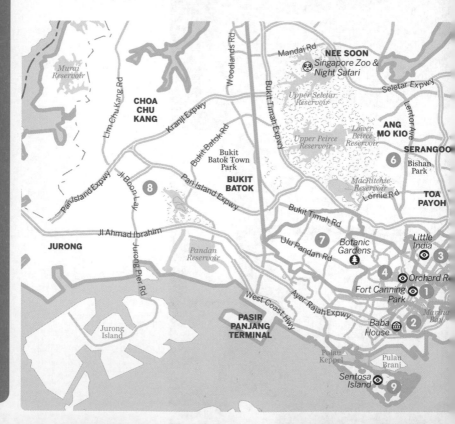

ples, all set against the financial heart that funds Singapore.

❸ Little India & Kampong Glam (p65)

Little India is Singapore trapped in its gritty past – it's frenetic, messy and fun. Spice traders spill their wares across five-foot ways and Indian labourers swarm into the area each weekend. Kampong Glam, the former home of the local Sultan, has been polished up, and is home to hip clothing shops and fantastic Malay restaurants.

❹ Orchard Road (p77)

If you worship the gods of retail, pay your respects at the thousands of shops spread out across 22 (and counting!) malls. Don't forget to seek solitude along Emerald Hill, a strip of beautifully restored Peranakan houses.

❺ Eastern Singapore (p85)

Geylang is a red-light district come sundown, but also has some of the best local cuisine. East Coast Park is perfect for cycling and picnics by the beach, while nearby Katong and Joo Chiat are steeped in rich Peranakan culture. At the extreme tip of the island, you'll find green in Pasir Ris Park, the moving exhibits at Changi Prison and the launching point for a trip to Pulau Ubin.

❻ Northern & Central Singapore (p96)

From treetop walks in MacRitchie to the wetlands of Sungei Buloh, there's plenty to keep outdoor lovers busy. If hiking isn't your thing, seek out grand temples and the Singapore Zoo and Night Safari.

❼ Holland Village, Dempsey Hill & the Botanic Gardens (p102)

Expats and the well-heeled flock here for good food and drinks after a massage and pedicure at a spa. The entire area is book-ended by the gorgeous, lush Botanic Gardens and the Bukit Timah nature reserve.

❽ West & Southwest Singapore (p109)

Tackle the stunning Southern Ridges walk to explore the western ridgeline of Singapore. The National University of Singapore houses art gems, and further west are the family-friendly attractions of the Jurong Bird Park and the Science Centre.

❾ Sentosa & Other Islands (p116)

Jump on a bumboat in Changi across to Pulau Ubin, where you'll find an island that retains a 1960s *kampung* (village) vibe. A ferry will get you to Kusu and St John's islands – both quiet little dots perfect for a quiet day on the beach. If you want something faster-paced, Sentosa ticks all the right 'amusement' boxes.

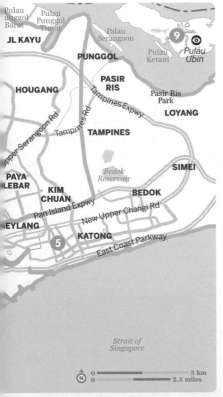

Colonial District, Marina Bay & the Quays

Neighbourhood Top Five

1 Getting a glimpse of Singapore's Colonial past set against its modern glamour via a **walking tour** (p44).

2 Learning about the rich Peranakan culture at the **Peranakan Museum** (p43).

3 There's just something that keeps people chugging back Singapore slings at the **Raffles Hotel** (p49).

4 Strolling in the early mornings or evenings across the Double Helix Bridge through the Marina Bay Sands into the brand-new landscaped **Gardens by the Bay** (p53).

5 Catching the stunning view of the bay, the Singapore River and tight web of the city from one of the many rooftop bars. **Ku Dé Tah** (p49) is hugely popular and a good place to start your night.

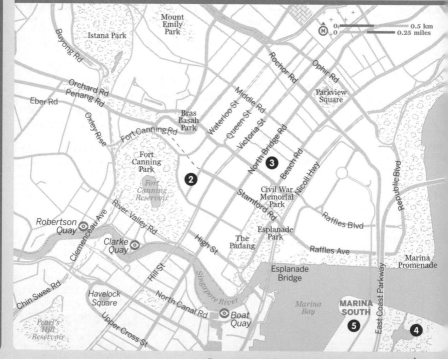

For more detail of this area, see Map p208 and p210 ➡

Explore Colonial District, Marina Bay & the Quays

This is the heart of Singapore: an urban treasure-trove of colonial buildings, museums, shopping centres, parks and riverside entertainment strips. The City Hall MRT station bolts the neighbourhood together and is a perfect starting point. Wander northwest off along Stamford Rd towards the museums.

Head in the opposite direction to the contemporary Esplanade and Marina Bay. Stroll through the rambling Gardens by the Bay, right behind the unmissable structure that houses the Marina Bay Sands.

Scope out the edifices of colonialism around the Padang. It's here you'll find the famous Raffles Hotel, a string of old churches, the old and new parliament houses, and the mouth of the Singapore River.

Save the three riverside quays for night time. Clarke Quay is a raucous cluster of bars and clubs, and Robertson Quay is where you should head if you want a nice meal. Set behind it all is idyllic Fort Canning Park.

Local Life

➡ **Food courts** The average local eschews the fine-dining options for food courts.

➡ **Foreign enclaves** The influx of migrants means that places such as Peninsula Plaza have turned into hubs for various groups of migrant workers. Don't be surprised to find Burmese food in a mall!

➡ **(Public) bus tours** Take a trip on bus 14. A double-decker doing the east–west route, it skirts the southern edge of downtown on the seven-storey East Coast Parkway, offering impressive views of the skyscrapers to the north and the harbour to the south.

Getting There & Away

➡ **MRT** The efficient subway service is centred on City Hall, an interchange station. The station is also connected via underground malls towards the Esplanade, from where you can cut across to Marina Bay. Raffles City is the next stop for the Quays. The Bayfront MRT station at Marina Bay Sands is scheduled to open some time in 2012.

➡ **Bus** The area is also well connected by bus to other parts of the island. Key bus stops are just outside the Raffles Hotel and outside St Andrew's Cathedral along North Bridge Rd. Bus 2 takes you down Victoria St and Hill St. Buses 51, 61, 63 and 80 go along North Bridge Rd. For Beach Rd, hop on bus 100, 107 or 961. Along Bras Basah Rd, get on bus 12, 14, 16, 77 or 111.

Lonely Planet's Top Tip

The National Museum and some galleries offer free entry from 6pm to 9pm every Friday, plus some museums offer combined tickets that save you a few bucks. Most bars in the area have 'happy hour' specials from 5pm to 8pm or 9pm. During these hours, drinks are either one-for-one or heavily discounted. Clubs have ladies nights where ladies get free entry and, sometimes, free booze (sorry boys). Unlike elsewhere, Singaporean ladies' nights tend to be sleaze free.

 Best Sights

➡ Peranakan Museum (p43)

➡ Asian Civilisatons Museum (p43)

➡ Fort Canning Park (p42)

For reviews, see p42 ➡

 Best Places to Eat

➡ DB Bistro Moderne (p45)

➡ Gluttons Bay (p46)

➡ Kilo (p45)

For reviews, see p45 ➡

 **Best Places to Drink**

➡ Loof (p49)

➡ Brewerkz (p48)

➡ 1 Altitude (p49)

For reviews, see p48 ➡

SIGHTS

RAFFLES HOTEL
HISTORICAL BUILDING

Map p208 (www.raffleshotel.com; 1 Beach Rd; ⓂCity Hall) Viewing the regal edifice that stands today, it's hard to believe that Raffles Hotel started life as a 10-room bungalow fronted by the beach (long gone thanks to land reclamation). It was opened in December 1887 by the Sarkies brothers, immigrants from Armenia and proprietors of two other grand colonial hotels, the Strand in Yangon (Rangoon) and the Eastern & Oriental in Penang.

The hotel's heyday began in 1899 with the opening of the main building, the same one that guests stay in today. Raffles soon became a byword for oriental luxury ('A legendary symbol for all the fables of the Exotic East', went the publicity blurb) and was featured in novels by Joseph Conrad and Somerset Maugham. The famous Singapore sling was first concocted here by bartender Ngiam Tong Boon in 1915, and (far less gloriously) the last Singaporean tiger, which escaped from a travelling circus nearby, was shot beneath the Billiard Room in 1902.

By the 1970s, the Raffles was a shabby relic, dodging the wrecking ball in 1987 with National Monument designation. In 1991 it reopened after a $160 million facelift. The hotel lobby is open to the public, and is a popular tourist attraction. Dress standards apply; so no shorts or sandals. Hidden away on the 3rd floor of the Raffles Hotel Arcade, the **Raffles Hotel Museum** (admission free; ☺10am-7pm) is worth hunting out. Here you'll find a fascinating collection of memorabilia including photographs and posters from bygone eras, and a fine city map showing how Noel Coward could once sip his gin sling and stare out at the sea from the hotel verandah.

SINGAPORE FLYER
OBSERVATION WHEEL

Map p208 (www.singaporeflyer.com.sg; 30 Raffles Ave; adult/child $29.50/20.65; ☺8.30am-10.30pm; ⓂCity Hall) People in cities around the world are paying money to get into a gigantic ferris wheel for glorious views, and why not? The Singapore Flyer currently holds the title as the world's largest 'observation wheel' – the pricey 30-minute ride offers views towards the Colonial District, CBD, Marina Bay, the high-rise housing landscape to the east and out to the south China Sea.

TOP SIGHTS
FORT CANNING PARK

When Raffles rolled into Singapore and claimed it for the mother country, locals steered clear of Fort Canning Hill, then called Bukit Larangan (Forbidden Hill) out of respect for the sacred shrine of Sultan Iskandar Shah, ancient Singapura's last ruler. Raffles built an *atap* (thatched roof) residence on the summit in 1822, which acted as Government House until the military built Fort Canning.

The park offers a wonderfully cool retreat from the hot streets below. Gothic gateways lead into the pleasant park, where gravestones from the old Christian cemetery are embedded in the brick walls. There's also a spice garden, on the site of Raffles' original botanical garden, where hollowed-out coconut shells on sticks offer samples of various spices for tasting. Look for an archaeological dig, where under a wooden roof you can see the 14th-century Javanese artefacts that have been uncovered there.

Visit the **Battle Box Museum** (Map p208; 2 Cox Terrace; adult/child S$8/5; ☺10am-6pm Tue-Sun), the former command post of the British during WWII, and get lost in the eerie and deathly quiet 26-room underground complex; life-sized models re-enact the fateful surrender to the Japanese on 15 February 1942. Japanese Morse codes are still etched on the walls.

DON'T MISS...

➡ Battle Box Museum
➡ Spice Garden

PRACTICALITIES

➡ Map p208
➡ www.nparks.gov.sg (search for the Fort Canning page for free downloadable walking tours)
➡ Admission free
➡ ⓂDhoby Ghaut

ST ANDREW'S CATHEDRAL   CHURCH

Map p208 (www.livingstreams.org.sg; 11 St Andrew's Rd; ☉visitors centre 9am-5pm, 9am-7pm Sat, 9am-1.30pm Sun) This peaceful cathedral stands in stark contrast against the buzzing cityscape. Completed in 1838 but torn down and rebuilt in its present form in 1862 after lightning damaged the original building (twice!), the cathedral has a 63.1m-tall tower, towering naves and lovely stained glass above the west doors. The grounds make a lovely place for a picnic or siesta on the grass.

ARMENIAN CHURCH   CHURCH

Map p208 (60 Hill St) Dedicated to St Gregory the Illuminator in 1836, Singapore's oldest church's neoclassical design is by eminent colonial architect George Coleman. Pushing up orchids in the graveyard is Agnes Joaquim, discoverer of Singapore's national flower – the *Vanda Miss Joaquim* orchid.

PERANAKAN MUSEUM   MUSEUM

Map p208 (39 Armenian St; adult/child $6/3; ☉1-7pm Mon, 9.30am-7pm Tue-Sun, to 9pm Fri; MCity Hall) Singapore's newest museum stands as a testament to the Peranakan (Straits-born locals) cultural revival in the Lion City. Opened in 2008, it has 10 thematic galleries and a variety of multimedia exhibits designed to introduce visitors to historical and contemporary Peranakan culture.

In addition to featuring traditionally crafted, beaded Peranakan clothing and exquisitely carved antique furniture, the museum also has a number of interactive exhibits. Our favourite is the diorama displaying a traditional Peranakan home, complete with two video-mounted portraits of elders who argue with each other about whether or not their descendants are leading culturally appropriate lives.

SINGAPORE ART MUSEUM   MUSEUM

Map p208 (www.singaporeartmuseum.sg; 71 Bras Basah Rd; adult/child $10/5; ☉10am-7pm Sat-Thur, till 9pm Fri; MCity Hall or Bras Basah) Two blocks west of Raffles Hotel is SAM, a fine museum housed in the former St Joseph's Institution, a Catholic boys' school that was relocated in 1987.

The reconstruction by local architect Wong Hooe Wai fuses historical charm with a strong contemporary feel. The gallery champions the arts in an economics-obsessed nation, with exhibitions ranging from classical Chinese calligraphy to electronic arts, though it sometimes seems content to hide away its permanent collection. A highlight is the Wu Guangzhong gallery, which features a rotating exhibition of $70 million worth of art donated by the father of modern Chinese painting.

Afterwards, it's worth stopping for coffee in the museum's genteel cafe, **Dôme**. Admission to the museum and 8Q SAM is free from 6pm to 9pm Fridays.

8Q SAM   MUSEUM

Map p208 (8 Queen St; adult/child $3/1.50, free with SAM ticket; ☉10am-7pm Sat-Thur, to 9pm Fri; MCity Hall or Bras Basah) Round the corner from SAM, the art museum's recent(ish) extension is named after its address and has a revolving-door focus on quirky installations, interactivity and contemporary art.

NATIONAL MUSEUM OF SINGAPORE   MUSEUM

Map p208 (www.nationalmuseum.sg; 93 Stamford Rd; adult/child $10/5; ☉history galleries 10am-6pm, living galleries 10am-9pm; MDhoby Ghaut) The grand dame of Singapore's museum scene is located in the history-drenched neoclassical 19th-century building that once housed the former Raffles Museum and Library. Perhaps the most magnificent feature of the building itself is the restored rotunda, which includes 50 carefully crafted pieces of stained glass. At once modern and classical, the museum features a wide variety of multimedia exhibits focused primarily on – naturally – Singapore's history, culture and overall glory. The engaging 'Singapore Story' exhibition begins on the top floor and spirals down over two floors. Visitors are greeted upon entry by a stunning two-storey-high *Koyaanisqatsi*-esque video installation.

ASIAN CIVILISATIONS MUSEUM   MUSEUM

Map p210 (www.acm.org.sg; 1 Empress Pl; adult/child $8/4, half price after 7pm Fri; ☉9am-7pm Tue-Sun, to 9pm Fri; MRaffles Place) Inside an impressive 1865 building named in honour of Queen Victoria, this museum is a must for any Singapore visit – escape the humidity, put your watch in your pocket and get lost inside. Ten thematic galleries explore traditional aspects of pan-Asian culture, religion and civilisation, with exquisite, well-displayed artefacts from Southeast Asia, China, India, Sri Lanka and even Turkey. The exploration of Islam and its influence in the region is particularly compelling, though the boys might

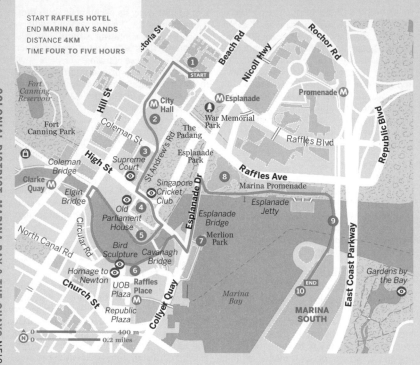

START **RAFFLES HOTEL**
END **MARINA BAY SANDS**
DISTANCE **4KM**
TIME **FOUR TO FIVE HOURS**

Neighbourhood Walk
Colonial & Modern Singapore

Start at the **1** **Raffles Hotel**. Wander around the cavernous lobby and shopping arcade before heading out along North Bridge Rd. Turn left into the magnificent **2** **St Andrew's Cathedral** and pop out the opposite side on St Andrews's Rd.

Continue past **3** **City Hall** and the old Supreme Court, both grand dames of Colonial Singapore. Nearby is the new Supreme Court, with its unmistakable spaceship design. Go all the way to the top for great views.

Below where St Andrew's Rd curves to the left you'll find a group of colonial-era buildings including the **4** **Victoria Theatre & Concert Hall**, in front of which you'll see the original Raffles statue, which once stood at the Padang.

Hang a right to walk along the northern bank of the Singapore River. The picturesque building with the multicoloured window frames, on the corner of Hill St, is the **5** **old Hill St police station**, which currently houses the Ministry of Communication and the Arts (MICA) and several good art galleries.

Cross the road at Hill St and head towards the river. This stretch is **6** **Boat Quay** and mostly filled with bars and restaurants. Look out for some great sculpture in this area. Continue the circuit by following the river further east to the point where it reaches Marina Bay. It's here where you'll find stairs leading into the bay, on top of which sits the famous **7** **Merlion statue**.

Head north along the Esplanade bridge towards **8** **Esplanade – Theatres on the Bay**, the world's largest and most expensive sculptural homage to the durian. Head east along the Marina Promenade till you get to the **9** **Helix bridge**. This bridge connects the promenade to the Marina Bay Sands complex and offers a great vantage point for photos across to the old Collyer Quay, Merlion and Fullerton buildings. Push on to your last stop at **10** **Marina Bay Sands**, and make your way to Ku Dé Tah for a well-deserved tipple.

be more interested in the large display of *krisses* (daggers). Visiting exhibitions – extra fees apply – have included the terracotta warriors.

FREE SINGAPORE TYLER PRINT
INSTITUTE   GALLERY
(www.stpi.com.sg; 41 Robertson Quay; ⊙1-5pm Sun & Mon, 9.30am-6pm Tue-Sat; ⬛54 from Ⓜ Clarke Quay) Established by the American printmaker Kenneth E Tyler, the institute features a gallery holding exhibitions on various aspects of printmaking, as well as a paper mill and an educational facility. Previous exhibitions have included luminaries such as David Hockney.

HONG SAN SEE TEMPLE   TEMPLE
(31 Mohamed Sultan Rd; ⊙6am-7pm; ⬛32, 54, 139, 195) This imposing Chinese temple was completed in 1913 and set up on a hill. The temple is built in a southern Chinese fashion, with sloping tiled roofs and ornamented columns. A major renovation in 2010 saw the temple restored to its full glory – the gold-gilded woodcarvings adorning the inner doors are impressive – hence its Unesco commendation for conservation.

MERLION   MONUMENT
Map p210 (One Fullerton, 1 Fullerton Rd; Ⓜ Raffles Place) Back in the 1980s, someone at the tourism board created a myth about a half-fish, half-lion, and the gawking Japanese tourists helped seal its status as an iconic (nobody said it was pretty) Singapore sight. While visiting it in itself isn't worth your time, the Marina Bay views it fronts make the trip here worthwhile. Don't forget to jump on a boat cruise (p51) for a complete circuit of Singapore's changing waterways.

MINT MUSEUM OF TOYS   TOY MUSEUM
Map p208 (26 Seah St; admission adult/child $15/7.50; ⊙9.30am-6.30pm Ⓜ City Hall) A slender blink-and-you-miss-it building houses a privately owned collection of 50,000 (!) toys spanning 100 years of history. From the oh-so-wrong golliwogs to tin toys from China, you'll probably see something that'll ignite childhood memories. Park yourself at the attached Mr Punch bar while the kids go ga-ga.

MARINA BARRAGE   PARK
(www.pub.gov.sg/marina; 8 Marina Gardens Dr; ⊙9am-9pm; Ⓜ Marina Bay then ⬛400) There's the pleasant – families flying kites while the sun sets in the background – and the hokey, in the form of the government's exhibition on NeWater (water purified from sewage). But you can't deny the brilliance at turning the flood-control dam of the Marina Channel into a gorgeous public park. Looking across the bay in the evenings, breeze on your face, is a particularly pleasant way to pass time in Singapore.

🍴 EATING

TOP CHOICE **KILO**   FUSION $$
(☎6467 3939; www.kilokitchen.com; 66 Kampong Bugis; mains from $28; lunch Sun, dinner Tue-Sat) Technically outside the limits of the Colonial District, but there are no boundaries when it comes to good food. Kilo is set on the second level of a nondescript industrial building – it's akin to stepping into someone's living room. Wall fans circulate air around the diners (there's no air-con). And the food, it's oh so good. The focus is on share plates of food prepared with fresh ingredients. Think garlic and cilantro pork belly, portobello and steak with white-wine spinach and ebi cappellini with stuffed mushrooms.

On the ground floor of the building is **Loysel's Toy** (66 Kampong Bugis; ⊙9am-6pm Tue-Fri, till 7.30pm Sat & Sun), serving up well-made lattes and sandwiches. The complex is hard to find, so take a taxi.

DB BISTRO MODERNE   FRENCH $$
Map p210 (☎6688 8525; The Shoppes at Marina Bay Sands, 2 Bayfront Ave; mains from $28; Ⓜ Promenade, Bayfront) French chef Daniel Boulud's Singaporean outpost is the best of the celebrity chef restaurants in the Marina Bay Sands complex, simply because service is top-notch and prices aren't inflated to ridiculous wallet-busting heights. The food itself: bistro-style French food with signature dishes such as the DB Burger (wagyu patty stuffed with foie gras) is not overly complex, but utterly enjoyable.

FOOD FOR THOUGHT   FUSION $$
Map p208 (8 Queen St; mains from $10; Ⓜ Bras Basah, City Hall) We admire the philosophy behind the restaurant – a portion of the proceeds go to aid projects. The food itself is a mix of familiar favourites: pastas, grilled meats and sandwiches, all with a twist:

THE PADANG & AROUND: THE HEART OF COLONIAL SINGAPORE

The open field of the **Padang** (MCity Hall) is where flannelled fools play cricket in the tropical heat, cheered on by members of the Singapore Cricket Club in the pavilion. At the opposite end of the field is the Singapore Recreation Club. Cricket is still played on the weekends.

This rather prosaic spot has darker historical significance, as it was here that the invading Japanese herded the European community together before marching them off to Changi Prison. Apart from the reconstructed monstrosity that is the Singapore Recreation Club (it looks like something made from kids' building blocks), the Padang is flanked by a handsome collection of colonial buildings and assorted monuments, all of which can be taken in on a leisurely stroll (see p44).

At the Padang's southern end, the **Victoria Theatre & Concert Hall** (1862), once the town hall, is now used for cultural events. The old **Parliament House** (1827) is Singapore's oldest government building. Originally a private mansion, it became a courthouse, then the Assembly House of the colonial government and, finally, the Parliament House for independent Singapore. It's now the Arts House, an arts centre.

Along St Andrew's Rd, the **Supreme Court**, built in 1939, is a relatively new addition and was the last classical building to be erected in Singapore. It replaced the Grand Hotel de L'Europe, which once outshone the Raffles as Singapore's premier hotel. Situated next door, and even newer, is the **new Supreme Court**, which opened in 2005.

City Hall, with its classical facade of Corinthian columns, is located next to the Supreme Court and dates from 1929. It was here that Lord Louis Mountbatten announced Japanese surrender in 1945 and Lee Kwan Yew declared Singapore's independence in 1965. Both the Supreme Court and City Hall are under renovation and will reopen as the National Art Gallery of Singapore in 2015. Completing the colonial trio is St Andrew's Cathedral (p43).

their chicken chop is coated in a lightly curried batter, for example. It's popular, so expect a wait during peak times.

MARINA BAY SANDS   INTERNATIONAL **$$$**
Map p210 (Marina Bay Sands, 2 Bayfront Ave; www.marinabaysands.com/Singapore-Restaurants; meals from $10-500; MPromenade, Bayfront) While the cluster of restaurants here don't warrant individual reviews, collectively, they're worth a mention. The lure of high rollers brought 'celebrity chefs' here quicker than it takes Gordon Ramsay to drop an F-bomb. Famed Aussie chef Tetsuya Wakuda opened **Waku Ghin**, Wolfgang Puck opened **Cut**, and Guy Savoy and Santi Santamaria both opened eponymous restaurants. In a little bit of morbid drama, Santi collapsed and died of a heart attack while hosting media at his restaurant. For modern Asian and great views, head to the rooftop for Justin Quek's **Sky on 57**. There are plenty of mid-range options including thin-crust pizzas at **Osteria Mozza** and Singapore's priciest food court, in the basement. Expect to splash out at least $300 (without alcohol) at the big-name restaurants.

GLUTTONS BAY   HAWKER CENTRE **$**
Map p210 (01-15 Esplanade Mall; mains $10-20; ⏰6pm-3am; MEsplanade) Selected by the *Makansutra Food Guide*, this bayside collection of the best hawkers (or street-food masters, as they call them) is a great place to start your exploration of the island's food culture. Everyone has their own favourites, but you can't go wrong with dishes such as oyster omelette, satay, and barbecue stingray. You have to try the divine *kaya* (coconut jam) fondue.

SEAH ST FOOD OUTLETS   LOCAL **$**
Map p208 (Seah St; MCity Hall) This short street next to the impeccable Raffles Hotel has a couple of good eating options. Standout places include **Hock Lam Beef Noodles**, where they serve rice noodles with beef coated with piquant thick sauce, **Sin Swee Kee** and **Swee Kee** (no relation to each other), for their chicken rice. Order the Hainanese pork chop at Swee Kee: fried, battered pork cutlet slathered with a spiced tomato-based sauce. YUM!

PURVIS ST FOOD OUTLETS LOCAL $

Map p208 (Purvis St; [M]City Hall) Not one to lose out to its neighbour Seah St, Purvis St packs it in with a whole heap of restaurants, many of them excellent. Those with deep pockets will want to splash out on Italian at **Garibaldi** or French at **Gunther's**. The chicken rice at old-school, 50-odd-year-old **Yet Con** is superb and you can shovel Thai food at **Jai Thai**. If you're in the area for brekkie, drop by **Killiney Kopitiam** or **YY Kafei Dian** for some *kaya* toast and thick coffee that'll knock your socks off.

RAFFLES CITY INTERNATIONAL $$

Map p208 (www.rafflescity.com.sg; 252 North Bridge Rd; [M]City Hall) You'll find several excellent eating options at this mall, most located in the confusing basement warren. **Handburger** makes gourmet (but somewhat small) burgers, **Skinny Pizza** is popular for its gourmet-topped pizzas made with flat cracker bread, punters queue out the door at **Din Tai Fung** for its divine *xiao long bao* (pork dumplings), or guzzle German beer and sausages at **Brotzeit**. Check out the deli counters at the basement **Marketplace** supermarket for a picnic basket.

CHEF CHAN'S RESTAURANT CHINESE $$

Map p208 (01-06 National Museum, 93 Stamford Rd; set meals from $38, dim sum from $4.80; [M]Dhoby Ghaut) Eponymous chef, sick of cooking for over 200 people in his large restaurant, closes shop and opens tiny restaurant with nine tables and a daily changing set menu. It's decked out with his exquisite, over-the-top antique furnishing, which pales in comparison to the food. He recently handed the reins to a disciple while he jaunts through China to collect recipes. The menu (but not the atmosphere) is less stuffy; there's now dim sum, and prices have tumbled.

EMPIRE CAFÉ LOCAL $$

Map p208 (Raffles Hotel, 2 Stamford Rd; mains $10-20; ⊙11am-11pm) Enjoy local favourites such as *char kway teow* (broad noodles, clams and eggs fried in chilli and black-bean sauce) and Hainanese chicken rice in this faux-1920s-style coffee house. With its genteel wooden chairs and marble-top tables, the Empire Café channels a colonial air synonymous with Raffles Hotel.

EQUINOX INTERNATIONAL $$$

Map p208 (✆6837 3322; level 70, Swissôtel, 2 Stamford Rd; mains $30-55) Adjectives struggle to describe the jaw-dropping views from this 70th-floor restaurant. Soaring ceilings, Asiatic wall hangings and plush fabrics are mere backdrops. The view rates a 10, the food a little less. Book early for a window seat. Retire for a drink at the neighbouring New Asia Bar or City Space afterwards.

ARTICHOKE MEDITERRANEAN $$

Map p208 (161 Middle Rd; mains $15-38; ⊙ dinner Tue-Sat, lunch Sat & Sun; [M]Bras Basah) Sequestered in a cosy little building behind an old church, Artichoke serves up share plates of Moorish food in cozy environs. Patrons hungrily dig into moussaka and slow-cooked beef cheeks while trying to decide what to order next.

WAH LOK CHINESE $$

Map p208 (2nd fl, Carlton Hotel, 76 Bras Basah Rd; mains over $20; [M]City Hall, Bras Basah). Long-running Cantonese restaurant popular with families. Staff are happy to offer suggestions if you can't make a decision past the exquisite Peking duck and dim sum.

HAI TIEN LO CHINESE $$

Map p208 (37th fl, Pan Pacific Hotel, 7 Raffles Blvd; mains from $25; [M]Esplanade) In preparation for a superb meal, savour the spectacular views while riding the external lift up to the 37th floor. A large range of nearly 30 set menus tailored to different tastes and requirements takes the headache out of ordering and allows you to concentrate on the scene outside. Or just have dim sum.

CENTRAL MALL INTERNATIONAL $$

Map p210 (6 Eu Tong Sen St; [M]Clarke Quay) This mall, conveniently set above the Clarke Quay MRT station, is home to a over 40 food and beverage outlets. Some of the more popular Japanese options include **Mautama Ramen**, **Ramen Santouka**, **Freshness Burger**, **Waraku** and **Watami**. If you fancy something local, try **No Signboard Seafood** for chilli crab and **Tung Lok Signatures** for dim sum.

KOPITIAM COFFEESHOP $

Map p208 (cnr Bencoolen St & Bras Basah Rd; ⊙24hr; [M]City Hall, Bras Basah) A top spot in the district for a late-night feed, this branch of the Kopitiam chain is brisk and blindingly bright, so if it's a late, boozy night grab a table outside where the light is more friendly. The food is uniformly good and you won't pay much more than $6 for a meal.

QUAYS OF THE CITY

The stretch of riverfront that separates the Colonial District from the CBD is known as the Quays. The Singapore River – once a thriving entryway for bumboats bearing cargo into the *godown* (warehouses) that lined the riverside – now connects the three quays together. A walk through the quays offers an eye-opening view to the changes that have impacted Singapore's trade through the years: from the dirt and grit of the once-filthy waterways to the gleaming steel and glass of today's financial district. To get a rundown on the area's history, visit the Asian Civilisations Museum (p43).

Boat Quay (Map p210; MRaffles Place) Closest to the former harbour, Boat Quay was once Singapore's centre of commerce, and remained an important economic area into the 1960s. By the mid-1960s, many of the shophouses were in ruins, business having shifted to high-tech cargo centres elsewhere on the island. Declared a conservation zone by the government, the area became a major entertainment district filled with colourful restaurants, bars and shops, though it has seen better days. It's on Boat Quay that you'll find riverfront restaurants serving all manner of Singaporean delicacies. Many visitors, however, find the restaurant touts a bit on the aggressive side. The streets behind the main strip are infinitely more interesting, with local restaurants and somewhat seedy bars.

Clarke Quay (Map p210; MClarke Quay) This quay, named after Singapore's second colonial governor, Sir Andrew Clarke, was, like Boat Quay, developed into a dining and shopping precinct in the early 1990s and subsequently redeveloped in the early 21st century. Its unique design has cemented its status as one of Singapore's most popular night haunts in the first decade of the 21st century. How much time you spend in Clarke Quay really depends upon your personal sense of aesthetics, for it's on this stretch of riverfront that Singapore's most whimsical designers have been given carte blanche to bring their dreams to life. Among the high (or low) lights: gumdrop railings done out in kids' paintbox colours, lilypad umbrellas straight out of a Dr Seuss colouring book, and many once-dignified shophouses now painted in too-bright shades. All this really seems moot, however, because the place is chock-a-block at night (when it's too dark to notice the garish design anyway). Clubs, bars, and restaurants jostle for the attention of punters. The best ones invariably have the longest queues.

Robertson Quay (off Map p210) At the furthest reach of the river, Robertson Quay was once used for the storage of goods. Now some of the old *godown* have been tarted up into flash members-only party places, and bars, though it's quieter and more low-key than its counterparts downriver (which is a good thing, really). You'll also find several good hotels and restaurants clustered around here.

DRINKING & NIGHTLIFE

Head to the three Quays (Clarke, Boat and Robertson) and wander along to Fullerton Bay and across to Marina Bay Sands to find some of the most up-and-coming (and priciest) clubs and watering holes in Singapore.

ZOUK
CLUB

(www.zoukclub.com; 17 Jiak Kim St; ☺Zouk & Phuture 10pm-4am Wed, Fri & Sat, Velvet Underground 9pm-3am Wed-Sat, Wine Bar 6pm-3am Tue-Sat) Twenty going on 21, Ibiza-inspired Zouk is still Singapore's hottest club. It features five bars, with the capacity to hold 2000, and a roomy dance floor with plenty of space to cut the rug – it's a world-class contender and a regular destination for globe-trotting DJs. You'll also find the alfresco **Zouk Wine Bar**, avant-garde **Phuture** and the Moroccan-inspired **Velvet Underground** hung with Keith Haring and Andy Warhol originals. Take a taxi, and be prepared to queue.

BREWERKZ
BAR

Map p210 (01-05 Riverside Point, 30 Merchant Rd; ☺noon-midnight Sun-Thu, noon-1am Fri & Sat; MClarke Quay) One of Singapore's gems, this sprawling microbrewery and restaurant offers a variety of superb beers brewed on site and varying in strength from 4.5% to 7%. The India Pale Ale is the most popular, but there's plenty to choose from. Those with adventurous palates will want to try the seasonal fruit beers (wildflower honey and dragon fruit!) and guest beers on tap. Pick up 5L or 30L kegs if you happen to want to take some home! Note: the earlier you arrive, the cheaper the beers.

LOOF
BAR

Map p208 (03-07 Odeon Towers Building, 331 North Bridge Rd; ⏲5pm-1am Sun-Thu, 5pm-3am Fri & Sat; MCity Hall) This rooftop bar gets its name from the Singlish mangling of the word 'roof'. Ambient beats soothe away the city noise, and comfy leather-clad seats are scattered around the deck...perhaps these are to blame for the mellow crowd? For privacy (and air-con), ask for one of the seven semi-enclosed seating areas. One-for-one happy hour lasts from 5pm to 8pm each weekday.

RAFFLES HOTEL
BAR

Map p208 (1 Beach Rd; ⏲10am-late; MCity Hall) Yup, it's a cliché, but still, few visit Singapore without at least stopping off for drinks at one of the several bars in the famous Raffles Hotel. **Bar & Billiard Room** features live jazz, a billiard table, and has a nice verandah for chilling out, Raj style. The courtyard **Gazebo Bar** is a tasty spot for a tipple below rattling palms. The most popular bar with tourists is the plantation-style **Long Bar** on the Arcade's second level, where you can throw peanut shells on the floor and enjoy a Singapore sling for a whopping $25... if you can stomach the terrible cover band at night.

KU DÉ TAH
BAR

Map p210 (Skypark, Marina Bay Sands North Tower, 1 Bayfront Ave; ⏲noon till late; MPromenade, Bayfront) While it's annoying that you're forced into the corner by the bar if you're only there for drinks ('Sorry sir, EMPTY seats are for those eating here'), you're still better off paying $20 for a drink than to access the heavily promoted Skypark. You get great views of Marina Bay and the city sprawl plus a drink. PS: no one will stop you from wandering down to the Skypark for some postdrink happy snaps.

BRUSSELS SPROUTS BELGIAN BEER & MUSSELS
BAR

(01-12 Robertson Quay, 80 Mohamed Sultan Rd; ⏲5pm-midnight Mon-Thu, noon-1am Fri & Sat, noon-midnight Sun) Cute restaurant bar that lays the Belgian theme on heavy with mussels, trappist ales galore and Tintin murals on the wall (the whole gang's there, down to Thompson & Thompson). Over a hundred beers on the menu.

LEVEL 33
BAR

(33-01 Marina Bay Financial Tower 1, 8 Marina Blvd; ⏲noon-midnight Sun-Thu, noon-2am Fri & Sat; MRaffles Place) In a country obsessed with unique selling points, this one takes the cake, no, keg. Laying claim to being the world's highest 'urban craft-brewery', Level 33 brews its own lager, pale ale, stout and porter. But we can live with the hyperbole as long as the views are good and the beer cold.

1 ALTITUDE
BAR

Map p210 (63rd Floor, 1 Raffles Place; ⏲6pm till late; MRaffles Place) Extreme Altitude might be a better name for this rooftop bar with the best city views, bar none (sorry, couldn't resist). Wedged across a triangle-shaped deck, the world's highest alfresco bar induces vertigo as well as crazy picture taking. Smart casual dress. If it rains, take cover downstairs at **282**. This sister bar has sports on the LCD screens and golf simulators.

LANTERN
BAR

Map p210 (Fullerton Bay Hotel, 80 Collyer Quay; ⏲8am till late; MRaffles Place) It may be lacking in height (it's dwarfed by the surrounding CBD buildings), and serves its drinks in plasticware (shame!), but it's certainly not lacking in popularity. White-collar types ring ahead to book tables for after-work drinks at this breezy bar at the top of the Fullerton Bay Hotel. The hotel sits at the edge of Marina Bay, looking directly across to Marina Bay Sands.

HARRY'S
BAR

Map p210 (www.harrys.com.sg; 28 Boat Quay; ⏲11am-1am Sun-Thu, 11am-2am Fri & Sat; MRaffles Place) The Harry's empire now spans 34 (!) bars all across Singapore. But this branch is loaded with history for those interested in financial scandals. Harry's is the one-time hangout of Barings' bank-breaker Nick Leeson. It's still a city-slickers' favourite, with the suits flocking here for happy hour until 8pm and the occasional live band. The upstairs lounge is quieter and a comfortable place to contemplate busting a bank. It has a free pool table.

NEW ASIA BAR
BAR

Map p208 (Swissôtel the Stamford, 2 Stamford Rd; entry Fri & Sat incl 1 drink $25; ◉3pm-late; Ⓜ City Hall) Save the $30 you would have spent on the Singapore Flyer and spend it on drinks here instead! The 70th floor and panoramic views help your booze go down a little easier. Come early for sundowners, and once you tire of the views, shake it on the dance floor. Smart casual dress.

PAULANER BRAUHAUS
MICROBREWERY

Map p208 (01-01 Times Square@Millenia Walk, 9 Raffles Blvd; ◉noon-1am Sun-Thu, noon-2am Fri & Sat; Ⓜ City Hall) A three-storey wood-and-brass German microbrewery bar and restaurant serving up brothy tankards of Munich lager and Munich dark brews and platters of sausage and cheese 'knacker'. There are also special seasonal brews like Salvator Beer, Mailbock Beer and Oktoberfest Beer. Beers are served in 300mL, 500mL and 1L (where's the loo?) steins.

MOLLY MALONE'S
IRISH PUB

Map p210 (53-56 Circular Rd; ◉11am-2am Tue-Sat, 11am-midnight Mon & Sun; Ⓜ Raffles Place) Well-travelled drinkers will have seen the mock-Irish interior and the genuine Irish stew and fish-and-chip menu a hundred times before, but that doesn't make it any less cosy or welcoming. It's just behind Boat Quay on Circular Rd. Make it a pint or three of Guinness, please.

PENNY BLACK
PUB

Map p210 (26/27 Boat Quay; ◉11am-1am Mon-Thu, 11am-2am Fri & Sat, 11am-midnight Sun; Ⓜ Raffles Place) Fitted out like a Victorian London pub (without the tuberculosis and dodgy gin), the Penny Black's interior was actually built in London and shipped to Singapore, so it has some claim to authenticity. Specialises in hard-to-find English ales for the swaths of expat Brits that work in the area. The upstairs bar is particularly inviting.

ARCHIPELAGO BREWERY
MICROBREWERY

Map p210 (79 Circular Rd; ◉3pm-1am Mon-Thu & Sun, 4pm-3am Fri & Sat) Asia Pacific Breweries (makers of Tiger) decided to jump on the microbrewery bandwagon with their line of yummy Asian-accented beers. This is their flagship pub on a Y-junction on mildly seedy Circular Rd.

OVER EASY
BAR

Map p210 (01-06 One Fullerton, 1 Fullerton Rd) The egg dishes on the menu aren't anything to shout about, but the drinks are easily done over, given the stunning Marina Bay views and 'one-for-one' happy-hour specials (6pm to 8pm).

EM BY THE RIVER
BAR

(01-05, 1 Nanson Rd; ☒51, 64, 123, 186) The outdoor riverside setting at Robertson Quay guarantees a quiet chill-out spot for drinks. Find a spot under one of the trees and settle in. An understaffed crew means that you might need to yell, scream or dance to get service.

HOME CLUB
CLUB

Map p210 (www.homeclub.com.sg; B1-01/06 The Riverwalk, 20 Upper Circular Rd; ◉6pm-2am Mon-Thu, 6pm-late Fri & Sat; Ⓜ Clarke Quay) Set right by the Singapore River in between Boat and Clarke Quays, this thumping venue features DJs spinning house, dubstep, drum and bass, and a wide variety of live rock and pop bands. Comedy nights on Tuesdays are a hoot!

BUTTER FACTORY
CLUB

Map p210 (www.thebutterfactory.com; 02-02 One Fullerton, 1 Fullerton Rd; admission incl 2 drinks from $21; ◉10pm-4am Wed, Fri & Sat) At 8000 sq ft, Butter Factory's as slick as it is huge. Street art on the walls of Bump, the hip hop and rhythm and blues room, betrays its young and overdressed crowd. Fash is its chilled-out 'art' bar, and walls are plastered with colourful pop-art reminiscent of underground comics (yes, the ones you hid from mum).

ZIRCA MEGA CLUB
CLUB

Map p210 (www.zirca.sg; 01-02 Block 3C River Valley Rd, The Cannery, Clarke Quay; admission incl 2 drinks men $16-30, women $16-28; ◉9.30pm-late Wed-Sat; Ⓜ Clarke Quay) The lines out the door don't seem to faze the gorgeous young things trying to get into Zirca. Mash with the mainly twenty-somethings under pulsating lights in Zirca (dance club) or Rebel (hip-hop arena).

ATTICA
CLUB

Map p210 (www.attica.com.sg; 3A River Valley Rd, 01-03 Clarke Quay; ◉5pm-3am Mon-Thu, 11pm-late Fri & Sat; Ⓜ Clarke Quay) One of the swankest clubs in town, Attica is where the

ORGANISED TOURS

Singapore is easy for self-navigation, but there are a number of worthwhile tours that can open up the city and its history, or simply offer a unique experience. Recommended:

Culinary Heritage Tour (☎6238 8488; www.eastwestplanners.com) These tailor-made tours are a good way of sampling the most famous dishes with someone showing you the best places to eat them. Aimed at the more affluent visitor. Prices and itineraries are available on request.

Imperial Cheng Ho Dinner Cruise (☎6533 9811; www.watertours.com.sg; adult/child daytime cruises $27/14, dinner cruises $55/29) Three daily tours on a replica Chinese junk picks its way from Marina South out to Sentosa or Kusu Island. The food is nothing spectacular, but the views are.

Original Singapore Walks (☎6325 1631; www.singaporewalks.com; adult/child from $30/15) Led by informed, enthusiastic guides, these walks through various parts of the city – including Chinatown, Little India and the Quays – provide a fascinating insight into Singapore's past, including the down-and-dirty stuff you won't hear about anywhere else. The WWII tour is excellent, too. No booking necessary, just check the website for meeting times and places, then turn up. Deals online.

Singapore Duck Tours (☎6333 3825; www.ducktours.com.sg; adult/child $33/17) A city tour so hokey you'll never forget it. Jump into a brighly coloured amphibious vehicle playing a tinny soundtrack, before plunging into the Marina Bay.

Singapore Nature Walks (☎6787 7048; serin@swiftech.com.sg) Singapore's natural assets are often overlooked and hard to find, but freelance guide Subaraj has a passion for nature and an intimate knowledge of the island's pockets of wilderness.

River Cruises

They're over quickly, but the bumboat cruises that ply the stretch between the Quays and Marina Bay are a pleasant way of soaking up some history. Festooned with Chinese lanterns, they are best taken at night, when they make a romantic pre-dinner excursion. Cruises depart from several places along the Singapore River including Clarke Quay, Raffles Landing and Boat Quay. They generally run between 8.30am and 10.30pm.

Singapore River cruise operators include the following:

City Hippo (☎6338 6877; www.ducktours.com.sg; tours from $15)

Singapore River Cruises (☎6336 6111; www.rivercruise.com.sg; tours from $15)

COLONIAL DISTRICT, MARINA BAY & THE QUAYS DRINKING & NIGHTLIFE

bold and beautiful meet to dazzle and be dazzled. When it gets too hot inside, cool down in the chic courtyard and ogle the eye candy. There's usually a line to get in, always a sign of pedigree in Singapore's club world.

CRAZY ELEPHANT BAR, LIVE MUSIC
Map p210 (www.crazyelephant.com; 01-03/04 Clarke Quay; ⏱5pm-1am Sun-Thu, 3pm-2am Fri & Sat; ⓂClarke Quay) Anywhere that bills itself as 'crazy' should set the alarm bells ringing, but you won't hear them once you're inside. This touristy rock bar is beery, blokey, loud, graffiti covered and testosterone heavy – rock on!

TIMBRE@SUBSTATION BAR, LIVE MUSIC
Map p208 (www.timbre.com.sg; 45 Armenian St; ⓂCity Hall) Young ones are content to queue for seats at this popular live-music venue. The food is of the lazy fried variety, but a daily rotating roster of local musicians keeps things interesting and the crowds distracted.

SOHO COFFEE CAFE
Map p208 (36 Armenian St; ⏱8am-6pm Mon-Fri, 9am-6pm Sat & Sun; ⓂCity Hall) Perfectly poised location in a central but quiet part of the colonial district. Soho Coffee does yummy burgers and superb coffees. It also operates also a coffee and sandwich bar in the Cheers convenience store round the corner at 61 Stamford Ct.

☆ ENTERTAINMENT

MICA BUILDING
GALLERIES

Map p210 (140 Hill St; MClarke Quay) Among the several galleries in the brightly coloured colonial MITA Building is **Art-2 Gallery** (www.art2.com.sg) and **Gajah Gallery** (www.gajahgallery.com), which both specialise in contemporary Southeast Asian work. **Soobin Art Gallery** (www.soobinart.com.sg) displays a lot of work from the region, plus avant-garde artists from China.

ESPLANADE – THEATRES ON THE BAY
THEATRE

Map p210 (☑6828 8377; www.esplanade.com; 1 Esplanade Dr; MCity Hall, Esplanade) The 1800-seater state-of-the-art concert hall at the Esplanade – Theatres on the Bay is the home of the highly respected Singapore Symphony Orchestra (SSO), but it also plays host to scores of music, theatre and dance performances. Check out their regularly updated website, especially for information on upcoming free shows and other programs.

MARINA BAY SANDS
THEATRE, CASINO

Map p210 (www.marinabaysands.com; 10 Bayfront Ave; MPromenade) While this complex makes most of its money from the casino ($100 entry for Singaporeans!), the **theatre** is worth visiting for its Broadway favourites. The **Artscience Museum** (admission $25) has interesting exhibitions, but the value you get from the entry fee is questionable. There's even an indoor **ice-skating rink**.

ACTION THEATRE
THEATRE

Map p208 (☑6837 0842; www.action.org.sg; 42 Waterloo St; MBras Basah) Set in a two-storey heritage house, this established theatre group shows local and international plays with contemporary themes in its small, 100-seat upstairs theatre and in the two open-air venues.

SINGAPORE REPERTORY THEATRE
THEATRE

(☑6733 8166; www.srt.com.sg; DBS Arts Centre, 20 Merbau Rd; MClarke Quay) Based at the DBS Arts Centre, but also performing at other venues, this theatre group offers up repertory standards such as works by Shakespeare, Tennessee Williams and Arthur Miller, as well as some modern Singaporean plays. Recent coups include bringing in Sam Mendes' *Richard III* staring Kevin Spacey.

THEATREWORKS
THEATRE

Map p208 (☑6737 7213; www.theatreworks.org.sg; 72-13 Mohamed Sultan Rd; MClarke Quay) This is one of the more experimental and interesting theatre companies in Singapore, led by enigmatic artistic director Ong Keng Sen. Performances are now housed in their headquarters. Check the website for details.

SINGAPORE DANCE THEATRE
DANCE

Map p208 (☑6338 0611; www.singaporedancetheatre.com; 2nd fl, Fort Canning Centre, Cox Tce; MDhoby Ghaut) This top dance company performs traditional ballets and contemporary works. The group's Ballet under the Stars season at Fort Canning Park is very popular. There are regular ballet and pilates classes conducted on site.

WILLOWSTREAM SPA
SPA

Map p208 (☑6339 7777; www.willowstream.com; Fairmont Hotel, 80 Bras Basah Rd; MCity Hall) This massive spa is a temple for the body. Think jacuzzis, plunge pools, rooms that puff aromatic steam and staff that will slather good stuff on your face before pushing, prodding and kneading the kinks out of your jetlagged body. An inhouse salon will style your hair, wax you, and give pedicures and manicures.

ULTIMATE DRIVE
CAR RIDE

Map p210 (☑6688 7997; www.ultimatedrive.com; Marina Bay Sands Hotel Tower 3, 1 Bayfront Avenue; rides from $128-388; MPromenade, Bayfront) Dress to kill, then make a show of getting into a Ferrari F430 (red!) or Lamborghini Gallardo (yellow!) before tearing out for a spin. A taste of luxury can be yours, if only for 12 to 30 minutes. One can dream, right?

G-MAX REVERSE BUNGY
THRILL RIDE

Map p210 (www.gmax.com.sg; 3E River Valley Rd; per ride $45; ☺3pm-late Mon-Fri, noon-late Sat & Sun; MClarke Quay) You and two other thrillseekers will be strapped into padded chairs enclosed inside a metal cage, which is propelled skyward to a height of 60m at speeds exceeding 200km/h before being pulled back down by gravity. Though the ride offers spectacular views to those who can keep their eyes open, it's best avoided by people prone to velocity-induced vomiting.

THE CHANGING FACE OF SINGAPORE

'Seriously, folks, I love Singapore. I can't wait to see what it looks like when they finish building it.'

With that line, Singapore-based comedian Jonathan Atherton describes succinctly the endless drive for expansion that in Singapore borders on mania. The area just southwest of the CBD, known as Marina Bay, once a mere gleam in the eyes of city planners, now sits as a shining example of land reclamation, boasting wide, palm-lined boulevards ringed with high-class condominiums, bars and restaurants and the Marina Bay Sands integrated resort. What's next?

The government embarked on creating a huge 101-hectare garden just across from it. **Gardens by Bay** (www.gardensbythebay.org.sg) will be Singapore's third botanic gardens (after Fort Canning and the Botanic Gardens at the end of Orchard Rd). It will have state-of-the-art greenhouses, large structures powered by solar energy and, of course, loads of flora. ETA for completion is 2012. It will essentially connect up the colonial district to the Marina Bay Sands and across to the Marina Barrage. Talk about civic planning!

That's not the end of it. The old Supreme Court and City Hall along St Andrew's Rd are being gutted and converted to Singapore's next major **National Art Gallery** (www.nationalartgallery.sg, not to be confused with the Singapore Art Museum) due to open in 2015. The collection will focus on 19th- and 20th-century Southeast Asian art. Next door, the Victoria Concert Hall is being glammed up for a reopening in 2013.

GX5
THRILL RIDE

Map p210 (☑6338 1146; www.gmax.com.sg; 3E River Valley Rd; per ride $45; ⊗3pm-late Mon-Fri, noon-late Sat & Sun; ⓂClarke Quay) A relatively gentle high ('relatively' is the key here) is offered right next door to the G-Max Bungy. Whereas the G-Max offers a straight-up face-peeling vertical trip, the GX5 swings riders up and over the Singapore River with somewhat less nauseating velocity. The trip also lasts longer, though which one provides more bang for your buck is a matter of personal choice.

 SHOPPING

The cluster of protected architecture around the Colonial District means it has been spared the consumerist blitzkrieg that consumed Orchard Rd, but the area still has its fancy malls.

RAFFLES CITY
MALL

Map p208 (www.rafflescity.com; 252 North Bridge Rd; ⓂCity Hall) The name and the soaring atrium give the impression of expensive exclusivity, but Raffles City is one of Singapore's best malls. There's a three-level branch of the excellent **Robinsons** department store, global fashion brands such as

Topshop, a top floor specialising in children's clothes and toys, the **Ode to Art** gallery, a clutch of handbag boutiques on the ground floor, plus a top-floor food court and a massive amount of basement restaurants.

RAFFLES HOTEL ARCADE
MALL

Map p208 (328 North Bridge Rd; ⓂCity Hall) Part of the hotel complex, stylish Raffles Hotel Arcade is firmly upmarket, with designer clothes and accessories, watchmakers, galleries, wine sellers and similarly refined places gently tempting you into credit-card wantonness. **Chan Hampe** and **Artfolio** galleries are worth a peek for local art, and **Elliot's Antiques** has exquisite pieces. Even if you can't afford its cameras, the **Leica Store** might have an exhibition worth seeing.

MARINA BAY SANDS
MALL

Map p210 (www.marinabaysands.com; 10 Bayfront Ave; ⓂPromenade, Bayfront) If you want a totally un-Singaporean shopping experience, drop by the 'Shoppes' at Marina Bay Sands. Most people visiting cloister themselves in the dungeonlike casinos, leaving the shopping mall empty, which is great because you'll have top brands all to yourself. A massive Louis Vuitton store, set on a floating island in the Bay, was set to open at time of writing.

CITYLINK MALL
MALL

Map p208 (1 Raffles Link; MCity Hall) The first underground mall in Singapore, designed by Kohn Pederson Fox from New York, this seemingly endless tunnel of retail links City Hall MRT station with Suntec City and the Esplanade. It's a tempting means of escaping searing sun or teeming rain, and a comfortable way of getting into the city from the Marina Bay hotels. It may be a bit disorienting, but there's a full range of fashion and food down here.

SUNTEC CITY
MALL

Map p208 (www.sunteccitymall.com; 3 Temasek Blvd; MPromenade, Esplanade) Vast and bewildering, and often frustratingly inaccessible, Suntec has everything under the sun, plus 60 restaurants, cafes and several food courts. One of the biggest crowd-pullers is the **Fountain of Wealth**, which was once accorded the status of World's Largest Fountain (though not, you'll observe, Most Attractive) in the *Guinness Book of Records*. Scan the media for one of Suntec's regular themed 'fairs', where you can pick up substantially discounted items such as cameras, electronics and computer gear.

MARINA SQUARE
MALL

Map p208 (www.marinasquare.com.sg; 6 Raffles Blvd; MEsplanade) Some 225 outlets, including loads of high-street brands, are packed into this massive shopping space. Centrally located in the Marina Centre area, it has easy access to and from CityLink Mall, Suntec City, Millenia Walk and the Esplanade.

MILLENIA WALK
MALL, FASHION

Map p208 (www.milleniawalk.com.sg; 9 Raffles Blvd; MPromenade) Small, often neglected mall sandwiched between Marina Square and Suntec City that is worth visiting for **Parco Next Next**. Japanese retail giant Parco supports local designers by giving them mentorship and reduced rents.

FUNAN DIGITALIFE MALL
COMPUTERS, ELECTRONICS

Map p208 (109 North Bridge Rd; MCity Hall) Hardware yourself across six floors of electronics, camera and computer stores. Funan is a better bet than Sim Lim Square if you don't know exactly what you're doing. Occupying the 6th floor, you can find almost anything at the massive **Challenger** Superstore. It's open 24 hours in case you need to buy an iPad at 3am. For cameras, visit family run **John 3:16** (05-46).

GRANNY'S DAY OUT
FASHION

Map p208 (www.grannysdayout.com; 03-25 Peninsula Shopping Centre, 3 Coleman St; ☺1-8pm Mon-Sat, 1.30-6.30pm Sun; MCity Hall) Great, ever-changing selection of vintage clothes, shoes and accessories from the '60s to the '80s. Sorry guys, unless you're into crossdressing, 90% of the stuff here is for women only.

PENINSULA SHOPPING CENTRE
MALL, CAMERAS

Map p208 (3 Coleman St; MCity Hall) The shopping centre that props up the Peninsula Excelsior Hotel has seen better days, but it's one of the best hunting grounds in Singapore for sporting goods and second-hand camera gear. Among the tennis rackets, bowling balls and football shirts are also plenty of unexpected and eccentric shops, from guitar repairmen to designer sneakers. The ground floor has several shops stocking all sorts of quality camera equipment, including Leicas.

PENINSULA PLAZA
MALL, CAMERAS

Map p208 (111 North Bridge Rd; MCity Hall) This place is almost 'little Burma', with floors crammed with Burmese grocery stores, and hole-in-the-wall Burmese eateries. There are moneychangers here, and Singapore's best-stocked camera store (though not necessarily the cheapest), **Cathay Photo**, is on the ground floor. Next door are several stores with displays packed with second-hand camera gear.

ROYAL SELANGOR
GIFTS

Map p210 (✆6268 9600; 01-01 Clarke Quay; www.royalselangor.com.sg; MClarke Quay) Malaysia's pewter specialists aren't high on the hip list – think the kind of personalised tankards your uncle uses for his real ale – but don't discount their jewellery, some items of which might even suit painfully fashionable teens. The best bit is the School of Hard Knocks (SOHN), at which groups of 12 bash pewter into malleable masterpieces. Thirty-minute courses cost $30; you get to keep the inscribed dish you make and your natty SOHN apron.

Chinatown & the CBD

Neighbourhood Top Five

1 Visit the fascinating **Chinatown Heritage Centre** (p57) and discover the unspeakable hardships that had to be endured by the immigrants who gave this part of town its name.

2 Meet the stars of the show in the unusually informal **Chinese Theatre Circle** (p63).

3 Skip the free brekkie at your hotel and head to **Ya Kun Kaya Toast** (p58) for a traditional Singaporean breakfast.

4 Share a lunchtime table with a stranger at the ever-popular **Maxwell Rd Hawker Centre** (p60).

5 Swank it up with Champagne cocktails at pretty much any bar on uberchic Ann Siang Hill. **Beaujolais** (p61) is one of our favourites.

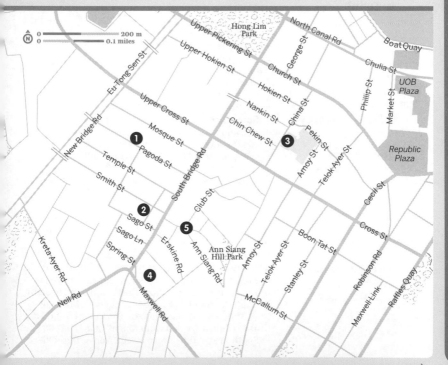

For more detail of this area, see Map p201

Lonely Planet's Top Tip

As with anywhere in Singapore, it's worth taking advantage of happy hours (usually until 9pm) at the fancy bars around Chinatown. If that's still too pricey for you, have a few beers at a hawker centre instead.

 Best Places to Eat

➡ Maxwell Rd Hawker Centre (p60)

➡ Blue Ginger (p58)

➡ Cumi Bali (p58)

➡ Lau Pa Sat (p60)

➡ Ya Kun Kaya Toast (p58)

➡ Dim Joy (p58)

For reviews, see p58 ➡

 Best Places to Drink

➡ Beaujolais (p61)

➡ Screening Room (p61)

➡ Nanyang Old Coffee (p60)

➡ Tantric Bar (p62)

➡ Maxwell Rd Hawker Centre (p60)

For reviews, see p61 ➡

Best Places for History & Culture

➡ Chinatown Heritage Centre (p57)

➡ Baba House (p57)

➡ Sri Mariamman Temple (p57)

For reviews, see p57 ➡

Explore Chinatown

With the possible exception of the Chinatown Heritage Centre, sights here are interesting rather than must-see, but that's a good thing. It leaves more time for visitors to focus on Chinatown's star attraction – food. Start early with a traditional Singaporean breakfast in a *kopitiam* (coffeeshop). For lunch join the crowds at one of Chinatown's bustling hawker centres. Come evening take your pick of fine restaurants from a huge variety of national cuisines (it's not just Chinese food in Chinatown, you know).

In between meals, poke your head into an antiques shop here or an art gallery there as you wander past beautifully renovated shophouses in the gentrified streets to the southwest (Duxton Hill area) and southeast (Ann Siang Rd area) of Chinatown's touristy heartland (the lanes fanning off Trengganu St).

Once the sun's gone down, unwind with a cocktail in one of Ann Siang Rd's rooftop bars or grab a cheap beer at a street-side stall.

Local Life

➡ **Hawker Centres** It's a wonder how any of Singapore's expensive restaurants stay in business because the cheap food at hawker centres is so goddamn good. Chinatown is no exception. Eat at as many hawker centres as you can while you're here, but if you've only time for one, make it Maxwell Rd (p60).

➡ **Coffee versus kopi** Fresh-ground Western-style coffee can be found across Chinatown – head to any swank bar or cafe around Ann Siang Rd or Duxton Hill – but locals prefer *kopi* (pronounced 'koh-pee') at a traditional *kopitiam*. Try Nanyang Old Coffee (p60), but read our *kopi* primer (p61) before you go.

➡ **Souvenirs** Skip the tourist tat in the lanes around Trengganu St and hunt down an antiques shop or a local art gallery for a souvenir with a difference. Our favourite is Tong Mern Sern Antiques (p64).

Getting There & Away

➡ **MRT** Not surprisingly the heart of Chinatown is served by Chinatown MRT station, which spits you out onto Pagoda St. Outram Park station is better for the Duxton Hill area, while Tanjong Pagar is a handy third alternative. Raffles Place is the station for the CBD.

➡ **Bus** From the Colonial District, hop on bus 61, 145 or 166, which takes you from North Bridge Rd to South Bridge Rd. From Hill St, buses 2, 12 and 147 run down New Bridge Rd. It's easy to walk from the river and the CBD to Chinatown, but from Raffles Quay, bus 608 goes to South Bridge Rd, or take bus C2 from Clifford Pier.

👁 SIGHTS

CHINATOWN HERITAGE CENTRE MUSEUM
Map p201 (www.chinatownheritagecentre.com.sg; 48 Pagoda St; adult/child $10/6; ⊘9am-8pm; MChinatown) An engaging museum housed across three floors of a converted shophouse, the Chinatown Heritage Centre focuses on the squalid living conditions that many Chinese immigrants once endured. Re-created kitchens, bedrooms and workshops are crammed with interesting artefacts from back in the day, and some of the old videos and recorded interviews that accompany displays can be quite moving.

BUDDHA TOOTH RELIC
TEMPLE BUDDHIST TEMPLE
Map p201 (www.btrts.org.sg; 288 South Bridge Rd; ⊘7am-7pm; MChinatown) This huge, eye-catching, five-storey, southern Chinese-style Buddhist temple was opened to great fanfare in 2008. Its main drawcard is what is reputed to be the left canine tooth of the Buddha, recovered from his funeral pyre in Kushinagar, in northern India. Its authenticity is put into question by similar claims from Buddha tooth relic temples in Sri Lanka, China, Japan and Taiwan. Nevertheless, the temple remains popular with tourists and devotees alike. The tooth is encased in a gold stupa, placed five metres behind a protective glass wall so you can't actually recognise it's a tooth without viewing it through binoculars. What? You didn't bring your binoculars?

SRI MARIAMMAN TEMPLE HINDU TEMPLE
Map p201 (244 South Bridge Rd; MChinatown) Paradoxically in the middle of Chinatown, this is the oldest Hindu temple in Singapore, originally built in 1823, then rebuilt in 1843. You can't miss the incredible, brightly coloured 1930s *gopuram* (tower) above the entrance, the key to the temple's South Indian Dravidian style. Sacred cow sculptures graze the boundary walls, while the *gopuram* is covered in kitsch plasterwork images of Brahma the creator, Vishnu the preserver and Shiva the destroyer.

Every October, the temple hosts the Thimithi festival; devotees queue along South Bridge Rd to hotfoot it over burning coals!

THIAN HOCK KENG TEMPLE TAOIST TEMPLE
Map p201 (www.thianhockkeng.com.sg; 158 Telok Ayer St; MRaffles Place, Chinatown) Its name translates as Temple of Heavenly Happiness and it's the oldest and most important Hokkien temple in Singapore. It was built between 1839 and 1842 on the site of the shrine to the goddess of the sea (Ma Cho Po), which was once the favourite landing point of Chinese sailors, back when Telok Ayer St ran along the shore line. All the materials came from China except the gates (from Scotland) and the tiles (from Holland). The temple was restored in 2000.

FREE SINGAPORE CITY GALLERY MUSEUM
Map p201 (www.ura.gov.sg/gallery; URA Bldg, 45 Maxwell Rd; ⊘9am-5pm Mon-Sat; MTanjong Pagar) This city-planning exhibition gallery provides a compelling insight into the government's resolute policies of high-rise housing and land reclamation. The highlight is an 11m-by-11m scale model of the city, which shows how Singapore should look once all the projects currently under development are finished.

CHINATOWN & THE CBD SIGHTS

WORTH A DETOUR

BABA HOUSE
....
A short walk west of Chinatown, along Neil Rd, is **Baba House** (off Map p201; ☏6227 5731; http://nus.edu.sg/museum/baba; 157 Neil Rd; admission free; ⊘2-3.30pm Mon, 10-11.30am Thu; MOutram Park), one of the best-preserved Peranakan heritage homes found anywhere in Singapore. This beautiful blue three-storey building was donated to the National University of Singapore (NUS) by a member of the family that used to live here. The NUS then set about renovating it so that it best matched how it would have looked in 1928, when, according to the family, Baba House was at its most resplendent. Period furniture has been added to original family photos and artefacts to create a wonderful window into the life of a wealthy Peranakan family living in Singapore a century ago. Baba House can only be visited on a 90-minute guided tour, held every Monday and Thursday, but the tour is excellent and costs absolutely nothing. Bookings, either online or by telephone, are essential as numbers for each tour are limited.

WAK HAI CHENG BIO TEMPLE TAOIST TEMPLE

Map p201 (cnr Phillip & Church Sts; ⓂRaffles Place) On the CBD edge of Chinatown, this small temple, whose name translates as Calm Sea Temple, dates from 1826. It's an atmospheric place, with giant incense coils smoking over its empty courtyard, and a whole village of tiny plaster figures populating its roof.

SENG WONG BEO TEMPLE TAOIST TEMPLE

Map p201 (113 Peck Seah St; ⓂTanjong Pagar) Tucked behind red gates next to the Tanjong Pagar MRT station, this temple, seldom visited by tourists, is dedicated to the Chinese City God, who is not only responsible for the well-being of the city but also for guiding the souls of the dead to the underworld. It's also notable as the only temple in Singapore that still performs ghost marriages, helping parents of children who died young to arrange a marriage for their child in the afterlife.

EATING

TOP CHOICE BLUE GINGER PERANAKAN $$

Map p201 (☎6222 3928; www.theblueginger.com; 97 Tanjong Pagar Rd; mains $10-30; ◷noon-2.15pm & 6.30-9.45pm; ⓂTanjong Pagar) Housed in an attractive shophouse, Blue Ginger is one of the few restaurants in Singapore that specialises in Peranakan food, a unique cuisine that developed in the 1800s thanks to interracial marriages between Chinese immigrants and local Malay women. You'll also find Indonesian influences in some of the dishes, such as the coconut milk used for the restaurant's mouth-watering grilled-chicken speciality *ayum panggang*. Bookings recommended.

TOP CHOICE CUMI BALI INDONESIAN $$

Map p201 (66 Tanjong Pagar Rd; mains $6-18; ◷11.30am-3pm & 6-9.30pm Mon-Sat; ⓂTanjong Pagar) Authentic Indonesian cuisine served up in unpretentious surroundings. Cumi Bali is named after its speciality squid dish, and it's as 'lickin' good' as the menu says it is. Also well worth trying is the mouth-watering *ikan bakar* (fish grilled in 18 different spices), the *sayur lodeh* (a coconut-flavoured vegetable curry), the *tahu telur* (a slightly spicy tofu and egg dish) and the *sate madura* (a Javanese-style chicken satay).

YA KUN KAYA TOAST COFFEESHOP $

Map p201 (01-01 Far East Sq, 18 China St; ◷7.30am-7pm Mon-Fri, 8.30am-5.30pm Sat & Sun; toast sets from $3.70; kopi from $1.30; ⓂChinatown, Raffles Place) A chain of Ya Kun outlets has mushroomed across Singapore, but this one, with terrace seating alongside it, is by far the most atmospheric and is the closest geographically to the 1944 original. Perfect for breakfast, the speciality is *kaya* (coconut jam) toast served with runny eggs (sprinkle them with black pepper like the locals do) and strong *kopi* (coffee).

DIM JOY DIM SUM $$

Map p201 (80 Neil Rd; dim sum $3-7, mains $6-9; ◷11am-2.30pm & 6-9.30pm Wed-Mon, closed Tue; ⓂChinatown) Delicious dim sum in a refined environment. Sit in the front courtyard or lap up the air-con inside. As well as dim sum, there's a small choice of noodle and rice dishes, a selection of Chinese teas and even some European wines. OK, so it's posh dim sum. But it's damn good.

CI YAN ORGANIC VEGETARIAN HEALTH FOOD VEGETARIAN $

Map p201 (8 Smith St; mains $5-8; ◷noon-10pm; ⓂChinatown) Excellent food, a very friendly manager and an informal atmosphere make this a fine choice for a no-fuss vegetarian meal in the heart of Chinatown. They tend to only have five or six dishes (when we ate here choices ranged from the delicious brown-rice set meal to wholemeal hamburgers, vegetarian Penang laksa and almond tofu), written up on a blackboard each day. They also have an interesting range of fruit drinks.

L'ANGELUS FRENCH $$$

Map p201 (☎6225 6897; 85 Club St; mains from $40; ◷midday-3pm & 7-11pm Mon-Fri, 7-11pm Sat; ⓂChinatown) Cosy, friendly, traditional French restaurant run by a couple of attentive French expats, who also run the excellent bar Le Carillon de L'Angelus, further up on Ann Siang Rd. The escargot are a speciality, but we like the cassoulet, an incredibly filling, hearty bean and meat stew. Bookings recommended.

LAN ZHOU LA MIAN CHINESE $

Map p201 (19 Smith St; mains $5; ◷noon-11pm; ⓂChinatown) They do rice dishes and dumplings here too, but this place is all about the noodles, pulled to perfection (sometimes at your table as you watch) and cooked with

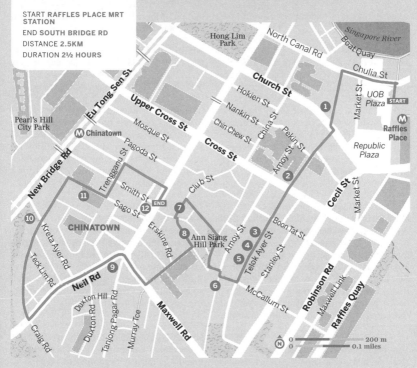

Neighbourhood Walk

Chinatown

Emerge from Raffles Place MRT station and head west along Chulia St then south down Phillip St to the ❶ **Wak Hai Cheng Bio Temple**. Cross over Church St to Telok Ayer St until you reach ❷ **Ying Fo Fui Kun**, a two-storey building established in 1822 for the Ying Fo Clan Association, which services Hakka Chinese.

At the junction with Boon Tat St is the ❸ **Nagore Durgha Shrine**, a mosque built between 1828 and 1830 by Chulia Muslims from South India. A little further on is the beautifully restored ❹ **Thian Hock Keng Temple** and the ❺ **Al-Abrar Mosque**, built in the 1850s.

Turn right into Amoy St where at No 66 you'll see the ❻ **Siang Cho Keong Temple** (1869). Left of the entrance is a small 'dragon well' into which you can drop a coin and make a wish. Close to the temple, you'll see a small archway marked Ann Siang Hill Park. Go through here, then follow the walkways upwards to what is Chinatown's highest point, before walking

down the other side to ❼ **Club St**, with its highly decorated terraces. Continue round the corner onto ❽ **Ann Siang Rd**. Some of the terraces here once housed Chinese guilds and clubs – note the art deco buildings at Nos 15, 17 and 21.

Work your way down to Maxwell Rd, passing the famous hawker centre of the same name. On the corner of Neil Rd and Tanjong Pagar Rd is the triangular ❾ **Jinriksha station**, once the depot for hand-pulled rickshaws. Walk along Neil Rd to Keong Saik Rd, a curving street of old terraces, clan houses, clubs and boutique hotels. At the junction with Kreta Ayer Rd is the small Hindu ❿ **Layar Sithi Vinyagar Temple**, built in 1925 with the five-tier *gopuram* over the entrance added in 2007.

Continuing along Keong Siak Rd, you'll soon hit the back of the ⑪ **Chinatown Complex**, where you can stop for a cheap bite to eat or carry on, through the market lanes, to ⑫ **Nanyang Old Coffee** for a cup of traditional Singaporean *kopi*.

a variety of soups and sauces. Good honest affordable nosh.

ANNALAKSHMI JANATHA   INDIAN VEGETARIAN **$**
Map p201 (www.annalakshmi.com.sg; 104 Amoy St; ⊗11am-3pm Mon-Sat; ⓂTanjong Pagar) This Indian eatery is an institution in more ways than one: first, because of the outstanding quality of the vegetarian food, served up buffet style; second, because it's a charity organisation staffed by volunteers. Eat your fill, then pay what you think it deserves at the cashier – $5 to $10 tends to be an appropriate amount.

NANYANG OLD COFFEE   COFFEESHOP **$**
Map p201 (www.nanyangoldcoffee.com; 268 South Bridge Rd; toast sets $3.50, kopi from $1.10; ⊗7.30am-6pm; ⓂChinatown) Along with nearby Ya Kun Kaya Toast, this is a smart choice for a traditional Singaporean breakfast of *kaya* toast, runny eggs and strong *kopi*. Sit outside in the breezy five-foot way or indoors where you'll also find a collection of coffee paraphernalia, rather optimistically marketed as the Singapore Coffee Museum.

L'ENTRECOTE   FRENCH **$$$**
Map p201 (www.lentrecote.sg; 36 Duxton Hill; steak & chips $29; ⊗noon-10.30pm Mon-Fri, 6-10.30pm Sat; ⓂTanjong Pagar) This place only does one dish – steak and chips – but it does it very well indeed, so if you're pining for a slice of French bistro action you could do a lot worse than trek up to this lovely cobblestoned section of Duxton Hill. There's a choice of starters and desserts and, as you would expect, an excellent selection of French wines to wash it all down with. Bookings recommended.

SPRING JU CHUN YUAN   CHINESE **$$$**
Map p201 (✆6536 2655; www.juchunyuan.com.sg; 130 Amoy St, 01-01 Far East Sq; mains $20-60; ⊗11.30am-2.30pm & 6-10pm; ⓂRaffles Place) In terms of atmosphere, this must be the most irresistibly romantic Chinese restaurant in Singapore. Done up like a 19th-century house, it specialises in Fuzhou classics like Buddha Jumps Over The Wall. It's pricy, for sure (the shark's fin stew will set you back more than $1000!), but worth a visit for a special occasion (we recommend you book).

YANTI NASI PADANG   INDONESIAN **$**
Map p201 (45 Keong Saik Rd; mains from $5; ⊗8am-10pm; ⓂOutram Park) Sit on wicker chairs in the five-foot way, overlooking the street, or inside under the fans as you tuck in to fabulously affordable curries from Indonesia, Sumatra specifically. It's buffet-style point-and-choose ordering, and extremely popular at lunchtimes.

SPIZZA   PIZZA **$$**
Map p201 (✆6224 2525; 29 Club St; pizzas $17-21; ⓂChinatown) Easygoing, friendly pizzeria – one of the most relaxed options on Club St. The wood-fired thin-crust pizzas are perfect, not too heavy on the toppings – and unlike many pizzerias in Singapore they're happy to load on the anchovies if you ask nicely. Deservedly popular, and they do take-out.

TOP HAWKER CENTRES IN & AROUND CHINATOWN

If you're new to Singapore, brush up on your Hawker Centre etiquette (p169) then head to one of the following venues for a cheap and cheerful dining experience you won't forget in a hurry. Expect to pay around $3 to $5 for a main dish.

Maxwell Rd Hawker Centre (Map p201; cnr South Bridge & Maxwell Rds; ⊗24hr; ⓂChinatown) One of Singapore's iconic hawker centres, Maxwell Rd is best viewed at lunchtime, when it's heaving with people. Its most famous resident is the **Tian Tian** chicken rice stall (No 10), but there are loads of great stalls here.

Lau Pa Sat (Map p201; 18 Raffles Quay; ⊗24hr; ⓂRaffles Place) *Lau pa sat* means 'old market' in Hokkien, which is appropriate since the handsome iron structure shipped out from Glasgow in 1894 remains intact. Cynics complain that a recent renovation sapped some of the 'old Asia' atmosphere, but we still love this place. Don't miss the very handy sign outside with its list of 10 must-try dishes.

Chinatown Complex (Map p201; 11 New Bridge Rd; ⊗8am-9.30pm; ⓂChinatown) Leave the Smith St evening food market to the tourists and join the locals for some Hainanese chicken rice at this no-nonsense hawker centre in the middle of Chinatown.

LOCAL KNOWLEDGE

ORDERING TRUE SINGAPOREAN COFFEE

A visit to a *kopitiam* (coffeeshop) to sample a thick-rimmed cup of *kopi* (coffee) – pronounced 'koh-pee' – is an essential part of the Singapore experience. Coffee enjoyed by the locals here differs slightly from the type of coffee you'll be used to back home. The key to the taste is the way the beans are prepared. Roasted with sugar and margarine, local coffee is dark, strong and retains the smooth caramel and butter character of its roasting companions. *Kopi* is either drunk black or mixed with condensed or evaporated milk. When it comes to ordering, there's a bit of a code involved, so to help you get your head round the terminology, try this *kopi* primer. Note that these terms can also be applied to *teh* (tea).

Kopi Coffee with condensed milk. No sugar, but the condensed milk makes it sweet.

Kopi-O Black coffee with sugar.

Kopi-O kosong Black coffee without sugar (*kosong* is Malay for nothing or zero).

Kopi-C Coffee with evaporated milk and sugar (the C is for Carnation, a popular evaporated milk brand).

Kopi-C kosong Coffee with evaporated milk, but no sugar.

Kopi peng Iced coffee with condensed milk.

Kopi gao Literally, 'thick' coffee (think double espresso).

Kopi poh A 'light' coffee.

TONG HENG
PASTRIES $

Map p201 (285 South Bridge Rd; snacks from $1; ⏰9am-10pm; ⓂChinatown) A pocket-sized pastry shop that's been in business for around 70 years. Specialises in pastries, tarts and cakes from the southern Chinese province of Guangdong. The egg tarts are particularly delicious.

KIM JOO GUAN
SNACKS $

Map p201 (257 South Bridge Rd; www.kimjooguan.com; ⏰9am-8pm; ⓂChinatown) This small, cold-meat outlet specialises in barbecued pork slices – a delicacy brought over with immigrants from China's Fujian province – and is hugely popular. It's generally cheaper than similar stores elsewhere in Singapore. Expect to pay around $12 for a 300g pack.

DRINKING & NIGHTLIFE

As well as trying the places listed below, don't forget that the coffeeshops and hawker centres listed in our eating section are great options for a quick caffeine fix or a cheap beer.

BEAUJOLAIS
BAR

Map p201 (1 Ann Siang Hill; ⏰noon-1am; ⓂChinatown) Tough to find a bar with a better location than this one. Get here early, grab a table on the terrace and watch this ultra-chic corner of Chinatown cruise by as you enjoy a glass or two of fine French wine (from $10 per glass).

SCREENING ROOM
BAR

Map p201 (www.screeningroom.com.sg; 12 Ann Siang Rd; ⏰6pm-2am; ⓂChinatown) Best known for its sofa-strewn minicinema (p63), Screening Room also has a hugely popular, extremely swanky rooftop bar. There's the usual choice of beers, but this is a venue fit for cocktails (from $15), sipped whilst admiring views of heritage buildings in one direction and the lights of CBD office towers in the other.

HOOD
BAR, LIVE MUSIC

Map p201 (www.hoodbarandcafe.com; 55 Keong Saik Rd; beer from $10; ⏰3pm-1am Sun-Fri, to 2am Sat; ⓂOutram Park, Chinatown) The live music every night from around 9.30pm attracts a large local crowd. It's mostly sing-along covers of Western chart-toppers, but the quality of the singers and bands tends to be decent and the atmosphere is fun. Beers go for $10, but you can get cheaper multibottle deals.

LOCAL KNOWLEDGE

SINGAPORE'S MUSIC SCENE: THE LOWDOWN

Local filmmaker and musician Kenny Png has played for some of Singapore's best-known underground bands. He filled us in on the local music scene.

How would you summarise the state of the local music scene in Singapore at the moment?

The music scene here is very diverse, with bands that range from funk, pop to even Vedic metal and Chinese Gothic rock. The majority are either independent or signed to very small labels. Finding good local gigs by established original bands can be troublesome, however, as there is not much demand for shows like that in Singapore, so bands tend to tour the neighbouring regions instead. Many original musicians hold full-time jobs as the cost of living in Singapore is very high, so music for them is just a very serious hobby. Full-time musicians are usually people who play cover songs at a music bar or club.

What are some notable bands to look out for while in Singapore?

The Observatory, In Each Hand a Cutlass, B-Quartet, Ugly in the Morning, La' Dies, Opposition Party, Lunarin, LGF, Meltgsnow, DJ Ko Flow, Analog Girl.

What are the hottest music venues in the city right now?

Timbre@Substation (p51) is a popular music venue for the office crowd. They have a different band on every night. It's mostly covers – pop and indie. The Prince of Wales (p73) is a backpacker hostel that has a laid-back bar with acoustic performances most nights. Hood (p61), by Chinatown, is an up-and-coming venue that regularly features one of Singapore's more popular bands, Timmy. Cover music there is more rock and pop. Home Club (p50), near Clarke Quay, is popular for original local bands to stage their own shows.

How do you see the music scene developing in the next few years?

The music scene will not change that much in the next few years as local and even regional demand for original local music remains low. The explosion of online media and distribution will ensure a healthy independent scene. An affluent class of musicians who do not need to live off their music fuels this scene. They simply seek an audience for their work and often distribute their original works for free. The cover-music scene, however, will continue to thrive as an alternative for the working crowd who prefer to chill out to live music they know.

PIGEON HOLE   CAFE

Map p201 (www.thepigeonhole.com.sg; 52-53 Duxton Rd; ◎10am-11pm Tue-Thu, 10am-1am Fri, 11.30am-1am Sat, 11.30am-8pm Sun; ⓜOutram Park, Chinatown) Arty cafe with friendly staff and great coffee. Has live music some weekends and runs open-mic evenings a couple of times a month (check the website) where you can listen to local musicians playing, well, anything they want.

TANTRIC BAR   BAR

Map p201 (78 Neil Rd; ◎8pm-3am; ⓜOutram Park, Chinatown) A peaceful spot to relax among the fountains, palm trees and Arabian chic in the courtyard, this is one of the most popular and classiest of a cluster of gay bars in this part of Chinatown.

TEA CHAPTER   TEAHOUSE

Map p201 (www.tea-chapter.com.sg; 9-11 Neil Rd; tea from $5; ◎11am-11pm; ⓜChinatown) Queen Elizabeth and Prince Philip dropped by here for a cuppa in 1989, and for a $10 fee you can sit at the table they once sat at. Otherwise, the charge is $6 per person, which includes tea of your choice up to that value. The selection of Chinese teas is excellent, and staff is on hand to give you advice on what to choose. Also has a wonderful collection of souvenir tea sets for sale (around $100).

YIXING XUAN TEAHOUSE   TEAHOUSE

Map p201 (www.yixingxuan-teahouse.com; 30/32 Tanjong Pagar Rd; ◎10am-9pm Mon-Sat, to 7pm Sun; ⓜChinatown) Probably the best place to start if you know nothing about Chinese tea. Former banker Vincent Low is on hand to explain all you need to know about sampling different types of tea, and can give you a tea-ceremony demonstration with tastings ($20, 45 minutes).

WONDERFUL FOOD & BEVERAGE
DRINKS STALL

Map p201 (6 Sago St; ☺10am-10pm; Ⓜ Chinatown) If you're fed up with the ridiculous prices for drinks in bars round here, head instead to this small, friendly street-side stall, grab a $5 beer and watch the Chinatown souvenir hunters whizz by. Also has an interesting selection of exotic fruit drinks, as well as satay snacks.

TOUCAN IRISH PUB
PUB

Map p201 (15 Duxton Hill; ☺11am-1am Mon-Thu, 11am-2am Fri, 4pm-2am Sat; Ⓜ Outram Park, Chinatown) With a pleasant garden area and a lovely location on the corner of the approach to cobblestoned Duxton Hill, this otherwise run-of-the-mill Irish pub is a decent choice for those who like their Guinness alfresco. Expect to pay at least $14 for a beer.

LE CARILLON DE L'ANGELUS
BAR

Map p201 (24 Ann Siang Rd; ☺5pm-2am Mon-Sat, 5pm-1am Sun) Run by the same people behind the quality French restaurant, L'Angelus. Expect fine wine and high prices.

PLAIN
CAFE

Map p201 (☎6225 4385; 50 Craig Rd; ☺7.30am-7.30pm daily; Ⓜ Tanjong Pagar) Neither plain nor set on a plain of any sort, this cafe is cool, stark minimalism. Its coffee, thick and rich. The service is of the 'if you don't have enough cash, pay next time' variety. Also serves decent brekkie.

 ENTERTAINMENT

CHINESE THEATRE CIRCLE
CHINESE OPERA

Map p201 (☎6323 4862; www.ctcopera.com.sg; 5 Smith St; Ⓜ Chinatown) Teahouse evenings organised by this nonprofit opera company are a wonderful, informal introduction to Chinese opera. Every Friday and Saturday at 8pm there is a brief talk ($20, in English) on Chinese opera, followed by an excerpt from an opera classic, performed by actors in full costume. Delicious lychee tea and little teacakes are included in the price. It lasts about 45 minutes and, although you aren't allowed to video the performance, you can take photos. Bookings recommended. For $35, turn up at 7pm and you can enjoy a Chinese meal beforehand.

SCREENING ROOM
FILM

Map p201 (☎6221 1694; www.screeningroom. sg; 12 Ann Siang Rd; tickets $20, food & film $55; ☺noon-2.30pm & 6.30pm-late; Ⓜ Chinatown) Get your ticket, order some food and drinks and sink into a comfy sofa to watch a film projected onto the pull-down screen. After the performance, head upstairs to the rooftop bar for some post-show drinks with a view.

SINGAPORE CHINESE ORCHESTRA
CLASSICAL MUSIC

Map p201 (☎6440 3839; www.sco.com.sg; Singapore Conference Hall, 7 Shenton Way; Ⓜ Tanjong Pagar) Performs classical Chinese concerts throughout the year, featuring traditional instruments, including the *liuqin, ruan* and *sanxian*. Occasionally collaborates with Japanese, jazz and Malay musicians.

TOY FACTORY THEATRE ENSEMBLE
THEATRE

Map p201 (☎6222 1526; www.toyfactory.com.sg; 15A Smith St; Ⓜ Chinatown) A cutting-edge bilingual (English and Mandarin) theatre company, which began its life in puppetry. Stages productions of well-known overseas plays as well as producing Singaporean works.

 SHOPPING

Pagoda St and its immediate surroundings have become a byword for tourist tat, but behind and beyond the stalls crammed with souvenir T-shirts and two-minute calligraphers there are small shops selling everything from contemporary Singaporean artwork to antique furniture. This area is also famous for its Chinese medicine centres.

EU YAN SANG MEDICAL HALL
CHINESE MEDICINE

Map p201 (269A South Bridge Rd; ☺8.30am-6pm Mon-Sat; Ⓜ Chinatown) Opened in the early 20th century and now tastefully refurbished, this is Singapore's most famous Chinese medicine centre and has spawned branches across the country. Looking like a modern Western chemist, the goods on the shelves are anything but familiar to Western eyes. Pick up some Monkey Bezoar powder to relieve excess phlegm, or Liu Jun Zi pills to dispel dampness. There are also herbal teas, soups and oils; most remedies come with easy-to-follow labels.

WORTH A DETOUR

ARTS DISTRICT BY THE DOCKS

A clutch of excellent art galleries can be found in the most unglamorous of places, a short walk southwest of Chinatown. **Tanjong Pagar Distripark** is an arts centre housed in the warehouses of the loading bays at the sprawling docks near the now disused Tanjong Pagar Railway Station. The warehouses are more used to hosting pallets of goods, but the high ceilings and reasonable rent have seen some notable galleries move in.

The biggest hitter is **Ikkan Art International** (www.ikkan-art.com; Ground fl, 01-05 Tanjong Pagar Distripark, 39 Keppel Rd; ⊙11am-6pm Mon-Sat; ⓂTanjong Pagar), which was showcasing work from various high-profile international artists when we last visited, including a collection by Chinese dissident Ai Weiwei.

Valentine Willie Fine Art (⌨8www.vwfa.net; 2nd fl, 02-04 Tanjong Pagar Distripark, 39 Keppel Rd; ⊙11am-7pm Tue-Sat, 11am-3pm Sun; ⓂTanjong Pagar) seeks out and displays the hottest Southeast Asian artists, while the unusual **Redot Fine Art Gallery** (www.redotgallery.com; 2nd fl, 02-06 Tanjong Pagar Distripark, 39 Keppel Rd; ⊙noon-7pm Tue-Sat; ⓂTanjong Pagar) is the only art gallery in Singapore specialising in indigenous Australian art.

To get here from Chinatown, walk south along Cantonment Rd until you reach the Ayer Raja Expressway, which is raised above Keppel Rd. Cross under this flyover and turn right. Walk along Keppel Rd for about 100m and the Distripark will be on your left. Bus 145 from St Andrew's Cathedral, by City Hall MRT station, also runs here.

TONG MERN SERN ANTIQUES　ANTIQUES
Map p201 (51 Craig Rd; ⊙9am-6pm Mon-Sat, 1-6pm Sun; ⓂOutram Park) Outside it's a beautifully renovated, three-storey shophouse; inside, an Aladdin's cave of dusty furniture, books, records, wood carvings, porcelain, and a multitude of other bits and bobs that we found hard to identify. A banner hung above the front door proclaims: 'We buy junk and sell antiques. Some fools buy. Some fools sell.' Better have your wits about you.

YONG GALLERY　ANTIQUES
Map p201 (260 South Bridge Rd; ⊙10am-7pm; ⓂChinatown) The owner here is a calligrapher, and much of his artwork is on sale. You'll also find jewellery, genuine jade products and antiques as well as more affordable gifts such as decorative bookmarks, Chinese fans and clocks. The shop is stuffed with goodies so it's fun browsing even if you're not in a buying mood.

UTTERLY ART　ART
Map p201 (☑6226 2605; www.utterlyart.com.sg; 229A South Bridge Rd; ⊙noon-8pm Mon-Sat, noon-5.30pm Sun; ⓂChinatown) This small, welcoming art gallery is an excellent introduction to Singapore's contemporary art scene. It's mostly paintings, although they exhibit sculpture and ceramics on occasion, and roughly half of the stuff they display is work from Singaporean artists. They also exhibit a lot of Filipino work too. Exhibitions are held every other week and usually last for one week. Call or check the website for what's on when you're in town.

PEOPLE'S PARK COMPLEX　MALL
Map p201 (1 Park Rd; ⊙10am-9.30pm; ⓂChinatown) Old-fashioned shopping mall housed at the foot of the garish green and yellow housing block that looms large over one end of Temple St. It's an interesting place to wander around if you're after some decent-quality Chinese souvenirs but don't feel like bargaining too hard for them, or if you're looking for traditional herbal remedies. There's all manner of Asian health gadgets and treatments here, from herbal tinctures and arthritis-curing marble hand balls to nondodgy massage parlours and even footbaths with tiny fish that suck the dead skin off your feet! They tickle.

YUE HWA
CHINESE PRODUCTS　DEPARTMENT STORE
Map p201 (70 Eu Tong Sen St; ⊙11am-9pm; ⓂChinatown) This store in an old six-storey building with echoes of Shanghai specialises in products from China. Downstairs you'll find medicine and herbs, clothes and cushions. Moving to level 5, you'll pass through silks, food and tea, arts and crafts and household goods, before ending up at the large (unattractively lit) furniture section.

Little India & Kampong Glam

LITTLE INDIA | KAMPONG GLAM | BUGIS

Neighbourhood Top Five

1 Bag a table at **Bismillah Biryani** (p69) and tuck into the best biryani and kebabs this side of the Bay of Bengal.

2 Shop for saris at the **Tekka Centre** (p75), before heading downstairs for a bite to eat at one of Little India's liveliest hawker centres.

3 Transport yourself to southern India by sampling thali served on a banana leaf at **Gandhi Restaurant** (p69), one of Little India's numerous no-frills canteens.

4 Take a back seat during *puja* (prayers) at **Sri Veeramakaliamman Temple** (p67), Little India's most atmospheric Hindu temple.

5 Sip strong Turkish coffee or puff on a sheesha at one of the many Middle Eastern–style cafes around **Arab St** (p68).

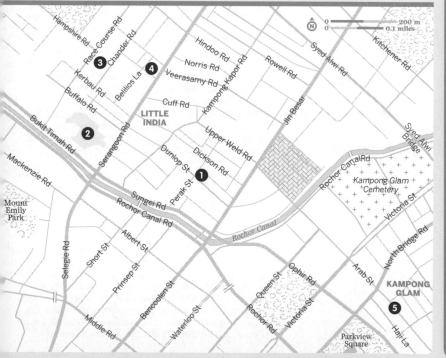

For more detail of this area, see Map p204 ➡

Lonely Planet's Top Tip

If you want to see Little India at its busiest, most Indian best, come on a Sunday. This is the only day off for many workers, particularly Indian labourers, and at times it feels like you're sharing the streets with half the subcontinent.

Best Places to Eat

➡ Bismillah Biryani (p69)

➡ Nan Hwa Chong Fishhead Steamboat Corner (p72)

➡ Café Le Caire (p72)

➡ Sankranti (p69)

➡ Ah-Rahman Royal Prata (p75)

➡ Jaggi's (p69)

For reviews, see p69 ➡

Best Places to Drink

➡ BluJaz Café (p74)

➡ Prince of Wales (p73)

➡ Countryside Cafe (p73)

➡ Zsofi Tapas Bar (p73)

For reviews, see p73 ➡

Best Places to Shop

➡ Tekka Centre (p75)

➡ Haji Lane (p69)

➡ Nali (p75)

➡ Celebration of Arts (p75)

➡ Mustafa Centre (p75)

For reviews, see p75 ➡

Explore Little India & Kampong Glam

The heart of Little India lies in the colourful, incense-scented lanes between Serangoon Rd and Jln Besar, stretching from Campbell Lane in the south to Syed Alwi Rd in the north. The best way to take in this area's wonderful sights, smells and sounds is to simply wander these lanes on foot. Shopping and temple hopping both rank highly here, but the main attraction is the fabulously authentic Indian food. Arm yourself with an empty stomach and dive in.

There's also great food – Middle Eastern, Malay, Chinese – to be had in Kampong Glam, an area sometimes just referred to as Arab St, where you'll find beautiful mosques, cute cafes and trendy boutiques dotted around quiet, brightly painted lanes.

Come evening, both Little India and Kampong Glam have fun drinking options. Little India is livelier, but Kampong Glam is trendier with its sheesha cafes and back-alley vibe. Unsure which to choose? Try both; they're only a 15-minute walk apart.

Local Life

➡ **Connect with your food** Using your fingers rather than cutlery is an integral part of the Indian eating experience. Wash your hands before and after (all Indian restaurants have sinks), and be sure to only use your right hand (the left is for toilet duties).

➡ **South Indian breakfasts** You'll soon tire of the free toast-and-tea breakfasts at your hotel, so head instead to one of Little India's many canteen restaurants and enjoy a scrummy south Indian breakfast of *dosa* (paper-thin lentil-flour pancake), *idly* (spongy, round, fermented rice cakes) or *uttapam* (thick, savoury rice pancake).

➡ **Park life** Skip the bars and do what many of the local Indian workers do by buying cans of Kingfisher from a corner shop and settling down with your mates for a drink at one of the small parks in Little India.

Getting There & Away

➡ **MRT** Little India station is right by the Tekka Centre. You can walk here from Bugis and Farrer Park stations. Bugis is best for Kampong Glam. It only takes 15 minutes to walk from Little India to Kampong Glam.

➡ **Bus** No 65 runs from Orchard Rd to Serangoon Rd. From the Colonial District, catch bus 131 or 147 on Stamford Rd. For Kampong Glam, take bus 7 from Orchard Rd to Victoria St (get off at the Stamford School, past Arab St). From the Colonial District, buses 130, 133, 145 and 197 go up Victoria St, and buses 100 and 107 run along Beach Rd from the Raffles Hotel to Bussorah St.

◉ SIGHTS

◉ Little India

SRI VEERAMAKALIAMMAN TEMPLE
HINDU TEMPLE

Map p204 (141 Serangoon Rd; ⊘5.30am-12.15pm & 4-9pm; MLittle India) This Shaivite temple, dedicated to Kali, is the most colourful and bustling in Little India. Kali, bloodthirsty consort of Shiva, has always been popular in Bengal, the birthplace of the labourers who built this temple in 1881. Images of Kali within the temple show her wearing a garland of skulls and ripping out the insides of her victims, and sharing more peaceful family moments with her sons Ganesh and Murugan. The temple is at its liveliest during each of the four daily *puja* (prayer) sessions. If you're lucky enough to visit at those times, do bear in mind that this is a place of worship, not a tourist attraction.

SRI SRINIVASA PERUMAL TEMPLE
HINDU TEMPLE

off Map p204 (✆397 Serangoon Rd; ⊘6.30am-noon & 6-9pm; MFarrer Park) Dedicated to Vishnu, this temple dates from 1855 but the striking, 20m-tall *gopuram* (tower) is a $300,000 1966 add-on. Inside is a statue of Vishnu, his sidekicks Lakshmi and Andal, and his bird-mount Garuda. The temple is the starting point for a colourful street parade during the Thaipusam festival.

SRI VADAPATHIRA KALIAMMAN TEMPLE
HINDU TEMPLE

off Map p204 (555 Serangoon Rd; MFarrer Park, Boon King) Dedicated to Kaliamman, the Destroyer of Evil, this south Indian temple began life in 1870 as a modest shrine, but underwent a significant facelift in the 1960s to transform it into the beautifully colourful structure you can see today. The carvings here – particularly on the domed *vimana* inside – are among the best temple artwork you'll see anywhere in Singapore.

LEONG SAN SEE TEMPLE
TAOIST TEMPLE

(371 Race Course Rd; ⊘6am-6pm; MFarrer Park) This relatively low-key temple, dating from 1917 and dedicated to Kuan Yin (Guanyin), is a surprisingly active place of worship. In fact, you'll often find more religious fervour here than at other, larger Taoist temples in Singapore. The name translates as Dragon Mountain Temple and it's beautifully decorated with timber beams carved with chimera, dragons, flowers and human figures, all of which were being given a long-overdue coat of paint when we visited.

To get here, walk north up Serangoon Rd then, opposite Beatty Rd, turn left through a decorative archway emblazoned with the Chinese characters for the temple (寺山龍), which is opposite you, at the end of the lane.

SAKAYA MUNI BUDDHA GAYA TEMPLE
BUDDHIST TEMPLE

off Map p204 (366 Race Course Rd; ⊘8am-4.45pm; MFarrer Park) Opposite the Leong San See Temple, the Sakaya Muni Buddha Gaya Temple, also known as the Temple of 1000 Lights, is dominated by a 15m-tall, 300-tonne Buddha that sits alongside an eclectic range of deities, including Kuan Yin (Guanyin), the Chinese goddess of mercy and, interestingly, the Hindu deities Brahma and Ganesh. The temple was founded by a Thai monk in 1927.

LITTLE INDIA & KAMPONG GLAM SIGHTS

INDIAN HERITAGE CENTRE

Plans for a $12 million state-of-the-art heritage centre in Little India were at an advanced stage as we were doing our research for this book. The designs certainly looked impressive, although the ultra-modern, slightly cubist structure will significantly change the face of this historic part of town.

Supposedly based on the look of a *baoli* (an Indian step well, which was traditionally a meeting place for Indian communities), the five-storey building will be covered in multi-faceted translucent hexagonal tiles, which will light up at night, creating a shimmering image not unlike that of Beijing's Water Cube, the eye-catching swimming venue of the 2008 Olympic Games.

As part of the redevelopment, there are plans to pedestrianise Campbell Lane, transforming it into a modern shopping precinct.

The Heritage Centre itself will house galleries and education spaces, and is due to open towards the end of 2013.

Flanking the entrance are yellow tigers, symbolising protection and vitality. On your left as you enter the temple is a huge mother-of-pearl footprint, complete with the 108 auspicious marks that distinguish a Buddha foot from any other 2m-long foot. It's said to be a replica of the footprint on top of Adam's Peak in Sri Lanka.

⊙ Kampong Glam

SULTAN MOSQUE   MOSQUE
Map p204 (3 Muscat St; ◷5am-8.30pm; ⓂBugis) Singapore's largest mosque is the golden-domed focal point of Kampong Glam. It was originally built in 1825 with the aid of a grant from Raffles and the East India Company, as a result of Raffles' treaty with the Sultan of Singapore that allowed him to retain sovereignty over the area. A hundred years later in 1928, the original mosque was replaced by the present magnificent building, which, interestingly, was designed by an architect who was from Ireland and worked for the same company that designed the Raffles Hotel.

Bear in mind that this is a functioning mosque and only go inside if there isn't a prayer session going on. Non-Muslims are asked to refrain from entering the prayer hall at any time, and all visitors are expected to be dressed appropriately. Pointing cameras at people during prayer time is never appropriate.

MALAY HERITAGE CENTRE   MUSEUM
Map p204 (✆6391 0450; www.malayheritage.org. sg; 85 Sultan Gate; adult/child $3/2; ◷10am-6pm Tue-Sun, 1-6pm Mon) The Kampong Glam area is the historic seat of the Malay royalty, resident here before the arrival of Raffles, and the *istana* (palace) on this site was built for the last sultan of Singapore, Ali Iskander

> ### ARAB STREET
> The area's traditional textile district centres on **Arab St** (Map p204; ⓂBugis), where you'll find several caneware shops near the junction with Baghdad St as well as all manner of textiles, clothes and carpets. Stop here for a well-deserved rest and some bread, dips and grilled lamb at the area's best Middle Eastern restaurant, Café Le Caire (p72), also known as Al Majlis.

Shah, between 1836 and 1843. An agreement allowed the palace to belong to the sultan's family as long as they continued to live there. Even though this was repealed in 1897, the family stayed on for over a century and the palace gradually slid into ruin.

In 1999 the family moved out and a long period of renovation ended in 2004 with the opening of the Malay Heritage Centre. The building and grounds are a delight and the museum itself is a sparse but interesting account of Singapore's Malay people, featuring a reconstructed *kampong* (village) house upstairs.

The museum was undergoing another round of renovations at the time of research, and was due to open again in June 2012.

CHILDREN LITTLE MUSEUM   TOY MUSEUM
Map p204 (42 Bussorah St; admission $2; workshops $15; ◷11am-6pm; ⓂBugis) This delightful personal collection of retro toys showcases how kids in Singapore once lived without games consoles. Can you imagine? Wonderfully enthusiastic owner Terry Chua will take you on a private tour of the museum, bringing to life the toys on show with tales of how he and his friends used to play with them. Toy-making workshops can also be arranged. There are also a number of toys for sale.

MALABAR MUSLIM JAMA-ATH MOSQUE   MOSQUE
Map p204 (471 Victoria St; ⓂLavender) The blue-tiled Malabar Muslim Jama-Ath Mosque, the only one on the island dedicated to Malabar Muslims from the South Indian state of Kerala, is one of the most distinctive in Singapore, but it didn't always look this way. Work on the building started in 1956, but it wasn't officially opened until 1963 due to cash-flow problems. The magnificent tiling on the mosque was only finished in 1995.

HAJJAH FATIMAH MOSQUE   MOSQUE
Map p204 (4001 Beach Rd; ⓂLavender, Bugis) Constructed in 1846, this mosque is named after a Melaka-born Malay woman, Hajjah Fatimah; the site was once her home. It has two unusual features. First is its architecture, which is British influenced, rather than traditional Middle Eastern. The second is its leaning minaret, which leans about six degrees off-centre.

HAJI LANE

This incredibly quaint, brightly painted narrow **lane** (Map p204; Ⓜ Bugis), running parallel to Arab St, is filled with cute boutique shops, chill-out cafes (sheesha smoking almost obligatory) and trendy (but not overly swanky) bars. It's a top spot for browsing, partying or just resting up, depending on what time of day you get here.

◉ Bugis

KUAN IM THONG HOOD CHO TEMPLE
BUDDHIST TEMPLE

Map p204 (178 Waterloo St; Ⓜ Bugis) A short walk south from Little India brings you to a pedestrianised section of Waterloo St, which is home to this popular, if slightly strange, Buddhist temple. Dedicated to the goddess of mercy Kuan Yin (Guanyin), the temple attracts a large daily crowd of devotees, but inside it feels more like a shopping mall than a temple, with air-con and polished tiled flooring. Devotees are often dressed in office attire, which adds to the modern flavour. Flower sellers can always be found outside the temple, which is particularly busy on the eve of Chinese New Year, when it stays open right through the night. Just up from the temple, near the South-East Asia Hotel, is a large money god, with a polished belly where the faithful rub their hands for good luck.

Next door is the recently renovated and even more polychromatic **Sri Krishnan Temple**, which also attracts worshippers from the Kuan Yin temple, who show a great deal of religious pragmatism by also burning joss sticks and offering prayers at this Hindu temple.

 **EATING**

✗ Little India

TOP CHOICE BISMILLAH BIRYANI
INDIAN $

Map p204 (50 Dunlop St; kebabs from $4; biryani from $6; ◔noon-8pm; Ⓜ Little India) There's a large red banner hanging outside the entrance to this place which explains how a customer found the restaurant by Googling 'best biryani in Singapore'. Google came up trumps because this place is magic. The mutton biryani is the speciality – and it is special – but even that is surpassed by the mutton *sheekh* kebab, which is melt-in-the-mouth good. Don't leave it too late in the day to get here. Most of the best dishes are long gone before 8pm.

SANKRANTI
SOUTH INDIAN $

Map p204 (100 Sayed Alwi Rd; mains from $8; ◔11.30am-4pm & 6pm-midnight; Ⓜ Little India) Like Andhra Curry, this excellent restaurant specialises in food from the south Indian state of Andhra Pradesh and is arguably the best of a cluster of good restaurants in and around Little India's 24-hour shopping hub, the Mustafa Centre. The extensive menu includes a number of north Indian dishes, too, and has an enticing choice of set-meal thalis, the pick of the bunch being the Sankranti Special, a 10-piece culinary extravaganza.

GANDHI RESTAURANT
SOUTH INDIAN $

Map p204 (29 Chander Rd; dishes from $2, set meals from $4; ◔11am-11pm; Ⓜ Little India) No-frills, canteen-style restaurant with non-attentive staff and cheap decor. But who cares when the food is this good? You'll probably have to share a table with strangers, who will probably be using their fingers to eat their delicious set-meal thali or their *dosa* (paper-thin lentil-flour pancake) or *uttapam* (thick, savoury south Indian rice pancake with finely chopped onions, green chillies, coriander and coconut). Wash your hands by the sink at the back, and tuck in.

JAGGI'S
INDIAN PUNJABI $

Map p204 (www.jaggis.com; 34-36 Race Course Rd; dishes $2.50-$5; ◔11.30am-3pm & 6-10.30pm; Ⓜ Little India) One of the few authentic, no-nonsense outfits in a string of otherwise touristy, overpriced Indian restaurants on Race Course Rd. Don't be put off by the school-canteen vibe. The Punjabi food here is delicious and this place is deservedly popular with the local Indian population. Point and choose, and mix and match until you have a meal's worth of dishes, then pay the boss and take your tray of goodies to your table which, again, you'll probably have to share with other hungry customers.

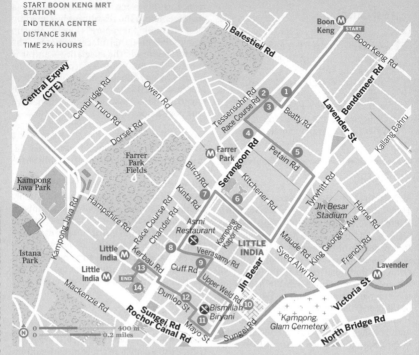

START BOON KENG MRT STATION
END TEKKA CENTRE
DISTANCE 3KM
TIME 2½ HOURS

Neighbourhood Walk

Little India

Walk south along Serangoon Rd, crossing over the Lavender St junction, until you reach ❶ **Sri Vadapathira Kaliamman Temple**, with its beautiful carvings. After the temple, turn right through a decorative archway marked with three Chinese characters, which mean Dragon Mountain Temple, or ❷ **Leong San See Temple**. Opposite this Taoist temple is the Buddhist ❸ **Sakaya Muni Buddha Gaya Temple**. Peek inside at its 15m-tall Buddha then head south along Race Course Rd and turn left down a pedestrian alleyway. This brings you back onto Serangoon Rd, beside the striking ❹ **Sri Srinivasa Perumal Temple**. Cross over Serangoon Rd and walk along Petain Rd with its terrace of beautifully restored ❺ **shophouses** by the corner of Surdee Rd. Turn right onto Jln Besar. After a short walk, turn right again onto Syed Alwi Rd: you're now entering the heart of Little India. You'll soon reach the hectic 24hr shopping hub known as the ❻ **Mustafa Centre**. Turn left at Serangoon Rd, walk past

❼ **Angullia Mosque** and look to your right at ❽ **Sri Veeramakaliamman Temple**, Little India's main Hindu Temple. Walk away from the temple, along Veerasamy Rd, then turn right down Kampong Kapor Rd to find the whitewashed 1929 ❾ **Kampong Kapor Methodist Church**. Turn left along Upper Weld Rd to its junction with Jln Besar where, ahead, you'll see the open-air ❿ **Sungei Rd Thieves Market**. After a quick browse, walk south along Jln Besar before turning right into Mayo St, site of the eye-catching ⓫ **Abdul Gaffoor Mosque**, with its intriguing mix of Arab and Victorian architecture. Continue to ⓬ **Dunlop St**, backpacker central, and home to the best biryani restaurant in Singapore, then cross over Serangoon Rd into Kerbau Rd where you'll be dazzled by a beautiful chemist, housed inside the brightly painted ⓭ **Tan House**. Walk through the alley between Tan House and the excellent Andhra Curry onto colourful Buffalo Rd before slipping into the back entrance of the ⓮ **Tekka Centre**, Little India's most famous hawker centre.

ANANDA BHAVAN SOUTH INDIAN VEGETARIAN **$**
Map p204 (Serangoon Rd, outside the Tekka Centre; set meals $6-8, dishes $3-5; ☺7am-10pm; ⓂLittle India) Great place to sample south Indian breakfast fare such as *idly* and *dosa* (written as 'thosai' on the menu here). It also does super-value-for-money *thali*, some of which are served on banana leaves. There are other branches around Little India; all just as no-frills as this one, and all with the same commitment to dishing up tasty, healthy, vegetarian food.

AZMI RESTAURANT (NORRIS RD CHAPATI) INDIAN MUSLIM **$**
Map p204 (1 Norris Rd; dishes $2-4, chapati $0.70; ☺7.30am-10.30pm; ⓂLittle India) Arguably the best place in Little India to sample freshly baked chapati, this corner restaurant is always popular. Choose from a selection of curries, displayed buffet-style, then decide how many chapatis you need to mop up your curry with. Seating is of the plastic-stool variety, so don't bother wearing your Sunday-best outfits. Drinks can be purchased from a separate Chinese-run stall in the corner of the seating area.

FRENCH STALL FRENCH **$$**
off Map p204 (☎6299 3544; 544 Serangoon Rd; mains from $16; drinks & desserts ☺3-6pm Tue-Sun, dinner ☺6-10pm Tue-Sun; ⓂFarrer Park) French chef Xavier Le Henaff married a Singaporean and set up this place as somewhere that ordinary folks could enjoy French food. Prices have risen in recent years, making it less of a bargain than it once was, but there's still a good wine selection, great food and even better deserts, while the street-side five-foot way makes for atmospheric outdoor dining.

ANDHRA CURRY SOUTH INDIAN **$$**
Map p204 (41 Kerbau Rd; mains $5-10, set meals from $8; ☺11am-11pm; ⓂLittle India) Housed in a brightly painted shophouse conversion next to the striking Tan House, this place specialises in dishes from the south Indian state of Andhra Pradesh. It's clean and efficient, and bridges the gap nicely between Little India's very cheap, salt-of-the-earth, canteen-style restaurants and its slick, sanitised and slightly overpriced tourist favourites. Biryanis are popular – the Hyderabad biryani is a speciality – while the tandoor

meat dishes are also very tasty. The large vegetarian set-meal thalis are good value.

WILD ROCKET INTERNATIONAL **$$**
Map p204 (☎6339 9448; hangout@mtemily, 10A Upper Wilkie Rd; mains $25-40; ☺noon-2.30pm & 6.30-10.30pm Tue-Sun; ⓂLittle India) Fancy Western food with a heavy Singaporean influence, Wild Rocket's menu is as stylish as it is unusual. The ambience is peaceful and refined; a stark contrast to most of the restaurants found down the hill in the heart of bustling Little India. Attached to the boutique hotel hangout@mt.emily.

MUSTARD INDIAN BENGALI **$$**
Map p204 (32 Race Course Rd; mains from $12; ☺11.30am-3pm & 6-10.45pm Mon-Fri, 11.30am-10.45pm Sat & Sun; ⓂLittle India) One of the most refined of the more upmarket Indian restaurants that line this end of Race Course Rd, this small restaurant with excellent service offers dishes – all cooked in mustard oil – hailing mostly from Bengal. Kebabs are the speciality, but there are a number of good curries and biryanis on offer too.

KOMALA VILAS SOUTH INDIAN VEGETARIAN **$**
Map p204 (76-78 Serangoon Rd; dishes $3-7; ☺7am-11pm & 6pm-midnight; ⓂLittle India) Similar to Ananda Bhavan (but slightly pricier) this bright yellow branch of the Komala Vilas chain also does good south Indian breakfasts. The set-meal lunchtime thalis (served

TEKKA CENTRE

Little India's most famous hawker centre, the **Tekka Centre** (Map p204; cnr Serangoon & Buffalo Rds; dishes $3-5; ⓂLittle India) has stalls serving the Hainanese chicken rice and *nasi goreng* (Indonesian fried rice) you can find in other food centres across Singapore but it focuses on Indian food too, which means plenty of biryani options, tandoor offerings and mutton curries galore. Well worth seeking out is **Ah-Rahman Royal Prata** (stall 01-248; murtabak $4-5; ☺7am-10pm), which serves even better *murtabak* (stuffed savoury pancake) than those you'll find at Zam Zam – really, they are impossibly good – and watching the chef mould, flip and fill them is like watching an artist at work.

on the second floor from 11am to 4pm) come with unlimited refills. Very popular.

USMAN
PAKISTANI **$**

Map p204 (cnr Serangoon & Desker Rds; dishes $1-10; ⊙noon-2am; MLittle India) This tiny corner restaurant only has room for seating in the five-foot way outside, making it a lively spot for a quick bite to eat. The meat dishes here are all decent, especially the tandoori chicken, but what we love at Usman is the *paneer* (soft, unfermented cheese made from milk curd), particularly the *pulak paneer* (paneer with a spinach gravy). Some of the other vegetable options are dirt cheap – you can eat dhal for $1! – so this isn't a bad choice for a quick lunchtime snack. Don't forget to mop up whatever you order with a freshly baked *naan* (tandoor-cooked flatbread).

AZMI RESTAURANT
INDIAN MUSLIM **$**

Map p204 (43 Dunlop St; snacks $1.20; ⊙8am-8pm; MLittle India) Located right next door to Abdul Gaffoor Mosque, this tiny Muslim snack shop fills up around prayer time, with punters spilling out onto the street. Finger food such as *samosa* (deep-fried pastry triangles filled with vegetable or meat) and *pakora* (bite-sized pieces of vegetable dipped in chickpea-flour batter and deep fried) is served in $1.20 portions and washed down with a cup of sweet tea or coffee.

COCOTTE
FRENCH **$$**

Map p204 (✆6298 1188; www.restaurantcocotte.com; Wanderlust, 2 Dickson Rd; mains $35-50; ⊙midday-2pm & 6.30-10pm; MLittle India, Bugis) The swish restaurant of the ultratrendy boutique hotel Wanderlust, Cocotte is completely out of place in Little India but makes a nice treat if you fancy a splurge. Expect high-quality rustic French cuisine and an excellent choice of wines. Bring a jacket, though; the air-con seems to be stuck on Arctic. Brrrrrrr.

✕ Kampong Glam

TOP CHOICE NAN HWA CHONG FISH-HEAD STEAMBOAT CORNER
CHINESE HOTPOT **$$**

Map p204 (812-816 North Bridge Rd; fish steamboats from $18; ⊙4.30pm-12.30am; MLavender) Arguably the best fish-head steamboat in Singapore. If you only try this unique dish once, you'd do well to make it here. The fish head is brought to you in the steaming broth of a large conical-shaped pot and is then shared by everyone at the table. One is enough for three or four people, and can stretch to more with rice and side dishes. There are four types of fish to choose from – we adored the red snapper ($20), which has less bone and more meat than the others. The atmosphere is hawker-centre-like; it's open-fronted and noisy, with plastic tables and chairs scattered about. Staff members are patient with those who don't know the steamboat drill so you won't feel pushed into ordering what you don't want, although you'll probably love it all.

TOP CHOICE CAFÉ LE CAIRE
MIDDLE EASTERN **$$**

Map p204 (39 Arab St; mains $10-20, snacks $6-10; ⊙10am-3.30am; MBugis) Arab St's true gem, this informal Egyptian hole-in-the-wall cafe, also known as Al Majlis, is housed in a beautiful shophouse conversion, with seating spilling out into the five-foot way (on both Arab St and Haji Lane). It does wonderful Turkish coffee so is perfect for a daytime pitstop, but the food here is worth making a special trip for, with hummus, olives, felafel, pita, salads, yoghurt and a variety of kebabs all featuring, either as side-dish snacks or as main courses.

TEPAK SIREH
MALAY **$$**

Map p204 (✆6396 4373; 73 Sultan Gate; lunch/dinner $16/20, children lunch/dinner $10/12; ⊙11.30am-2.30pm & 6.30-9.30pm Mon-Sat; MBugis) Considering the surroundings – located next to the former Sultan's palace (now the Malay Heritage Centre) and inside the beautiful house of the former *bendahara* (an important administrative position in pre-colonial Malay kingdoms) – this place is surprisingly informal. Customers pay a set price, then help themselves to as much as they like from the fabulous buffet spread, which is a virtual encyclopaedia of Malay specialities.

ZAM ZAM
MUSLIM **$**

Map p204 (699 North Bridge Rd; dishes from $3.50; ⊙8am-11pm; MBugis) These guys have been here since 1908 so they know what they're doing. Tenure hasn't bred complacency, though – the touts still try to herd customers in off the street while frenetic chefs inside whip up delicious *murtabak*, the restaurant's speciality savoury pancakes that are filled with mutton, chicken, beef and even venison.

> ### SINGAPORE'S MINI THAILAND
> If you've just been on the southeast Asia overland haul and are pining for some authentic Thai cuisine, you've just hit the jackpot. **Golden Mile Complex** (Map p204; 5001 Beach Rd; dishes $3-6; ☺10am-10pm; Ⓜ Lavender, Bugis) is Singapore's mini Thailand, full of Thai shops, grocers, butchers and eateries. The signs are in Thai, the customers are mostly Thai and the food, clustered on the ground floor, is 100% magnificent like-mother-makes Thai. The atmosphere is often boisterous and drunken and a little roughhouse for some. The Isan (northeast) food is best – try **Nong Khai** (stall 01-74; dishes from $5, beer from $7; ☺10am-10pm) on the ground floor. Look for the orange sign. Golden Mile is also known for its nightlife, with punters coming to drink themselves silly at Thai-style discos. Prices are much cheaper than at the average bar in Singapore, but the atmosphere can be seedy.

GOLDEN MILE FOOD CENTRE
HAWKER CENTRE $

Map p204 (505 Beach Rd; ☺10am-10pm) Not to be confused with the Thai-centric Golden Mile Complex across the road, this hawker centre promotes the government's 'Ask for Healthier Changes' policy (less oil, syrup, fat etc), but the famous *tulang* soup from basement stalls 4, 15 and 28 doesn't really comply: meaty bones stewed in a rich, spicy, blood-red tomato gravy. Gnaw off the flesh, suck out the marrow, and sop up the sauce with bread. Also try the famous *ah balling* (rice balls with sweet fillings) and *char kway teow* (fried flat rice noodles) on the 2nd floor.

DRINKING & NIGHTLIFE

As well as the places listed below, remember you can also just grab a beer at one of the hawker centres. Haji Lane in Kampong Glam is dotted with cutesy cafe-bars that come and go in the blink of an eye according to the latest drinking trends. It's worth having a wander round there to see if one takes your fancy.

 Little India

PRINCE OF WALES
BAR

Map p204 (101 Dunlop St; ☺9am-1am; 🛜; Ⓜ Little India) The closest thing to a pub in Little India, this knockabout Australian drinking den, which doubles as a backpacker hostel (p147), is friendly, very popular and has live music pretty much every night (from 9pm).

Has a small beer garden, a number of sports screens and a pool table. Various drinks promotions help to keep prices reasonably affordable; normal prices start at $10 for a beer.

COUNTRYSIDE CAFE
CAFE

Map p204 (71 Dunlop St; ☺9.30am-midnight; 🛜; Ⓜ Little India) The cutest and most popular Western-style cafe in Little India is run by welcoming owners, has free wi-fi and serves an excellent cup of coffee. Well-priced alcoholic drinks (beer from $6.50, wine from $7.50), and a prime location beside the Inn Crowd youth hostel, ensure it remains busy in the evenings too. Also does some decent Western-friendly food.

ZSOFI TAPAS BAR
BAR

Map p204 (68 Dunlop St; ☺5pm-1am Mon-Thu, to 2am Fri & Sat, to 11pm Sun; 🛜; Ⓜ Little India) It's all about the rooftop here, a wonderful and highly unusual space for this part of town, and big enough to (nearly) always find a seat on. Drinks are anything but cheap – expect to pay at least $12 for a beer – but every one of them comes with free tapas, which goes some way to softening the blow when you get the bill.

KERBAU RD BEER GARDEN
DRINKS STALL

Map p204 (Kerbau Rd; ☺10am-11pm; Ⓜ Little India) Little more than a couple of drinks stalls with plastic tables and chairs scattered beside them, this 'beer garden' is packed every night with Indian drinkers who come for the Bollywood movies that are shown on the small TV as much as for the cheap booze (beer from $3).

Kampong Glam

TOP CHOICE BLUJAZ CAFÉ
BAR, LIVE MUSIC

Map p204 (www.blujaz.net; 11 Bali Lane; beer from $6; ☺noon-midnight Mon-Thu, noon-2am Fri, 4pm-2am Sat; ☎; MBugis) Decorated in a rather eccentric fashion and located next to an artists' studio that spills its works into the laneway, this is as close as you'll get to a bohemian hangout in Singapore, though it attracts a diverse crowd. There's live music (not always jazz) downstairs at weekends and often on Mondays, and a funky lounge upstairs. There's also prime outdoor seating in the side alley that links Bali Lane with Haji Lane. Prices are decent, with small glasses of beer starting at $6.

If it's too crowded or noisy here, you could try nearby **Piedra Negra** (cnr Beach Rd & Haji Lane; ☺noon-midnight Mon-Thu, noon-2am Fri, 5pm-2am Sat & Sun), a Mexican-style bar-restaurant, which shares owners with BluJaz, and which also has outdoor seating.

★ ENTERTAINMENT

★ Little India

WILD RICE
THEATRE

Map p204 (☑6292 2695; www.wildrice.com.sg; 65 Kerbau Rd; MLittle India) Singapore's sexiest theatre group is based in Kerbau Rd, but organises shows elsewhere in the city (as well as abroad). Productions range from farce to serious politics, and fearlessly wade into issues not commonly on the agenda in Singapore.

★ Kampong Glam

BIAN CAFE
BEIJING OPERA

Map p204 (www.singopera.com.sg; 52 Kandahar St; ☺11am-10pm; MBugis) This small cafe, adorned with Chinese Opera memorabilia, is a pleasant-enough place to come for coffee (from $2.50) or a beer (from $6.80), but if you visit on Thursday afternoons, between 3pm and 6pm (admission $8), you'll be treated to short bursts of Beijing Opera

songs. It's singing only – no make-up, no costumes, no acrobatic dances – but this is an unusual way to experience the art form. They'll even let you have a go yourself; Chinese Opera karaoke, anyone? On the first floor of the building, and accessed through the cafe, is the grandly named **Singapore Chinese Opera Museum** (admission $5), which houses more opera memorabilia.

ST GREGORY JAVANA SPA
SPA

Map p204 (☑6505 5755; www.stgregoryspa.com; Level 3, The Plaza, 7500A Beach Rd; treatments $30-170; ☺10am-10pm Mon-Fri, 9am-9pm Sat & Sun; MBugis) With spas all over Asia, St Gregory's is a major player in relaxation. It has three facilities in Singapore, all inside top-end hotels. This one is at the Park Royal on Beach Rd and offers ayurvedic therapies as well as all the usual luxury massage treatments. Non-guests of the hotel can also swim in the gorgeous pool (per day $50).

SANCTUM
SPA

Map p204 (☑6299 0170; www.sanctumsg.com; 2nd fl, 66A Haji Lane; ☺11.30am-8pm Mon-Sat; 1hr classes $80-150; MBugis) 'Nourishment for mind, body and soul' is how this place bills itself, and with tarot readings, meditation events, past-life regression, shiatsu and reiki, we see no reason to argue. Sanctum has three beautiful and uniquely set up rooms for sessions and chilling out, and offers online booking.

★ Bugis

NRITYALAYA AESTHETICS SOCIETY
MUSIC & DANCE

Map p204 (☑6336 6537; www.nas.org.sg; Stamford Arts Centre, 155 Waterloo St; MLittle India) Runs classes and workshops in traditional Indian arts such as classical dance, music, yoga and meditation. Also holds occasional performances. The website isn't always kept up to date so call or pop in to the Stamford Arts Centre to see what's on when you're here.

SHOPPING

Little India's streets are a browser's delight – a treasure trove of art, antiques, textiles, food and music. Kampong Glam, with its mix of boutiques shops and cute cafes, is quieter and more relaxed.

Little India

TEKKA CENTRE   CLOTHING
Map p204 (cnr Serangoon & Buffalo Rds; ⊙10am-10pm; ⓂLittle India) On the first floor here, above the bustling hawker centre, you'll find an array of Indian textile and sari shops. This is probably the cheapest place to pick up an Indian outfit. Prices are labelled, but bargaining is of course possible.

NALI   CLOTHING
Map p204 (32 Buffalo Rd; ⊙10am-9pm; ⓂLittle India) For better quality cotton and silk saris, try this small shop on colourful Buffalo Rd. You can pick up cotton saris for as little as $20. The beautiful silk versions, most of which are upstairs, go for between $100 and $1000.

CELEBRATION OF ARTS   HANDICRAFTS
Map p204 (2 Dalhousie Lane; ⊙8.30am-9pm; ⓂLittle India) Pick your way through beautiful wood-carved Indian furniture, statues and ornaments, lampshades, bedspreads and pashmina shawls.

INDIAN CLASSICAL MUSIC CENTRE   MUSIC
Map p204 (✆6291 0187; www.sitar.com.sg; 26 Clive St; ⊙10am-7pm Mon-Sat, 10am-3pm Sun; ⓂLittle India) Well stocked with pretty much every instrument in the Indian musical firmament. Quality is geared towards playing rather than just hanging on the wall, but some pieces would make great souvenirs nonetheless. Enthusiasts can sign up for classes. Also sells Indian music CDs.

MUSTAFA CENTRE   DEPARTMENT STORE
Map p204 (145 Syed Alwi Rd; ⊙24hr; ⓂFarrer Park) The bustling 24-hour Mustafa Centre in Little India is a magnet for budget shoppers, most of them from the subcontinent. This place has just about everything (electronics, jewellery, household items, shoes, bags, CDs), all at bargain rates. There's also a large supermarket with a superb range of Indian foodstuffs. If you can't handle crowded places, it's probably best to avoid Sundays.

SUNGEI RD THIEVES MARKET   MARKET
Map p204 (Sungei Rd, Weld Rd, Pasar Lane & Pitt St; ⊙afternoon; ⓂLittle India, Bugis) How and why the authorities allow this kerbside jumble sale to exist is a mystery, but happily it remains, spread out across four streets around a patch of open ground. The array of old geezers hawking random collections of used items makes it an interesting place to wander around and mingle with Singapore's iPad-free underbelly.

SIM LIM SQUARE   COMPUTERS
Map p204 (1 Rochor Canal Rd; ⊙10am-8.30pm; ⓂBugis) A byword for all that is cut-price and geeky, Sim Lim is jammed with stalls selling motherboards, soundcards, games consoles, laptops and cameras. If you know what you're doing, there are some bargains to be had, but the untutored are more likely to be taken for a ride. Hard bargaining is essential.

SIM LIM TOWER   ELECTRONICS
Map p204 (✆6295 4361; 10 Jln Besar; ⊙9am-6pm; ⓂBugis) A big electronic centre with everything from capacitors to audio and video gear – not far removed from Sim Lim Square. Again, arm yourself with knowledge, and be prepared to bargain hard.

Kampong Glam

LITTLE SHOPHOUSE   GIFTS
Map p204 (43 Bussorah St; ⊙10am-5pm; ⓂBugis) Traditional Peranakan beadwork is a dying art, but it's kept very much alive in this little shop on lovely Bussorah St. Whatever you think of the gaudy colours and elaborate patterns of Peranakan fashion, you can't deny the handiwork is exquisite. You might also fancy popping into the Children Little Museum next door, where you can buy retro Singapore toys.

STRAITS RECORDS   MUSIC
Map p204 (24 Bali Lane; ⊙2-10.30pm Mon-Sat, to 9.30pm Sun; ⓂBugis) One of the few alternative music stores in Singapore, Straits stocks hip hop, hardcore and reggae CDs, as well as some old vinyl, T-shirts and books. CDs from local bands start at around $10.

LITTLE INDIA & KAMPONG GLAM SHOPPING

BLOG SHOP
FASHION

Map p204 (35 Haji Lane; ⊙ 1-9pm Mon-Fri, noon-10pm Sat & Sun; Ⓜ Bugis) One of a number of trendy boutiques that dot fashionable Haji Lane. Sells women's clothing and accessories as well as some cute gifts.

Bugis

BUGIS JUNCTION
MALL

Map p204 (200 Victoria St; ⊙10am-10pm; Ⓜ Bugis) One of Singapore's more distinctive malls, featuring two streets of re-created shophouses, covered with a glass ceiling and air-conditioned. Expect lots of 'here today gone tomorrow' fashion stores. Also houses a cinema complex.

BUGIS ST MARKET
MARKET

Map p204 (Victoria St; ⊙9am-10pm; Ⓜ Bugis) A far cry from its seedy past as Singapore's most notorious red-light area, the Bugis St Market is now a teeming open-fronted three-level hive of stalls selling clothes, shoes and accessories, plus a few manicurists and nail bars, food stalls and, in a nod to the area's past, a sex shop. Don't expect much quality here, but it's a fun place to shop.

Orchard Road

Neighbourhood Top Five

1 Witness the future of shopping at **ION Orchard** (p83), Singapore's space-age wonder of a mall, and the epitome of retail cool.

2 Hunt for Indian antiques, barter for an Oriental rug or pore over ancient maps of Asia in the fascinating **Tanglin Shopping Centre** (p83).

3 Slow down your shopping spree with a leisurely stroll along historic **Emerald Hill Rd** (p79).

4 Treat yourself to a $250 slap-up meal at **Iggy's** (p79), arguably Singapore's very best restaurant.

5 Come back down to earth with a traditional Singaporean breakfast at **Killiney Kopitiam** (p79), the original locals' coffeeshop.

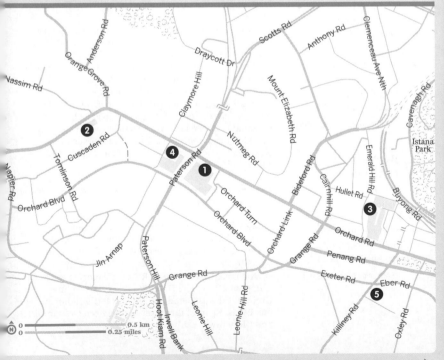

For more detail of this area, see Map p212

Lonely Planet's Top Tip

It's hard to believe it as you walk from mall to mall, but there is a rainforest within 2km of Orchard Rd, inside the grounds of the wonderful Botanic Gardens. So, if you fancy a green escape from the concrete jungle, hop on bus 7 or 77 from the Orchard MRT exit on Orchard Blvd, and you'll be there in 10 minutes.

Best Places to Eat

➡ Killiney Kopitiam (p79)
➡ Wasabi Tei (p79)
➡ Iggy's (p79)
➡ Salt Grill (p80)
➡ Takashimaya Food Village (p80)

For reviews, see p79 ➡

Best Places to Drink

➡ Que Pasa (p82)
➡ No 5 (p82)
➡ Dubliners (p82)
➡ KPO (p82)
➡ Curious Teepee (p82)

For reviews, see p81 ➡

Best Places to Shop

➡ ION Orchard (p83)
➡ Tanglin Shopping Centre (p83)
➡ One Price Store (p84)
➡ 313 Somerset (p83)
➡ Ngee Ann City (p83)

For reviews, see p83 ➡

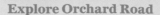

Explore Orchard Road

You would need the best part of a week to explore every floor of every mall in the Orchard Rd area, so do some shopping-mall homework before you go, using our lowdown on p34, along with this handy introductory website: www.orchardroad.sg.

Most malls don't open until 10am, but if you arrive early, fear not; you have the perfect excuse to kill some time in Killiney Kopitiam, a salt-of-the-earth, Singapore-style coffeeshop, before diving into the shopping madness.

Whichever malls you've chosen to explore it won't be long before your shopping-weary legs will be pining for a well-earned break. Try to time it so that you're close to Emerald Hill Rd and relax to the max at one of the beautiful bars on this lovely side street. Alternatively, head to Midpoint Orchard for a foot massage.

Local Life

➡ **Crowds** Retail therapy is serious business in Singapore, and the shopping malls on Orchard Rd can get exceedingly busy. That can be half the fun, but if you prefer to avoid crowds of shoppers get to the malls as they open (usually around 10am) and enjoy bustle-free shopping for about an hour or so before the hordes arrive.

➡ **Food courts** Don't turn your nose up at shopping mall food courts. Believe us – they are *so* much better than the food courts back home. You'll find cuisine from countries right across Asia, it will often be freshly cooked and will always be far cheaper than any of the restaurants you've been passing all day.

➡ **Fresh air** Air-con-cooled shopping malls are all well and good, but after a while it's nice to get a blast of good old-fashioned fresh air. So take your coffee break outside Curious Teepee (p82), on the roof terrace at KPO (p82) or at a streetside table at any of the bars on Emerald Hill Rd (p82).

Getting There & Away

➡ **MRT** Orchard Rd is served by no less than three MRT stations: Orchard, Somerset and Dhoby Ghaut, so there's really no need to use any other form of transport to get here.

➡ **Bus** Bus 7 links Orchard Rd with Victoria St (for Kampong Glam) and Holland Village, bus 65 links Orchard Rd with Serangoon Rd (for Little India), while bus 190 is the most direct service between Orchard Rd and Chinatown.

◉ SIGHTS

EMERALD HILL ROAD · ARCHITECTURE
Map p212 (Emerald Hill Rd; MSomerset) Take some time out from your shopping to wander up Emerald Hill Rd, where some of Singapore's finest terrace houses remain, many of which have been restored immaculately. The quiet residential atmosphere feels a million miles from the bustling malls of Orchard Rd. There are dozens of I-wish-I-could-afford-to-live-here homes to gawp at, but worth seeking out are No 56 (built in 1902, and one of the earliest buildings here), Nos 39 to 45 (with unusually wide frontages and a grand Chinese-style entrance gate) and Nos 120 to 130 (with art deco features dating from around 1925).

At the Orchard Rd end of the hill is a cluster of bars housed in beautiful shophouse renovations (see the boxed text p82); one of the swankiest places to drink in this area.

ISTANA · PALACE
Map p212 (www.istana.gov.sg; MDhoby Ghaut) The grand, whitewashed, neoclassical home of Singapore's president, set in 40 acres of grounds, was built by the British between 1867 and 1869 as Government House, and is open to visitors five times a year; on Labour Day (May 1), National Day (7 August), Chinese New Year (January or February), Diwali (October or November) and Hari Raya Puasa (or Eid-ul Fitr, the festival marking the end of Ramadan; dates vary). Only on these days will you get the chance to stroll past the nine-hole golf course, through the beautiful terraced gardens and into some of the reception rooms. The rest of the time, the closest you'll get are the heavily guarded gates on Orchard Rd.

FREE CATHAY GALLERY · MUSEUM
Map p212 (www.thecathaygallery.com.sg; 2nd fl, 2-16 The Cathay, 2 Handy Rd; ⊙11am-7pm Mon-Sat; MDhoby Ghaut) Film buffs will go ga-ga at this cinematic museum housed in Singapore's first high-rise building. The displays here trace the history of the Loke family, early pioneers in film production and distribution in Singapore and founders of the Cathay Organisation. You'll see old movie posters, cameras and programs that capture the golden age of local cinema.

TAN YEOK NEE HOUSE · ARCHITECTURE
Map p212 (101 Penang Rd; MDhoby Ghaut) Near Orchard Rd, on the corner of Penang Rd, Tan Yeok Nee House was built in 1885 as the townhouse of a prosperous merchant, and is the sole surviving example in Singapore of a traditional Chinese mansion. Today it's part of the Asian campus of the University of Chicago Graduate School of Business, and is not open to the public, but you can still admire its fine roof decoration from outside.

NGEE ANN FOOT REFLEXOLOGY · MASSAGE
Map p212 (☑6235 5538; 4th fl, Midpoint Orchard, 220 Orchard Rd; ⊙11am-9pm; MSomerset) This small, friendly and refreshingly unpretentious massage centre has been around for more than 15 years and offers foot, head and body massages by visually impaired masseuses. If you're the luxury spa type, this place probably isn't for you. If you just fancy a good, well-priced massage (treatments from $30), walk this way.

EATING

TOP CHOICE KILLINEY KOPITIAM · COFFEESHOP $
Map p212 (67 Killiney Rd; mains $4-6; ⊙6am-11pm Mon & Wed-Sat, 6am-9pm Tue & Sun; MSomerset) This original local coffee joint, which spawned a host of imitations and an empire of franchises, is still *the* place to come for a Singaporean breakfast of toast, soft-boiled eggs and strong coffee. If you're here later in the day, you can tuck into the likes of chicken curry, laksa or *nasi lemak* (coconut rice, dried anchovies and spices wrapped in a banana leaf) before sampling one of the three types of sweet-dumpling desserts.

WASABI TEI · JAPANESE $$
Map p212 (05-70 Far East Plaza, 14 Scotts Rd; dishes $5-15; ⊙noon-3pm & 5.30-9.30pm Mon-Fri, noon-4.30pm & 5.30-9.30pm Sat; MOrchard) Join the queue snaking out of this hugely popular pocket-sized sushi bar. The chef is Chinese, but he sure can slice raw fish. One word of warning: you'd better make your choices before you sit down because there's no seconds or post-order amendments allowed.

IGGY'S · INTERNATIONAL $$$
Map p212 (☑6732 2234; www.iggys.com.sg; Level 3, Hilton International, 581 Orchard Rd; lunch $85, dinner $250; ⊙noon-1.30pm & 7-9.30pm Mon-Fri, 7-9.30pm Sat; MOrchard) What is arguably Singapore's best restaurant is now housed

FOOD COURTS

Burrow into the basement of most shopping malls on Orchard Rd and you'll find a food court with stall upon stall selling cheap, freshly cooked dishes from all over the world. These are the best two:

Food Republic (Map p212; Level 4, Wisma Atria, 435 Orchard Rd; ◉10am-10.30pm; ⓂOrchard) OK, so not actually in the basement, this one, but that's one of the reasons we like it because this is one of the few Orchard Rd food courts where you actually get a bit of a view. Food Republic offers traditional hawker classics, as well as Thai, Indian and Japanese. Muck in with the rest of the crowd for seats before joining the longest queues. Roving 'aunties' push around trolleys filled with drinks and dim sum.

Takashimaya Food Village (Map p212; B2 Takashimaya, Ngee Ann City, 391 Orchard Rd; ◉10am-9.30pm; ⓂOrchard) A crazy but oh-so-good mishmash of stalls selling Japanese pancakes, *bibimbap* (Korean rice dish), ice cream, sweet cream puffs and more.

at the Hilton International after a long run at the Regent. The setting is swankier here, and the food as incredible as it always was: Japanese and European sensibilities meshed together in a tasting menu of epic proportions (eight courses for dinner!). The wine list is as impressive as it is extensive.

SALT GRILL INTERNATIONAL $$$
Map p212 (✆6592 5118; www.saltgrill.com; 55-01 & 56-01 ION Orchard, 2 Orchard Turn; mains from $40; ◉11.30am-2pm & 6-10pm; ⓂOrchard) Owned by renowned Aussie chef Luke Mangan, Salt combines good honest Australian hospitality with quality Western cuisine infused with Asian ingredients, all served up with fabulous 56th-floor city views. Drink at the bar if you don't want to splash out for a meal.

DIN TAI FUNG CHINESE $
Map p212 (B1-03 Paragon, 290 Orchard Rd; dim sum from $3.50, noodles from $5.50; ◉11am-10pm; ⓂOrchard) Now with branches across the island (including another on Orchard Rd, inside 313 Somerset), this outlet of Din Tai Fung – Taiwan's oldest dumpling and noodle chain – was the first to open in Singapore. The food here, carefully prepared by the large team of chefs, visible through the full-length glass of the kitchen, is top-notch. Among the highlights is the simple pork and shrimp dumpling soup in a delicate broth, and the juicy *xiao long bao* (steamed pork dumplings). The free-flowing jasmine tea is a bonus too.

CHATTERBOX (TOP OF THE M) CHINESE $$
Map p212 (✆6831 6291; 5th Fl, Mandarin Orchard, 333 Orchard Rd; mains from $20; ◉5am-midnight Mon-Sat; ⓂSomerset) Chatterbox,

the actual restaurant, is on the 5th floor of this building, but it's much more fun eating in the top-floor bar, known as Top of the M, which has magnificent views of the city. The menu is the same, and the restaurant's famous chicken rice loses none of its fabulous flavour on its trip up to the 38th floor.

BOMBAY WOODLANDS RESTAURANT INDIAN VEGETARIAN $$
Map p212 (B1-01/02 Tanglin Shopping Centre, 19 Tanglin Rd; mains from $9; ◉noon-3pm & 6-10.30pm; ⓂOrchard) Tucked away below street level in the Tanglin Shopping Centre, Bombay Woodlands is the sort of place you'd pass by without a glance. Don't. The food is magnificent and cheap for this end of town; go for the lunchtime buffet or order à la carte for south Indian delights such as *idly* (spongy, round, fermented rice cakes) or *dosa* (paper-thin lentil-flour pancake), washed down with a cool *lassi* (yoghurt and iced-water drink).

GORDON GRILL INTERNATIONAL $$$
Map p212 (✆6730 1744; Goodwood Park Hotel, 22 Scotts Rd; mains from $40; ◉noon-2.30pm & 7-9.45pm; ⓂOrchard) With its old military club atmosphere, complete with 'family' portraits, and its famed steaks, Gordon Grill, housed inside the colonial-era Goodwood Park Hotel, is an olde worlde oasis in the middle of ultramodern Orchard Rd. It's as much an experience as it is a meal, so this is perhaps the best place for splashing out on the wagyu beef, ordered by weight.

CANTEEN INTERNATIONAL $$
Map p212 (01-01 Shaw Centre, 1 Scotts Rd; mains $6-12; ⓂSomerset) Modern, clean-cut cafe with a good choice of both Western and lo-

cal food, so if you don't fancy the laksa or the *mee siam* (sweet and sour rice noodles), you can go for the bangers and mash instead.

SUN WITH MOON
JAPANESE $$
Map p212 (⚡6733 6636; 03-15 Wheelock Place, 501 Orchard Rd; mains from $15; ⊙11.30am-11pm Sun-Thu, 11.30am-midnight Fri & Sat; Ⓜ Orchard) Bag a window seat overlooking a leafy section of Paterson Hill and tuck into the *kamameshi* (rice dish cooked in an iron pot) followed by some tofu cheesecake (playfully served up in a bird cage). Hanging Japanese lanterns and shag carpets add to the Far East charms of this very pleasant restaurant.

CRYSTAL JADE LA MIAN
XIAO LONG BAO
CHINESE $
Map p212 (04-07 Ngee Ann City, Takashimaya Shopping Centre; 391 Orchard Rd; dumplings from $3.50, noodles from $7; ⊙11.30am-9.45pm; Ⓜ Somerset) The Lanzhou *la mian* (pulled noodles) and the Shanghai *xiao long bao* are the specialities in this branch of the popular Crystal Jade chain. There are also plenty of dim sum options.

ORIOLE CAFE & BAR
CAFE
Map p212 (01-01 Pan Pacific Serviced Suites, 96 Somerset Rd; mains $10-18; Ⓜ Somerset) Oriole's modern bistro slant is reflected in a wide-ranging menu that will induce dining indecision. Do you get the beef-cheek tagliatelle, good old fish and chips or a Philly steak and cheese? Staff pull perfect espressos behind the impressive La Marzocco machine.

🍷 DRINKING & NIGHTLIFE

Shopping is thirsty work. Thankfully, there are many places on or near Orchard Rd in which to refuel. You won't find bargain beer prices (with one notable exception), but you will find cool cafes and swanky cocktail action. You can also grab a cheap beer at many of the food courts in Orchard Rd's shopping malls.

LOCAL KNOWLEDGE

DURIAN: THE KING OF (SMELLY) FRUITS

Durians get a bad rap in Singapore. They're banned from pretty much all forms of public transport, most notably from the MRT; few hotels will allow you to bring one through their front doors, and any shopping mall worth its salt will have a strict 'no durians' policy. Why? It's simple.

They stink. Even before the formidable thorn-covered husk is removed, they stink. And once you've opened one: pooh-whee! And yet durians are still known throughout Southeast Asia as the King of Fruits (largely because of their enormous size and those crownlike thorns) and are still loved by so many Singaporeans that you really should give one a go before you leave. The taste is an acquired one. Aficionados say the flavour of the soft, mushy edible flesh is like custard with a hint of almond. Others are less complimentary.

Tucking into a durian is a messy affair, usually done beside an over-sized paper bag, which is used to dispose of as much of the mess as possible. If the smell of durian lingers on your hands, try soaking your fingers in a glass of Coca-Cola; apparently it gets rid of the stench.

You can buy durian from markets and street stalls around Singapore, but if you're looking for somewhere to actually eat the thing too, trek out to **Durian Culture** (www.durianculture.com; 23 Teck Chye Terrace; ⊙11am-10.30pm; Ⓜ Ang Mo Kio, then ☐24) where manager Koh Chang Heng (who claims he can tell the quality of a durian from one whiff) will advise you on what to pick and how to eat it. He stocks five or six different grades of durian as well as a variety of other tropical fruit, all of which can be washed down with the contents of a fresh coconut.

Take bus 24 from Ang Mo Kio MRT station. Get off at Serangoon Stadium and keep walking straight on to Upper Serangoon Rd. Turn left and Teck Chye Terrace will be on your left, set back from the main road. You could also walk (about 1km) from Serangoon MRT station, northeast along Upper Serangoon Rd, but it's a busy road.

DUBLINERS
IRISH PUB

Map p212 (165 Penang Rd; ⊘11.30am-1am Sun-Thu, 11.30am-2am Fri & Sat; MSomerset) In a quieter section of Orchard Rd, Dubliners is one of the friendliest Irish pubs in Singapore, with the usual range of beers (from $12), including Irish stouts, and an excellent pub menu with generously sized mains starting at a very reasonable $6.50. The front verandah is a great spot for balmy nights and the service is spot on.

KPO
BAR

Map p212 (1 Killiney Rd; ⊘3pm-1am Mon-Thu, 3pm-2am Fri & Sat, 3-10pm Sun; MSomerset) Surely the quirkiest drinking set-up in Singapore, KPO is the only bar in the city with an attached post office. Stamp selling by day, cocktail mixing by night! The bar – so called because is sits at the junction of Killiney, Penang and Orchard Rds – is a funky, modern renovation of the former postmaster's house and has a lovely roof terrace overlooking a small, leafy park as well as a good selection of single-malt whiskeys. There's pub grub too, but, like the beers they sell here, it's not cheap (mains from $13).

CURIOUS TEEPEE
CAFE

Map p212 (02-24 Scape, 2 Orchard Link; ⊘noon-9pm; MOrchard) A cafe-cum-gift-shop selling funky knick-knacks, very good coffee and a few beers (from $11). Sit inside and browse the shelves, or drink out on the terrace overlooking youngsters risking life and limb in the Scape skate park below.

CUSCADEN PATIO
BAR

Map p212 (B1-11 Ming Arcade, 21 Cuscaden Rd; ⊘3pm-1am Sun-Thu, 3pm-3am Fri & Sat; MOrchard) This rundown basement bar with a small, open-air patio shouldn't be any good, but extra friendly staff and extra cheap drinks ensure it's as popular as any of the posh bars round Orchard Rd. The half-price beer deals mean you can sink a bottled lager for as little as $5 if you come before 10pm. Bargain. And the chicken wings go down very well indeed.

TWG TEA
CAFE

Map p212 (www.twgtea.com; 02-21 ION Orchard, 2 Orchard Rd; ⊘10am-10pm; MOrchard) For true tea connoisseurs; TWG stocks more than 450 varieties of tea from all over the world. Enjoy a pot at your table – with some scones perhaps? – or take away a pack for later.

DRINKS ON EMERALD HILL RD

Undoubtedly one of the nicest places to drink in the Orchard Rd area, Emerald Hill Rd is a peaceful residential oasis with a cluster of bars housed in beautifully renovated, 100-year-old Peranakan shophouses.

Que Pasa (Map p212; 7 Emerald Hill Rd; ⊘6pm-2am Sun-Thu, 6pm-3am Fri & Sat; MSomerset) An extremely pleasant wine and tapas bar with a convincingly shabby interior reminiscent of a real Spanish bar – except for the icy air-con (don't worry if you didn't bring a jacket; there's outdoor seating too). The wine list is impressive and, in keeping with the rest of Emerald Hill, extravagantly expensive. Expect to pay $14 for a glass of the cheapest wine. Tapas ($6–16) are uniformly excellent – try the mushrooms and the ubiquitous spicy sausage. Like all the bars on this strip, beers start from $12.

No 5 (Map p212; 5 Emerald Hill Rd; ⊘noon-2am Sun-Thu, noon-3am Fri & Sat; MSomerset) This one's been around for more than 20 years and remains a fine place for a drink, especially if you grab a seat outside on the terrace. Does good coffee, a range of single-malt whiskys and some pub grub too.

Alley Bar (Map p212; 2 Emerald Hill Rd; ⊘5pm-2am Sun-Thu, 5pm-3am Fri & Sat; MSomerset) The focal point of Alley Bar has to be the large gilded mirror hanging at the far end of the room, while the decor reflects the name of the bar, which has been done up to look like a street, with fake shopfronts, parking meters and street signs.

Ice Cold Beer (Map p212; 9 Emerald Hill Rd; ⊘6pm-2am Sun-Thu, 6pm-3am Fri & Sat; MSomerset) A more raucous, boozy establishment at the top of the Emerald Hill bar strip, offering a huge range of chilled beers from around the world to a rock soundtrack. Like the others it's housed in a 1900s Peranakan shophouse, though the frontage is pretty much all that remains.

TOP OF THE M
BAR

Map p212 (Level 38 Orchard Wing, Mandarin Singapore; ⊘5am-midnight Mon-Sat; ⓂSomerset) Sip cocktails (from $18) or a beer (from $15) and enjoy the view as the bar revolves slowly around the top floor of the Mandarin, 137m above Orchard Rd. You also can order food from the excellent Chatterbox restaurant on the 5th floor and eat it up here too.

TAB
LIVE MUSIC

Map p212 (www.tab.com.sg; 02-29 Orchard Hotel, 442 Orchard Rd; ⊘5am-1am Sun-Thu, 5pm-3am Fri & Sat; ⓂOrchard) Mid-sized live-music venue where local bands are encouraged to play their own stuff as well as covers. Foreign acts occasionally play here too. There are normally two gigs a night; the first starting at around 8pm, the second at around 11pm, although sometimes it's a DJ rather than a live band, and there are normally no live acts on Sundays. Many of the shows are free. Sometimes there's a cover charge (typically $20) that includes one or two drinks.

 SHOPPING

ION ORCHARD
MALL

Map p212 (www.ionorchard.com; 2 Orchard Turn; ⊘10am-10pm; ⓂOrchard) Orchard Rd's new centre of gravity, futuristic ION, with its much photographed facade, is undoubtedly the best-looking of all the malls here. But it's also a beautiful place to shop. Cleverly designed floors, rising directly above Orchard MRT Station, are always busy but never feel packed. You'll find an array of top-end brands as well as more affordable high-street labels and plenty of food options. There are also jewellery and watches galore. The attached 56-storey tower boasts a top-floor viewing gallery, **ION Sky** (ticket counter on level 4; child/adult $8/16; ⊘10am-noon & 2-8pm). You can also dine on posh nosh up here, at the excellent Salt Grill.

TANGLIN SHOPPING CENTRE
MALL

Map p212 (www.tanglinsc.com; 19 Tanglin Rd; ⊘9.30am-9pm; ⓂOrchard) A one-of-a-kind for Orchard Rd, this mall specialises in Asian art and is *the* place to come for rugs, carvings, ornaments, jewellery, paintings, furniture and the like. The fascinating **Antiques of the Orient** (www.aoto.com.sg; 02-40 Tanglin Shopping Centre; ⊘10am-6pm) is housed here, with its wonderful old books, photographs and genuinely ancient maps from all parts of Asia. You'll also find **Select Books** (03-15 Tanglin Shopping Centre; ⊘9am-6.30pm Mon-Sat, 10am-4pm Sun), an Asian book specialist, as well as some decent Asian-food options.

313 SOMERSET
MALL

Map p212 (www.313somerset.com.sg; 313 Orchard Rd; ⊘10am-10pm; ⓂSomerset) The new and hugely popular 313 has a great location above Somerset MRT Station and houses a cool mix of clothes shops such as **Zara**, music stores, restaurants, cafes and the always busy Apple shop, **EpiCentre**.

NGEE ANN CITY
MALL

Map p212 (www.ngeeanncity.com.sg; 391 Orchard Rd; ⊘10am-9.30pm; ⓂOrchard) You could spend days inside the megalithic Ngee Ann City. Well, not quite, but it is massive – seven floors of retail mayhem housed inside a downright ugly, brown-coloured marble and granite building. Inside, things are more modern with well-known luxury brands competing for space with the likes of **Kinokuniya** (southeast Asia's second-largest bookstore) and the Japanese department store **Takashimaya**, which houses Takashimaya Food Village, one of Orchard Rd's best food courts, and the reason locals call the mall 'Taka'.

WISMA ATRIA
MALL

Map p212 (www.wismaonline.com; 435 Orchard Rd; ⊘10am-10pm; ⓂOrchard) Five floors of street fashion plus the large Japanese department store **Isetan** and excellent food options including **Food Republic** and a branch of **Din Tai Fung**. Linked via underground walkway to ION Orchard shopping mall and, in turn, Orchard MRT Station.

SCAPE
MALL, SKATE PARK

Map p212 (www.scape.com.sg; 2 Orchard Link; ⊘10am-10pm; ⓂSomerset) The coolest teen hangout in Orchard Rd, Scape is more sprawling youth club than traditional shopping mall, although its mishmash of venues does include a mall of sorts, housing skatewear shops, gaming stores and cool cafes such as Curious Teepee, as well as dance studios, music centres and art galleries. It's the **skate park**, though – a sprawling, 3,000-square-metre concrete playground – that really draws the kids by the gang-load.

PLAZA SINGAPURA
MALL

Map p212 (www.plazasingapura.com.sg; 68 Orchard Rd; ⊘10am-10pm; ⓂDhoby Ghaut) As

WORTH A DETOUR

SHOPPING IN AN ACTUAL SHOP!

If you fancy a break from wall-to-wall malls, but still want to shop, slip away from Orchard Rd and walk up the impossibly quaint Emerald Hill Rd where you'll find a delightful antiques shop called **One Price Store** (Map p212; 3 Emerald Hill Rd; ⊕10am-4pm). Run most of the time by an old Chinese guy who speaks very little English, this 1900s Peranakan shophouse conversion is filled with Chinese art and antiques, including woodcarvings, porcelain snuff boxes and delicate glass jars. Prices are all marked, and some of the smaller items go for as little as $7 or $8.

popular as it is vast, Plaza Singapura was Singapore's original multistorey shopping mall. Teens come here to go to the movies and to check out the gaming arcades, while parents shop in Carrefour hypermarket. Loads of eating options here too.

WHEELOCK PLACE
MALL

Map p212 (501 Orchard Rd; ⊕10am-10pm; ⓂOrchard) A classy, cone-domed number housing brands including **Nike** and **Birkenstock**. Linked to ION Orchard and the MRT by an underground walkway.

FAR EAST PLAZA
MALL

Map p212 (www.fareast-plaza.com; 14 Scotts Rd; ⊕10am-10pm; ⓂOrchard) Detour a couple of hundred metres off Orchard Rd for a suit, a second-hand book or a tattoo at this old-fashioned but slightly leftfield mall containing 80-plus fashion outlets.

ORCHARD CENTRAL
MALL

Map p212 (www.orchardcentral.com.sg; cnr Orchard & Killiney Rds; ⊕11am-11pm; ⓂSomerset) One of Orchard Rd's more recent creations, this eye-catchingly modern shopping monster has 12 floors of retail outlets, a roof garden and is scattered with public art, but remains surprisingly quiet; possibly because everyone's in nearby 313 Somerset instead.

MIDPOINT ORCHARD
MALL

Map p212 (220 Orchard Rd; ⊕10am-9pm; ⓂSomerset) This ageing mall is the place to come for some camera haggling or reflexology. There are a few seedy-looking massage parlours in here, but one you can trust is Ngee Ann Foot Reflexology.

PARAGON
MALL

Map p212 (www.paragon.com.sg; 290 Orchard Rd; ⊕10.30am-9.30pm; ⓂSomerset) Sassiness defined, with timeless luxury brands sharing this stylish retail space with high-end fashion labels such as Burberry and Jimmy Choo.

HILTON SHOPPING GALLERY
MALL

Map p212 (581 Orchard Rd; ⊕10am-7pm; ⓂOrchard) Rolex, Bulgari, Issey Miyake, Paul Smith, Donna Karan. You get the picture; one of Orchard Rd's most glamorous malls.

TANGLIN MALL
MALL

Map p212 (www.tanglinmall.com.sg; 163 Tanglin Rd; ⊕9.30am-9pm; ⓂOrchard) Unashamedly marketing itself towards 'expats and yuppies', Tanglin Mall is a small, well-laid-out centre where you'll find cute clothing boutiques, quaint cafes, posh toy shops and good-quality homeware stores, plus throngs of expat mums pushing around designer buggies.

HEEREN
MALL

Map p212 (www.heeren.com.sg; 260 Orchard Rd; ⊕10am-10pm; ⓂSomerset) Teen heaven, with plenty of skate- and surf-fashion stores among four floors of well-known sports shops and trendy microboutiques.

FORUM
MALL

Map p212 (www.forumtheshoppingmall.com.sg; 583 Orchard Rd; ⊕10am-10pm; ⓂOrchard) One for the young ones, this; with toys and babygoods stores as well as a handful of designer kids' clothing stores.

EXOTIC TATTOO
TATTOO SHOP

Map p212 (☎6834 0558; 04-11 Far East Plaza, 14 Scotts Rd; ⊕noon-9pm Mon-Sat, noon-6pm Sun; ⓂOrchard) Visitors looking for a tattoo shop with a definite pedigree should know about this place, for it's here that you'll be able to get exquisite work from Sumithra Debi. One of the few female tattoo artists in Singapore, Sumithra is the granddaughter of Johnny Two-Thumbs, probably Singapore's most legendary tattoo artist. Though there's another shop in the plaza bearing the Two-Thumbs name, Exotic Tattoo is the actual heir to the Two-Thumbs lineage. In addition to ink work, the shop also does piercing.

Eastern Singapore

GEYLANG | KATONG | EAST COAST PARK | CHANGI | PASIR RIS

Neighbourhood Top Five

1 Do your own gastronomic walking tour around the numerous **food joints in Katong/Joo Chiat** (p90).

2 Discovering the rich Peranakan culture at **Katong Antique House** (p87) and **Rumah Bebe** (p95).

3 Night-time crab *bee hoon* and people-watching at **Sin Huat Eating House** (p90) in Geylang.

4 Learning about Singapore's sombre brush with the Japanese during WWII at **Changi Prison Museum & Chapel** (p89).

5 Riding a bicycle or rollerblading along **East Coast Park** (p88) before plonking yourself down for a dinner and Tiger beer by the beach-fronting **East Coast Lagoon Food Village** (p92).

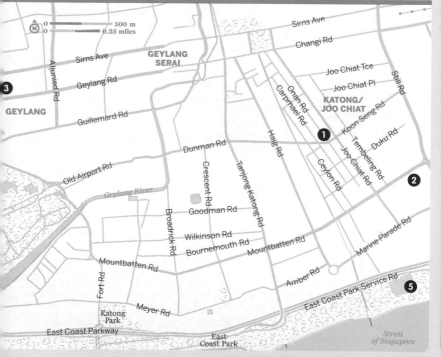

For more detail of this area, see Map p214 and p222

EASTERN SINGAPORE

Lonely Planet's Top Tip

The problem with Katong and Geylang being a culinary centre of Singapore is that restaurants come and go. Find out about the latest and greatest with a web search for local food blogs.

 Best Sights

➡ Changi Prison Museum & Chapel (p89)

➡ Katong Antique House (p87)

➡ Sri Senpaga Vinayagar Temple (p87)

For reviews, see p87 ➡

 Best Places to Eat

➡ Guan Hoe Soon (p91)

➡ Sin Huat Eating House (p90)

➡ Maeda (p91)

➡ Saveur (p90)

➡ Chin Mee Chin Confectionery (p90)

For reviews, see p89 ➡

 Best Places to Drink

➡ Sunset Bay Garden Beach Bar (p93)

➡ Cider Pit (p93)

For reviews, see p93 ➡

Explore Eastern Singapore

Though comprising a fair swath of the island, the neighbourhoods of the east receive far less attention from tourists than do those of the city centre. It's a shame, really, because whereas a district such as Chinatown is in danger of becoming a museum piece for tourists, the neighbourhoods of the east are vibrant, alive and, on the whole, more reflective of Singapore culture, both today and of days past. Closest to the city is the Geylang district, at once notorious as a red-light district, yet spiritual with myriad temples and mosques. The staggering amount of food outlets here is also a big draw.

Further east is Katong (also known as Joo Chiat), a picturesque neighbourhood of restored multicoloured shophouses that in recent years has come into its own as the spiritual heartland of Singapore's Peranakan people. Bordering Katong, and stretching for several kilometres along the seafront from the city right up to Tanah Merah, is East Coast Park. The well-paved waterfront paths offer plenty of space to skate and ride bicycles, as well as numerous spots for eating and drinking.

Don't discount a visit to Changi and Pasir Ris, the city's easternmost regions. Here's where you'll find the moving Changi Prison Museum and Chapel, a few resorts and theme parks for kids, a range of malls and the launching point for bumboats to Pulau Ubin and Johor in Malaysia.

Local Life

➡ **Food where it counts** Katong can lay claim to being the culinary centre of Singapore. There's everything from Peranakan to laksa and even French food in a coffeeshop. Geylang has several famed restaurants too.

➡ **People watching people** Locals flock to Geylang for its fantastic food, true, but just as many go there to gawk at the sex workers trawling the streets.

➡ **East Coast Park** Locals love this beachside park for barbecues, camping, cycling, sea sports and great food.

Getting There & Away

➡ **MRT** The east isn't well served by the MRT. Aljunied is Geylang's closest station; Paya Lebar and Eunos take you to the north end of Joo Chiat. Pasir Ris has its own station. Otherwise, buses are a better bet.

➡ **Bus** Buses 33 and 16 go to the centre of Joo Chiat, passing through Geylang; 14 goes from Orchard Rd to East Coast Rd. Buses 12 and 32 go to East Coast Rd from North Bridge Rd. Bus 2 from Tanah Merah MRT goes to Changi Village.

➡ **Taxi** Flag from the road. Taxi is best for East Coast Park.

◉ SIGHTS

◉ Geylang

AMITABHA BUDDHIST
CENTRE
BUDDHIST CENTRE

(☑6745 8547; www.fpmtabc.org; 44, Lorong 25A; ◉10am-6pm Tue-Sun; Ⓜ Aljunied) This seven-storey Tibetan Buddhist centre holds classes on dharma and meditation (check its website for the schedule), as well as events during religious festivals. The upstairs meditation hall, swathed in red-and-gold cloth, is open to the public and filled with beautiful statues and other objects of devotion. In addition to being involved with community outreach, the centre also operates a store selling religious and spiritual items such as prayer flags, spinning wheels, and other items associated with Tibetan Buddhism.

PU JI SI BUDDHIST RESEARCH
CENTRE
BUDDHIST CENTRE

(☑6746 6211; www.pujisi.org.sg; 39, Lorong 12; Ⓜ Aljunied) Inside this four-storey building, which is part educational facility, part house of worship, visitors will find meditation halls, Buddhist libraries filled with books and scripture, and a seemingly endless well of serenity. Take the elevator up for a seat by the fountain in the rooftop garden. Breathe in the air of serenity while pondering the eternal. Across the street from the centre sits a nameless jungle park for post-meditation contemplation.

◉ Katong/Joo Chiat

KATONG ANTIQUE HOUSE
MUSEUM

Map p214 (☑6345 8544; 208 East Coast Rd; 🚍10, 12, 14, 32) Part shop, part museum, the Katong Antique House is a labour of love for owner Peter Wee. A lifelong resident of the area, Peter displays (and occasionally sells) Peranakan antiques, artefacts and other objets d'art. A noted expert on Peranakan history and culture, Peter will happily regale you with tales as you browse. By appointment only, though it's sometimes open to the public (try your luck).

SRI SENPAGA VINAYAGAR
TEMPLE
HINDU TEMPLE

Map p214 (19 Ceylon Rd; 🚍10, 12, 14, 32) Easily among the most beautiful Hindu temples in Singapore, Sri Senpaga Vinayagar has an intricate yet understated facade. The temple eschews colour on the exterior and instead stuns visitors with its colourful devotional art inside. All the temple's devotional art is labelled in a number of languages. It has a number of unique features that make it well worth a visit even if you weren't in the neighbourhood already, especially the *kamalapaatham,* a specially sculptured granite foot-stone found in certain ancient Hindu temples. The roof of the inner sanctum sanctorum is covered in gold.

PERANAKAN TERRACE
HOUSES
ARCHITECTURE

Map p214 (Koon Seng Rd & Joo Chiat Place; Ⓜ Eunos) These two streets just off Joo Chiat Rd are where you'll find some of the finest Peranakan terrace houses in Singapore. Exhibiting the typical Peranakan enthusiasm for ornate design, they are decorated with stucco dragons, birds, crabs and brilliantly glazed tiles. *Pintu pagar* (swinging doors) at the front of the houses are another typical feature, allowing in breezes while retaining privacy. After falling into disrepair in the 1980s, the government designated them heritage buildings and all were restored to, some say, an overglossed state. They still look stunning. Many have been lavishly renovated inside and have become trendy homes, now worth around $2.5 million. For background information on the Peranakan people, see p170.

GEYLANG SERAI WET MARKET
MARKET

Map p214 (Geylang Serai; Ⓜ Paya Lebar) Hidden behind some older-style housing on Geylang Rd, this is a bustling Southeast Asian market, crammed with stalls selling fresh produce, fabrics and other wares. Upstairs is a popular food centre with great Malay and Indian stalls. Some say its continued existence defies the odds: as real-estate prices in the area skyrocket these older shopping areas are being razed and replaced with more Disney-esque areas such as the nearby (and thoroughly avoidable) Malay Cultural Village. The market is busiest during Ramadan, when the whole area is alive with evening market stalls. North of the market is a small park (next to the elevated MRT) where you can eat your durian in peace.

GEYLANG: NOT JUST A RED-LIGHT DISTRICT

What you may have heard about Geylang being an open-air meat market filled with a Dante-esque assortment of brothels, girlie bars, cheap hotels and alley after alley lined with prostitutes from all over Southeast Asia is all true. But strange as it may seem, the area is also one of the Lion City's spiritual hubs, with huge temples and mosques, and picturesque alleys dotted with religious schools, shrines and temples. A daytime stroll through the *lorongs* (alleys) that run north to south between Sims Ave and Geylang Rd offers surprising charm for those who take the time to look.

Several pretty side streets well worth checking out include tree-lined Lorong 27, a small street chock-a-block with colourful shrines and temples. Picturesque Lorong 24A is lined with renovated shophouses, from which the sounds of chanting often emerge; this is because many of these houses have actually been taken over by numerous smaller Buddhist associations in the area. Gorgeous Lorong 34 boasts both restored and unrestored shophouses painted in varying hues, as well as a number of colourful shrines and braziers for burning incense. One house on the street even boasts a street-side bamboo garden.

Take an MRT to Aljunied station and head south along Aljunied Rd. Once you get to Geylang Rd, you can head east or west. All the Lorongs snake out from Geylang Rd.

KUAN IM TNG TEMPLE   BUDDHIST TEMPLE

Map p214 (www.kuanimtng.org.sg; cnr Tembeling Rd & Joo Chiat Lane; MPaya Lebar) A beautiful temple dedicated to Kuan Yin, goddess of mercy, this Buddhist temple is home to many festivals throughout the year. Of particular interest to temple-lovers is the ornate roof ridges, adorned with dancing dragons and other symbols important to worshippers of the goddess.

CHURCH OF THE HOLY FAMILY   CHURCH

Map p214 (6 Chapel Rd; 10, 12, 14, 32) With its gracefully curving roof, stained glass and gleaming white edifice, this Catholic church displays an interesting mixture of Western and Asian architecture. Though not the original building (the original chapel on this spot was built in 1923, and the origins of the congregation go back further), the edifice is worth a look. Keep an eye out for the unusual stained-glass window featuring the image of a 16-pointed star over the altar.

◉ East Coast Park

EAST COAST PARK   PARK

Map p214 This 11km stretch of seafront park is where Singaporeans come to swim, windsurf, kayak, picnic, bicycle, rollerblade and, of course, eat. The whole park has been superbly designed so that the many leisure facilities don't crowd the green space. In this single, narrow strip, there are several bird

sanctuaries, patches of unmanaged bushland, golf driving ranges, tennis courts, a resort, several ponds and a lagoon, sea sports clubs, hawker centres, and some excellent bars and restaurants.

Renting a bicycle or rollerblades and gently pedalling from one end to the other, enjoying the sea breezes, watching the veritable city of container ships out in the strait and capping it off with a meal and a few beachfront beers is one of the most pleasant ways to spend a Singapore afternoon.

East Coast Park starts at the end of Tanjong Katong Rd in Katong and ends at the National Sailing Centre in Bedok, which is actually closer to the Tanah Merah MRT station. At the western end of the park, the bicycle track continues right through to Katong, ending at the Kallang River.

On weekends only, bus 401 from Bedok Bus Interchange, outside Bedok MRT, takes you directly to East Coast Park. On weekdays, take bus 197 from Bedok and stop along Marine Pde Rd (ask the bus driver where to get off). Walk 250m south to an underpass, which will take you into East Coast Park.

MARINE COVE
RECREATION CENTRE   RECREATION CENTRE

Map p214 (East Coast Park Service Rd) Midway along the park, near the end of Still Rd South, this outdoor leisure complex has tenpin bowling, squash, crazy golf and a large selection of restaurants, food stalls and bars, plus a McDonald's (only worth mentioning because it's Singapore's only one with a skate-through window). On the beach side of the complex there are a couple of bicycle and rollerblade rental stations and a kayak and sailboat rental place on the beach itself. There have been rumours of the centre's redevelopment, so fingers crossed it's still there when you visit. To get here on public transport, follow the same instructions as East Coast Park.

⊙ Changi & Pasir Ris

FREE **CHANGI PRISON MUSEUM & CHAPEL**   MEMORIAL, MUSEUM
Map p222 (☑6214 2451; www.changimuseum. com; 1000 Upper Changi Rd North; guided tour adult/child S$8/4; ☺9.30am-5pm; ☑2) A steady stream of visitors makes its way to this quiet, moving museum commemorating the Allied POWs who were captured and imprisoned and suffered horrific treatment at the hands of the invading Japanese forces during WWII. It was shifted from the original Changi prison site in 2001 when Singapore Prisons reclaimed the land to expand its operations. Inside stories are told through photographs, letters, drawings and murals; tales of heroism and celebration of peace temper the mood. There are also full-sized replicas of the famous **Changi Murals** painted by POW Stanley Warren in the old POW hospital. The originals are off limits in what is now Block 151 of the nearby Changi Army Camp.

Former POWs, veterans and historians will feel the loss of the actual site most keenly, but to the architects' credit the understated design of the new building is well suited to its dual role as a shrine and history museum. The square white facade is reminiscent of a concrete bunker, yet the greenery hints at healing and renewal. The gaping entrance and open-plan design is welcoming. The museum's centrepiece is a replica of the original Changi Chapel built by inmates as a focus for worship and presumably as a sign of solidarity. Tucked into the walls beside the altar, with its cross made of ammunitions casings, are little mementos left by visitors – white crosses, red poppies, fresh flowers and handwritten notes. Services are held on Sundays (at 9.30am and 5.30pm), but the shadeless courtyard heats up like an oven.

Bus 2 from Victoria St or Tanah Merah MRT station will take you past the entrance. Get off at bus stop B09, just after the Changi Heights condominium. The bus terminates at Changi Village.

PASIR RIS PARK   PARK
Map p222 (Pasir Ris Dr 3; Ⓜ Pasir Ris) Stretching along a couple of kilometres of the northeast coast, a short walk from Pasir Ris MRT station, this peaceful place is the third-largest park in Singapore and certainly among the best. The 71-hectare waterside park has family-friendly activities galore. Rent a bike or in-line skates to get around. Or hoof it and explore the 6-hectare mangrove boardwalk – go during low tide to see little crabs scurrying in the mud. Speaking of hooves, kids will love the pony rides at **Gallop Stables** (☑6583 9665; 61 Pasir Ris Green; rides $10; ☺8am-noon, 2-7pm Tue-Sun). Make it over to Downtown East (p95) to grab a bite or look out for several bars within the park.

LOYANG TUA PEK KONG TEMPLE   TEMPLE
Map p222 (20 Loyang Way; ☑9 from Ⓜ Bedok) The embodiment of the Singaporean approach to spirituality, this temple hosts three religions, Hinduism, Buddhism and Taoism, under one vast roof. There's even a shrine devoted to Datuk Kung, a saint of Malay mysticism and Chinese Taoist practices. This temple is new and grand with large handcrafted wooden cravings, swirling dragons on large granite pillars and hundreds of colourful effigies of deities, gods and saints. It's a bit off the beaten path, but worth the trip if you're en route to Changi Village. Get off bus 9 at the Loyang Valley condominium and walk in.

EATING

Few visitors spend a great deal of time in eastern Singapore, but we're hoping that will change, because the area is not only rich in history, culture and architecture but also is home to some exceptional food, from the Peranakan delights of Katong/Chiat to the superb seafood along East Coast. Hardier souls might brave the nightly, never-sleeping sleaze of Geylang, where some great food lurks among the prostitutes and punters. Look out for durian stalls along the way. You pick your durian, then it's split open for you. Eat it at the plastic tables and chairs in front of the stall.

✕ Geylang

SIN HUAT EATING HOUSE
SEAFOOD $$$

Map p214 (Lorong 35, Geylang Rd; ☺11am-late; MPaya Lebar) The best seafood in Singapore, or a victim of its own fame? Famous food writers have come here in legions and declared Chef Danny's crab *bee hoon* (rice vermicelli noodles) to be one of the greatest dishes on earth. Inevitably, it's very expensive, usually busy, and the service is notoriously rude, but as much as you're itching to criticise it, the food is fantastic. Ask for prices before committing if you don't want sticker shock later.

NO SIGNBOARD SEAFOOD
SEAFOOD $$

(414 Geylang Rd; dishes from $15; ☺noon-1am; MAljunied) Madam Ong Kim Hoi famously started out with an unnamed hawker stall (hence 'No Signboard'), but the popularity of her seafood made her a rich woman, with five restaurants and counting. Principally famous for its white-pepper crab, No Signboard also dishes up delightful lobster, abalone and less familiar dishes such as bullfrog and deer. Other branches are at East Coast Seafood Centre (p92), Esplanade – Theatres on the Bay (p52) and VivoCity (p115).

LOR 9 BEEF KWAY TEOW
NOODLES $

(Lorong 9, Geylang Rd; ☺dinner; MKallang) Once you've stopped gawking at the sights across the road in this red-light district, order the beef *hor fun* (flat rice noodles wok-fried with tender slices of beef in black-bean sauce) and some *tian ji zhou* (frog's leg porridge). The frog is cooked in a claypot with dried chilli, spices, spring onion and soy sauce. It tastes like chicken, only crunchier. Wash it all down with copious amounts of Tiger beer.

✕ Katong/Joo Chiat

TOP CHOICE CHIN MEE CHIN CONFECTIONERY
BREAKFAST $

Map p214 (204 East Coast Rd; dishes from $4; ☺8am-4pm Tue-Sun; 💺10, 14) *Kaya* (jam made from coconut and egg) toast like grandma used to make. A nostalgic trip for many older Singaporeans, old-style bakeries like Chin Mee Chin are a dying breed, with their mosaic floors, wooden chairs and strong coffee. One of the few Singaporean breakfast joints that still makes its own *kaya,* apparently.

TOP CHOICE SAVEUR
FRENCH $

Map p214 (Ali Baba Eating House, www.saveur.sg; 125 East Coast Rd; mains $9-12; ☺lunch Mon-Sat, dinner Thu-Mon; 💺10, 12, 14, 32) Duck confit for $9? Angel-hair pasta or duck rillettes for $4? Meats cooked sous-vide? It's the (low) price you pay for French dining in a coffee-shop sans linen and air-con. Go on a weekday, as it's madness otherwise. Don't forget to get *tau kaw pau* (fried bean curd stuffed

---

WORTH A DETOUR

FAR EAST: CHANGI VILLAGE

On the far northeast coast, Changi Village is an escape from the hubbub of the city. A wander around the area offers a window into a more relaxed side of Singapore, where vests, bermuda shorts and flip-flops (the quintessential heartlander uniform) is the look, and people are slightly less accustomed to seeing *ang moh* (Europeans) in their midst. The atmosphere is almost village-like, and a browse around the area will turn up cheap clothes, batik, Indian textiles and electronics.

En route, look out for the interesting old black-and-white colonial bungalows along Loyang Ave. Most locals make a beeline for the lively and renowned Changi Village Hawker Centre (p93) next to the bus terminus. Across from the bus terminal is Changi Beach, where thousands of Singaporean civilians were executed during WWII. It's lapped by the polluted waters of the Straits of Johor and lousy for swimming, but there's a good stretch of sand for a romantic stroll. It's popular on weekends but almost deserted during the week. Next to the bus terminal is the Changi Point Ferry Terminal, where you can catch bumboats to Pulau Ubin or Johor Bahru.

For a different kind of Singapore day, combine a few hours here with a trip to Pulau Ubin and round the day off with a meal at the Changi Village Hawker Centre, then a few beers at Charlie's Corner (p92).

with cucumber, yam pieces, chopped egg and mince meat) from a neighbouring stall. We fear its popularity means that it might outgrow its location soon, so check the website just in case.

JAI THAI
THAI $

Map p214 (205 East Coast Rd; mains from $5; ⊙lunch & dinner; 🚌10, 12, 14, 32) Service might be abysmally slow (they're always busy), but we muck in with the rest of the locals because it's 'cheap and good', as they all say. The *tom yum goong* is spicy enough to knock your socks off, though the $5 Singhas will easily quell the fire in your belly and mouth. If you don't do spicy, there are 81 other items on the menu certain to sate every palette.

328 KATONG LAKSA
LAKSA $

Map p214 (53 East Coast Rd; laksa from $4; 🚌10, 12, 14, 32) Several laksa stalls along this stretch have long been bickering over who was first and best. You won't go wrong at any of them, but this joint is, commercially at least, the most successful. The namesake dish is a bowl of thin rice noodles in a light curry broth made with coconut milk and Vietnamese coriander, and topped with shrimps and cockles. Order some *otah-otah* (spiced mackerel cake grilled in a banana leaf) to accompany the laksa. Compare notes with a competition stall just across the road. Another branch at 216 East Coast Rd.

NAÏVE
VEGETARIAN $$

Map p214 (99 East Coast Rd; mains from $10; ⊙lunch & dinner; 🚌10, 12, 14, 32) We were a little naive to think that the vegetarian food here would be dull. It's not. The menu features meatless variations on local favourites such as Golden Oat, where tofu (instead of prawns) is deep-fried and coated with sweet oats. The cosy dining room has communal tables, so you can enjoy a feel-good vegetarian fix with your fellow diners.

ENG SENG COFFEESHOP
SEAFOOD $$

Map p214 (247-249 Joo Chiat Pl; ⊙5-9pm; dishes from $15; Ⓜ Eunos) One of Singapore's signature dishes – black-pepper crab – is so good here that locals are (1) willing to queue over an hour to order and (2) happy to be rudely told how many crabs they can order by the proprietress. The sticky, honeylike peppery sauce makes it worth arriving at 4.30pm for an early dinner.

GUAN HOE SOON
PERANAKAN $$

Map p214 (38 Joo Chiat Pl; mains from $12; 🚌33) Famously, this is Singapore's oldest Peranakan restaurant (established 1953) and Lee Kuan Yew's favourite, but even boasts like that don't cut much ice with picky Singaporeans if the food doesn't match up. Fortunately, its fame hasn't inspired complacency and the Nonya food here is top notch. The definitive Peranakan *ayam buah keluak* (chicken with black nut) is a standout.

CHILLI PADI
PERANAKAN $$

Map p214 (11 Joo Chiat Pl; dishes from $6; 🚌33) Outstanding Peranakan food in its spiritual home of Joo Chiat – and so popular it's spawned a range of home-cook pastes. Try the sour *assam* fish head and or sambal *sotong* (squid), and don't miss the *kueh pie ti* (flour cups filled with prawn and turnip).

MAEDA
JAPANESE $$$

Map p214 (✆6345 0745; 467 Joo Chiat Rd; dishes from $10; 🚌16) Superlatives aren't enough to describe the authentic Osaka-style cuisine served up by owner and chef Maeda Hiroaki. Delicate slices of sashimi are dotted with chrysanthemum flowers for effect, and the menu features uncommon dishes such as squid guts. Maeda works the sushi counter and is more than happy to down some sake with you. If you can't decide what to order, spring for the *omakase* menu ($90 to $150). Portions are generous. Bookings recommended.

TONNY RESTAURANT
CHINESE $$

Map p214 (327 Joo Chiat Rd; dishes from $8; 🚌16) Chef Tonny Chan dishes up clever riffs on Cantonese food. Dishes such as deep-fried, finely shredded yam drizzled with truffle oil, creamy cold crab, and a mousse of lobster, scallops and egg whites give diners plen'tonny to be happy about.

TIAN TIAN CHICKEN RICE
CHICKEN RICE $

Map p214 (443 Joo Chiat Rd; dishes from $4; ⊙10.30am-9.30pm Tue-Sun; 🚌16) Fans of the original branch at Maxwell Rd will inevitably scoff and put it down, but this eastern outpost of Singapore's most famous Hainanese chicken rice stall is actually good. Tender boiled chicken served over fragrant rice with the best chilli sauce around. Save room because you need to order the Hainanese pork chop too.

EASTERN SINGAPORE EATING

TWO FAT MEN
THAI **$$**

Map p214 (376 East Coast Rd; dishes from $8; 5pm-3am daily; 🖳16) The outdoor decking is great, but the draft beer options are fairly limited – only Kronenbourg blanc and Singha – though it doesn't matter, because we rate this bar more for its Thai food. Forget the fried food and burgers – flip the menu round and home in on the Thai food. Juicy pork neck with tamarind sauce, creamy spicy green curry, basil chicken fried rice and other mouth-watering favourites are probably the reason you'll feel like two fat men when you leave.

MARINE PARADE FOOD CENTRE
HAWKER CENTRE **$**

Map p214 (Block 84, Marine Parade Central; dishes from $3; 🖳15, 31, 36, 196, 197) This longstanding hawker centre has over 50 stalls stretching in an L-shape. You'll probably end up spending more time deciding what to eat than on the meal itself! The standout stall is **Seremban Beef Noodles** at 01-184. The thick gravy, studded with beef, tendon and tripe, is intense. The *char kway teow* (broad noodles, clams and eggs fried in chilli and black-bean sauce) stall along the same row has erratic hours but is good too.

KATONG SHOPPING CENTRE
FOOD COURT **$**

Map p214 (865 Mountbatten Rd; 🖳10, 12, 14, 32) Head to the basement of what must be Singapore's most depressing mall (maid agencies line the corridors) for some good food-court grub. The **Delicious Boneless Chicken Rice** stall is particularly good. There's a little bakery, **Dona Mani**, tucked away in the basement, that serves up delectable banana pie. Follow your nose.

SIGLAP NEIGHBOURHOOD
INTERNATIONAL **$**

off Map p214 (Upper East Coast Rd; 🖳10, 12, 14) This strip of road is a hit with locals because of its laid-back vibe and decent (but not stellar) range of food options. Grab Thai food at **Porn's** (81 Upper East Coast Rd), Japanese at **Megumi** (77 Upper East Coast Rd), Turkish at **Turkish Cuisine** (162 Upper East Coast Rd), or just hunker down at the food centre across from Starbucks.

ROLAND RESTAURANT
SEAFOOD **$$**

Map p214 (🖉6440 8205; Block 89, 06-750 Marine Parade Central; crabs from $14; 🖳15, 31, 36, 196, 197) Located on top of a car park, but don't let that put you off. If the chilli crab (the restaurant lays claim to inventing it) and

USA duck in this giant restaurant are good enough for the prime minister, they're good enough for us, though eating in huge dining rooms is a little impersonal.

JIA WEI
CHINESE **$$**

Map p214 (2nd fl, Grand Mercure Roxy Hotel, 50 East Coast Rd; mains from $15; 🖳10, 14) Top spot in the East Coast area for dim sum, popular with business lunchers. Don't be put off by the remarkable ugliness of the hotel building – the service and the food here is excellent. If you've acquired a taste for durian, try the fried ice cream or pureed version for dessert. There's a take-away outlet just outside the lobby for those who want a meal on the run.

🍴 East Coast Park

EAST COAST LAGOON FOOD VILLAGE
HAWKER CENTRE **$**

Map p214 (1220 East Coast Parkway; dishes from $3; 🕙10.30am-11pm) There are few hawker centres with a better location. Tramp barefoot off the beach and order up some satay, seafood, or the uniquely Singaporean satay *bee hoon* from **Meng Kee** at stall 17. Expect to queue. Cheap beer and wine (!) available.

EAST COAST SEAFOOD CENTRE
SEAFOOD **$$**

Map p214 (1202 East Coast Parkway; mains $15-75; 🕙dinner) Overlooking the Straits of Singapore in the salty breeze, this renowned seafood centre boasts several excellent restaurants, all with outdoor seating. Don't miss the chilli crab, black-pepper crab and the intoxicating 'drunken' prawns. Standout places include **Jumbo**, **Long Beach**, **No Signboard** and **Red House**.

🍴 Changi & Pasir Ris

CHARLIE'S CORNER
INTERNATIONAL **$$**

Map p222 (01-08 Changi Village Hawker Centre, 2 Changi Village Rd; dishes from $10; lunch & dinner Tue-Sun; Ⓜ Tanah Merah then 🖳2) Charlie's Corner is something of an institution, run by an old fella who's been a fixture here for years. The endless varieties of beer and the fish and chips are the main draws, attracting people from far afield. The prices are a little high for a hawker-centre stall, but after a few beers you won't notice. Bottled beers come encased in a stubby holder…a nice touch!

THE INVENTION OF CHILLI CRAB

In 1956, Mr and Mrs Lim opened a seafood restaurant called the Palm Beach. It was here that Mrs Lim first concocted the now-famous tomato, chilli and egg sauce that makes the quintessential Singapore chilli crab. At least that's the story according to her son Roland, who is the proprietor of the eponymous Roland Restaurant (p92). Singaporean food outlets love their rags-to-riches tales.

The Lims emigrated to New Zealand in the 1960s, but Roland returned to Singapore to find his mum's dish a huge hit. He opened his own restaurant in 1985, and since moving to its present location along Marine Pde in 2000, the 1300-seater place has built up a solid reputation – so much so that former prime minister Goh Chok Tong dines here on National Day.

CHANGI VILLAGE HAWKER CENTRE MALAY $
Map p222 (2 Changi Village Rd; dishes from $3; ◷10.30am-11.30pm; MTanah Merah then ◻2) Row after row of stalls offering a plethora of food might bewilder most. But there's only one thing the locals come here for – the *nasi lemak*. Fragrant coconut rice is topped with fried chicken or fish, *ikan bilis* (fried anchovies) and sambal chilli. The original stall at 01-57 has spawned neighbouring imitators if you can't be bothered to queue (and the queues are sometimes insane).

DRINKING & NIGHTLIFE

Katong/Joo Chiat

CIDER PIT BAR
Map p214 (382 Joo Chiat Rd) A nondescript concrete structure houses an easy-to-miss little watering hole. Cider on tap and a wide range of imported British $10 pints (think London Pride and Hobgoblin) make this a perfect place to work your way into a drunken state. Avoid the seats inside unless you want to become mosquito bait.

FATBOY'S THE BURGER BAR BAR, RESTAURANT
Map p214 (www.fatboys.sg; 465 Joo Chiat Rd; ◷4pm-midnight Mon-Thu, noon-midnight Fri-Sun) We won't blame you for rolling out feeling like a fat boy, because the massive burgers here threaten to steal the show from the beer. Stella and Hoegaarden are on tap, along with a modest selection of bottled international brews. Sports TV completes the experience.

East Coast Park

SUNSET BAY GARDEN BEACH BAR BAR
Map p214 (1300 East Coast Park, Car Park F2) What could be finer than relaxing with cocktails or a pint in a car-free beachside park in the early evening? While the night away to the far-off thrumming of hundreds of cargo ships moored just off Singapore's southern shore. The food here is average so eat at the nearby East Coast Lagoon Food Village before retiring here.

Changi & Pasir Ris

CALIFORNIA JAM BAR
Map p222 (Block 1, Changi Village Rd; ◷4.30pm-midnight daily; ◻2) A little rock 'n' roll bar in Changi Village. Jimi Hendrix posters, beer on tap and the occasional transvestite sex worker gives this place a 'Walk on the Wild Side' vibe. California Jam is part of the strip of bars on Changi Village Rd that's somewhat popular with locals and expats looking to escape the trendy crush of central Singapore.

BAMBOOZE BAR
Map p222 (Block 5, Changi Village Rd; ◷3pm-1am daily; ◻2) Inside it's your typical low-key bar – TVs with the sports channel on, dark moody interiors and a long bar. But the expats who frequent the joint seem content to crowd the tables outside. Its $6 pints of Stella are probably the best draw. If you get sick of the crowd, head to any coffeeshop nearby for cheap $6 Tigers.

EASTERN SINGAPORE DRINKING & NIGHTLIFE

MUST-TRY TOURS

➡ Operated by Tony Tan (owner of the Betel Box Hostel and expert on all things Singapore), **Real Singapore Tours** (☑6247 7340; www.betelbox.com) is one you won't soon forget. Tony offers food tours (generally on Thursdays at 6pm), taking his charges on a veritable gastronomic odyssey through the historic Joo Chiat neighbourhood, where participants can sample over 20 authentic dishes from all over Southeast Asia. Other tours on offer include a superb cycling trip along the coastline of Singapore into the CBD. Prices start at $60 including food, equipment and the services of one of the most knowledgeable tour guides in Singapore.

➡ When it comes to selecting a guide to show you the sights and sounds of the Lion City, you won't find anyone more idiosyncratic than **Jeffery Tan** (☑9784 6848; http://jefflimo.tripod.com/jefflimo.htm). Known as 'Singapore's Singing Cabbie', Tan can croon in nine languages and will happily serenade you in the language of your choice while showing you the city's attractions. A native Singaporean, Tan's tours include any sights that you'd like; he also does a food tour, ensuring that all your senses are stimulated. If you feel like singing along, Jeff can accommodate you: the limo is equipped with the latest in video karaoke systems.

➡ **Geraldene Lowe-Ahmad** (☑6737 5250; geraldenestours@hotmail.com) and **Diana Chua** (☑9489 1999; dianachua1999@yahoo.com.sg) are the venerable dynamic duo of the Singapore guide scene, offering a wide variety of tours to suit all interests. Geraldene's knowledge of Singapore's history, cuisine, architecture, botany, ethnic diversity, religions and festivals is second to none. She also does amazing WWII tours, popular among veterans. In addition to cultural and historical tours, Diana also specialises in more esoteric areas, such as excursions examining Singaporean feng shui, cemeteries and other less-examined facets of the Lion City. Both offer time-specific tours, taking advantage of various religious and cultural festivities. Tours can be conducted in English, Malay, Chinese, Italian or French.

⭐ ENTERTAINMENT

NECESSARY STAGE   THEATRE

Map p214 (☑6440 8115; www.necessary.org; B1-02 Marine Parade Community Bldg, 278 Marine Parade Rd; 🚌12, 14 or 32) Since the theatre's inception in 1987, current artistic director Alvin Tan has collaborated with resident playwright Haresh Sharma to produce over 60 original works. Innovative, indigenous, and often controversial, the Necessary Stage is one of Singapore's best-known theatre groups.

SKI360°   WATER SPORTS

Map p214 (www.ski360degree.com; 1206A East Coast Parkway; per hr weekdays/weekends $32/42; ⊙10am-9.45pm Mon-Thu, till 11.45pm Fri, 9am-11.45pm Sat, till 9.45pm Sun) What better way to cool off than by strapping on some waterskis, a kneeboard or a wakeboard and getting dragged around a lagoon on the end of a cable? OK, you could just go swimming, but where's the fun in that? Best visited on weekday mornings, when there's usually hardly anyone there. The

poseur quotient goes through the roof at weekends, when it's just as entertaining sitting around hoping someone will come a cropper on the ramps. On weekends, take bus 401 from Bedok MRT. On weekdays, take bus 197, stop along Marine Pde Rd and walk through an underpass.

ESCAPE THEME PARK   THEME PARK

Map p222 (Downtown East, cnr Pasir Ris Dr 3 & Pasir Ris Close; www.escapethemepark.com.sg; adult/child/family $20/11/45; ⊙5-10pm Mon-Fri, 10am-10pm Sat & Sun; Ⓜ Pasir Ris) Who doesn't love a tropical water slide, roller coasters, go-karts, bumper boats and wave pools? The wet-and-wild flume ride is said to be Asia's highest. Price of admission allows access to unlimited rides: go-kart, slide, ride and splash around till you're wrinkled, sunburnt and sore.

WILD WILD WET   THEME PARK

Map p222 (Downtown East, cnr Pasir Ris Dr 3 & Pasir Ris Close; www.wildwildwet.com; adult/child/family $16/11/44; ⊙1-7pm Mon & Wed-Fri, 10am-7pm Sat & Sun; Ⓜ Pasir Ris) Part of the same Downtown East complex occupied by Escape Theme Park, this water fun-park offers eight rides in a similar vein.

PASIR RIS SPORTS & RECREATION CENTRE SWIMMING

Map p222 (120 Pasir Ris; adult/child $1.50/1; ☺8am-9.30pm Tue-Sun; ⓂPasir Ris) This $40 million (!) public swimming complex has jacuzzis, water slides and, yes, swimming pools of several varieties, including Olympic-sized monstrosities.

 # SHOPPING

The narrow lanes of shophouses and affluent residential suburbs of eastern Singapore are more renowned for their food than their shopping, and rightly so. Indeed, some of the better shopping options in the area are food related, though there are a couple of decent malls to divert the mind from its culinary pursuits.

KIM CHOO KUEH CHANG FOOD

Map p214 (109 East Coast Rd; 🚍10, 14) Joo Chiat is stuffed with bakeries and dessert shops, but Kim Choo retains that old-world atmosphere, selling its traditional pineapple tarts and other brightly coloured Peranakan *kueh* (bite-sized snacks) from a wooden counter that looks more like an apothecary's shop. Ask for recommendations, or buy one of each! Head upstairs to catch demonstations of how to make *bak chang* (rice dumplings) and pick up some Peranakan souvenirs.

RUMAH BEBE PERANAKAN CLOTHING

Map p214 (113 East Coast Rd; ☺9.30am-6.30pm Tue-Sun; 🚍10, 14) Bebe Seet is the owner of this 1928 shophouse and purveyor of all things Peranakan. She sells traditional *kebayas* (Nonya-style blouses with decorative lace) and beautifully beaded shoes. If you've got time and the inclination, you can take shoe-beading classes run by Bebe. Don't forget to buy some *kueh* before you go.

ISAN GALLERY GALLERY

Map p222 (www.isangallery.com.sg; 42 Jln Kambangan; ⓂKembangan) The home gallery of Percy Vatsaloo showcases intricately crafted and exquisitely beautiful clothing and other textiles made by tribal craftspeople of Isan in northeast Thailand. Visitors are welcome by appointment, and most of the items on display are also for sale. Percy works closely with the craftspeople themselves, and half of the sale price goes directly to them.

PARKWAY PARADE MALL

Map p214 (www.parkwayparade.com.sg; 80 Marine Parade Rd; 🚍15, 31, 36, 76) A tremendously popular mall in the east, Parkway houses anchor tenants such as **Isetan** department store, plus a range of electronics and fashion retailers and the customary onslaught of food outlets.

TAMPINES MALL MALL

Map p222 (4 Tampines Central 5; ⓂTampines) One of Singapore's largest and most-crowded suburban shopping centres, conveniently located right next to the Tampines MRT station. Aimed at middle-class heartlanders, you'll find another branch of the **Isetan** department store, a **cinema** and several bookshops inside this bottle-green monster. There are two smaller malls next door: **Century Square** and **Tampines 1**. The latter has chain and independent clothing stores targeted at young people.

DOWNTOWN EAST MALL

Map p222 (www.downtowneast.com.sg; cnr Pasir Ris Dr 3 & Pasir Ris Close; ⓂPasir Ris). Yes, it's the building with the ferris wheel built inside (rides $6.50). The mall itself has OK shops but the **cinema** is popular, as are the numerous food outlets and the **Orchid bowling alley**. It's connected to Wild Wild Wet and Escape Theme Park.

Northern & Central Singapore

Neighbourhood Top Five

❶ Trek to Singapore's steamy heart of darkness in the primary rainforest of the **Bukit Timah Nature Reserve** (p98).

❷ Treat your kids to breakfast with orang-utans at the magical **Singapore Zoo** (p99).

❸ Spot leopards and dodge bats as you give the tram tour the slip and walk around the **Night Safari** (p100).

❹ See the forest from a dizzying new angle on the 25m-high Treetops Walk at peaceful **MacRitchie Reservoir** (p99).

❺ Visit Singapore's last remaining *kampong* (village), at **Lorong Buangkok** (p101), before city developers get their hands on it.

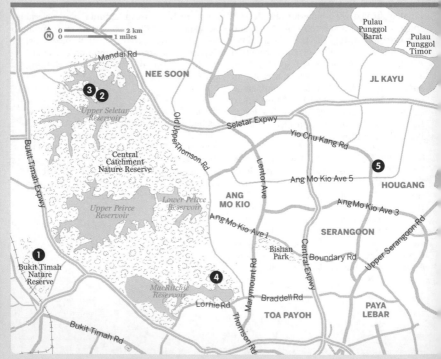

For more detail of this area, see Map p207 ➡

Explore Northern & Central Singapore

This wonderfully wild and gloriously green part of Singapore is packed with sights and activities that take time to see and do, so unless you're here for an extended stay you're going to have to pick and choose carefully among the main attractions.

If you fancy taking advantage of the excellent walking trails round here, then try to get your hiking done early in the morning. The weather will be cooler, and it will leave you most of the rest of the day to do other sightseeing.

The zoo and the night safari are both crammed with restaurants and cafes, but if you're visiting the other sights mentioned in this chapter, you might have to do some pre-planning around meal times. Eat before you set off or bring some food with you (especially if you're planning to trek round MacRitchie Reservoir). Alternatively, grab a meal at one of the MRT stations you'll be passing through. Both Ang Mo Kio and Toa Payoh stations are large transport hubs and have popular, well-stocked food courts as well as buses that go out to some of the main sights.

Local Life

➡ **Bus it** It's tempting to take cabs to all the out-of-the-way sights round here, but there's no need: A combination of MRT and bus rides will get you anywhere you need to go, and save you money.

➡ **Zoo tucker** Most of the food options in and around the zoo and the night safari are pricey, Western-friendly chains, but there is one locals' coffeeshop by the entrance to the zoo. Take advantage of it while it's still here and grab a *kopi* (coffee) and some *kaya* (coconut jam) toast, or a simple bowl of noodles before you dive into the animal magic.

➡ **Monkeys** Singapore's laws are as strict as anywhere on the planet and they're applied just as stringently when it comes to protecting animals. Get caught feeding wild monkeys in places like Bukit Timah and, not only should you feel ashamed of yourself, but you'll also be left to consider remortgaging your house to pay the potentially astronomical fines.

Getting There & Away

➡ **MRT** Northern and central Singapore is encircled by the North South Line. None of the stops is close to the nature reserves, but they're close enough to limit your taxi costs, or shorten your bus rides.

➡ **Bus** Bus 170 goes from Queen St Bus Terminal to Bukit Timah in less than half an hour. Other buses depart from the hubs at Toa Payoh or Ang Mo Kio MRT stations.

Lonely Planet's Top Tip

Places like Bukit Timah and MacRitchie Reservoir are by no means remote, but they can get exceedingly hot and humid, and once you're out on those walking trails there's nowhere to buy anything. So as well as remembering to don a hat and slap on some mosquito repellent, make sure you carry plenty of water, and perhaps a few snacks to keep you going.

Best Places for Adventure

➡ Bukit Timah (p98)
➡ MacRitchie Reservoir (p99)
➡ Night Safari (p100)

Best Places for History

➡ Lorong Buangkok (p101)
➡ Sun Yat Sen Nanyang Memorial Hall (p101)
➡ Cheng Huang Temple (p100)

Best Places for Kids

➡ Singapore Zoo (p99)
➡ Night Safari (p100)
➡ MacRitchie Reservoir (p99)

TOP SIGHTS
BUKIT TIMAH NATURE RESERVE

Singapore's only remaining area of primary forest, once teeming with tigers, is just a short bus ride from the centre and provides the ultimate busy-city antidote.

The last tiger was shot here in the 1920s, but you'll still find plenty of troops of monkeys (long-tailed macaques) to focus your camera lens on. Remember they are wild, though, and should not be fed.

There are four well-established walking trails (35 minutes to two hours return) within the reserve – plus a popular mountain-bike trail, although nowhere to rent bikes. Maps of all the routes can be found on wooden signboards, and the trails are colour-coded with markers.

The quickest and most popular hike is the one that leads straight up to the summit of Bukit Timah, which at 163m is the highest point in Singapore. Try to find time to venture off the main trails along some of the smaller paths. Look out for Rock Path, which will leave you clambering on your hands and knees in places, over rocks and tree roots; it all adds to the adventure.

Get off your bus at Bukit Timah Shopping Centre, continue walking the way the bus was going and you'll soon find Hindhede Dr up to your right.

DON'T MISS...

➡ Bukit Timah summit
➡ Rock Path
➡ Long-tailed macaques

PRACTICALITIES

➡ Map p207
➡ www.nparks.gov.sg
➡ 177 Hindhede Dr
➡ Admission free
➡ ⊗6am-7pm
➡ ⓂOrchard or Newton, then 🚍171; or 🚍170 from Little India's Queen St bus station

⊙ SIGHTS

MACRITCHIE RESERVOIR   NATURE RESERVE

Map p207 (www.nparks.gov.sg; Lornie Rd; ⊙6.30am-6pm; MToa Payoh, then 🚌571) Not quite as wonderfully wild as Bukit Timah, MacRitchie Reservoir does, nevertheless, allow you to really stretch your legs, with much longer walking trails skirting the water's edge and snaking through parts of the surrounding forest.

You'll almost certainly encounter monkeys (long-tailed macaques) in the forest and may be lucky enough to spot one of the huge monitor lizards that dart around the shallows of the reservoir with frightening speed.

You can rent kayaks at the **Paddle Lodge** (✆6344 6337; www.scf.org.sg; per 2hr $20; ⊙9am-6pm Tue-Sun), but most people come here for the excellent 10km walking trail – and its various off-shoots – that circumnavigates the reservoir. As at Bukit Timah, no maps are available (for environmental reasons), but all the trails are well signposted, and are illustrated in detail on wooden signboards dotted around the reserve.

The most popular place to aim for is **Treetop Walk** (⊙9am-5pm Tue-Fri, 8.30am-5pm Sat & Sun, closed Mondays), the highlight of which is traversing a 250m-long suspension bridge, perched 25m up in the forest canopy. Trails then continue through the forest and around the reservoir, sometimes on dirt tracks, sometimes on wooden boardwalks.

It takes three to four hours to complete the main circuit. From the service centre (which has changing facilities and a small cafe, although no tourist office), near where bus 157 drops you off, start walking off to your right (anti-clockwise around the lake) and you'll soon reach the Paddle Lodge. Treetop Walk is about 3 or 4km beyond this.

Young kids will have fun paddling on the submerged boardwalk, off to the left of the service centre in the small, landscaped MacRitchie Reservoir Park.

MEMORIES AT OLD FORD FACTORY   MUSEUM

Map p207 (✆6462 6724; www.s1942.org.sg; 351 Upper Bukit Timah Rd; admission $3; ⊙9am-5.30pm Mon-Sat; MBukit Batok, then 🚌173)

NORTHERN & CENTRAL SINGAPORE SIGHTS

TOP SIGHTS
SINGAPORE ZOO

Even if you're a bit anti-zoo, don't dismiss this one. It's one of the world's best, and the enclosures here do a fabulous job of keeping the animals happy (as far as we can tell) and the visitors enthralled (that, we are sure of). You won't see any cages; just clever use of moats and ditches and plenty of space for the animals to roam. The layout of the zoo is excellent, making it extremely visitor-friendly. And it's situated on a lush peninsula that juts out onto the waters of the Upper Seletar Reservoir, so the surrounding scenery is stunning.

Highlights for the youngsters include Kidzworld, where they can ride horses, feed farmyard animals and splash around in the wet-play area, and the Jungle Breakfast with Wildlife, where you and your family can have breakfast with orang-utans!

Walking is the best way to see everything, but there are also tram rides and boat trips. The new River Safari was due to open in 2012.

You can save money by buying a three-in-one ticket for the zoo, the Night Safari and Jurong Bird Park.

DON'T MISS...
➡ Jungle Breakfast with Wildlife
➡ Kidzworld
➡ Great Rift Valley of Ethiopia

PRACTICALITIES
➡ Map p207
➡ ✆6269 3411
➡ www.zoo.com.sg
➡ 80 Mandai Lake Rd
➡ adult/child $20/13, extra fee for some activities
➡ ⊙8.30am-6pm
➡ MAng Mo Kio then 🚌138

TOP SIGHTS
NIGHT SAFARI

Next door to the zoo, but completely separate, is the unusual Night Safari, where visitors can walk or ride past 120 different species of animals that are more active once the sun's gone down. In the darkness the moats and other barriers seem to melt away and it actually looks like these creatures – tigers, lions, leopards – could walk over and take a bite out of you. More docile animals such as antelope sometimes pass within inches of the electric trams.

Almost everyone heads straight for the tram queue as they enter. And you should too; the ride comes with a guide whose commentary is a good introduction to the park. But don't forget to walk around after you've done your loop of the park on the tram. Some of the walking trails take you past enclosures that the tram doesn't drive past, and the experience is even creepier on foot.

Kids enjoy the 30-minute show Creatures of the Night (⊙7.30pm, 8.30pm & 9.30pm, plus 10.30pm on Fridays and Saturdays).

When returning from the safari you should catch a bus at around 10.45pm as the last MRT train leaves Ang Mo Kio at 11.30pm. Otherwise, there's a taxi stand out front. Food and drink options abound outside the entrance.

DON'T MISS...

➡ Electric Tram Tour
➡ East Lodge Walking Trail
➡ Creatures of the Night

PRACTICALITIES

➡ Map p207
➡ ☏6269 3411
➡ www.nightsafari.com.sg
➡ 80 Mandai Lake Rd
➡ Adult/child $32/21
➡ ⊙7.30pm–midnight
➡ Ⓜ Ang Mo Kio then ⍾138

Complementing well a visit to Reflections at Bukit Chandu (p111), this museum charts Singapore's three years of Japanese occupation during WWII. Originally a car assembly plant of Ford Motors, this site is most remembered as the place where the British surrendered Singapore to the Japanese on 15 February 1942.

The art-deco-style building now houses a WWII exhibition gallery focusing on the experiences the local population had to endure during occupation. Photographs, ration books, diaries, prisoner drawings and a large interactive map provide insight into Singapore's darkest years. There is also a small garden with crops that were commonly grown during the period, along with storyboards explaining how each was used for sustenance.

Bus 170, from Little India's Queen St Bus Terminal, stops here just after Bukit Timah Nature Reserve.

FREE LIAN SHAN SHUANG LIN
MONASTERY   BUDDHIST TEMPLE
Map p207 (184E Jln Toa Payoh; ⊙7am–5pm; ⒨Toa Payoh) Nestled in a corner of the Toa Payoh

HDB estate this photogenic monastery, also known as the Siong Lim Temple, is a little out of the way, but makes an unusual off-the-tourist-trail diversion.

Shaded pathways lead from bonsai-filled courtyards to large halls decorated in golds, reds and blues. A huge reclining Buddha greets visitors in one room. Alongside it, 12 large mythical-style paintings tell the story of the temple's founding abbots. Attractive though it undoubtedly is, this largely modern building does lack a certain atmosphere, something that certainly cannot be said of the ageing **Cheng Huang Temple** (⊙9am–5pm) next door.

This place, dedicated to the Town God, who administers justice in the netherworld, is constantly buzzing with locals paying their respects. The main hall was built in 1912 and has thick beams, stained from decades of incense smoke, soaring up to red-and yellow-hued ceilings.

The monastery and temple are about a 1km-walk east of Toa Payoh MRT station – follow the signs down Kim Keat Link, off Lg 6 Toa Payoh, or take bus 238 three stops.

SUN YAT SEN NANYANG MEMORIAL HALL
MUSEUM

Map p207 (12 Tai Gin Rd; adult/child $4/3; ⊙9am-5pm Tue-Sun, MToa Payoh, then ⊑145) This national monument, built in the 1880s, was the headquarters of Dr Sun Yat Sen's Chinese Revolutionary Alliance in Southeast Asia, which led to the overthrow of the Qing dynasty and the creation of the first Chinese republic. Dr Sun Yat Sen briefly stayed in the house, which was donated to the Alliance by a wealthy Chinese businessperson, while touring Asia to whip up support for the cause. It's a fine example of a colonial Victorian villa and houses a museum with items pertaining to Dr Sun's life and work. A magnificent 60m-long bronze relief depicting the defining moments in Singapore's history runs the length of one wall in the garden.

The memorial hall was undergoing extensive renovations at the time of research, but will have reopened by the time you read this.

Next door is the **Sasanaramsi Burmese Buddhist Temple** (14 Tai Gin Rd; ⊙6.30am-9pm), a towering building guarded by two *chinthes* (lionlike figures) and housing a beautiful white-marble Buddha statue, decorated somewhat bizarrely with a 'halo' of different-coloured LED lights.

Bus 145 from the Toa Payoh bus interchange stops on Balestier Rd near the villa and temple, or else it's a 15-minute walk, heading south and crossing over the Pan-Island Expressway and the canal that runs parallel to it.

LORONG BUANGKOK
VILLAGE

As if willed into existence from an old black-and-white photograph from the 1950s, the *kampong* at Lorong Buangkok is mainland Singapore's last blip of resistance against the tide of modern development.

Hidden behind a wall of trees, this little swath of land houses a ramshackle collection of wooden houses, many with simple corrugated-iron roofs. The few residents live a seemingly idyllic existence, not unlike how many Singaporeans did before the development frenzy. Chickens roam the grounds, dogs flick flies away with a flap of their ears, crickets and birds hum and chirp in the background, and the 28 families here seem to have carefree sensibilities not commonly found in the general populace (the $30 per month rent probably helps).

The *kampong* is busiest during weekends when curious locals and photo clubs descend for a slice of nostalgia.

Sadly, the owner of the land, Sng Mui Hong, might not be able to preserve this family legacy. Master plans by the Urban Redevelopment Authority of Singapore have revealed that the land the *kampong* stands on is slated for redevelopment, although at the time of research this had been the case for a few years and so far the bulldozers have stayed away.

To get here, take bus 88 from Ang Mo Kio MRT station in the direction of Pasir Ris, and get off on Ang Mo Kio Ave 5 (10 minutes), just after Yio Chu Kang Rd. Walk north up Yio Chu Kang Rd and, after about 50m, turn right onto Gerald Drive. After about 200m, turn right into Lorong Buangkok. 50m later you'll see a dirt track on your left that leads to the village.

Holland Village, Dempsey Hill & the Botanic Gardens

Neighbourhood Top Five

1 Picnic on the lawns of the lush **Botanic Gardens** (p104) before venturing off into the rainforest.

2 Marvel at the beauty, diversity and sheer quantity of orchids on display at the **National Orchid Garden** (p104), housed inside the Botanic Gardens.

3 Bargain hunt your way through the array of **antique shops** (p108) on Dempsey Hill.

4 Satisfy your Western-food cravings with a visit to one of this area's excellent gourmet delicatessens. **Jones the Grocer** (p105) is a good place to start.

5 Sink a few beers on **Lorong Mambong** (p106), Holland Village's lively bar strip.

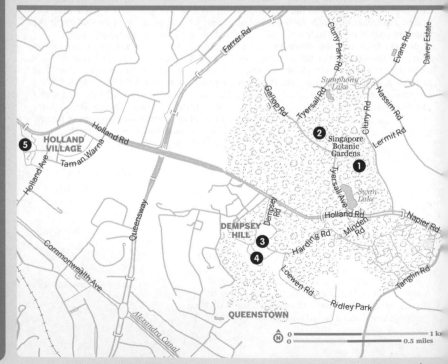

For more detail of this area, see Map p216

Explore Holland Village, Dempsey Hill & the Botanic Gardens

The standout, must-see sight here is the Botanic Gardens and you'd do well to set aside a few hours to fully soak up its charms. Making a picnic out of your visit can be fun, especially if you have kids in tow.

If you want to stock up on picnic goodies before you go, you could do a lot worse than the gourmet delis found in upmarket Holland Village or leafy (and even more upmarket) Dempsey Hill. Our favourite is Jones the Grocer.

Whilst there are plenty of pleasant food and cafe options within the Botanic Gardens itself, for a change of scene walk over to Dempsey Hill to grab a coffee before browsing around the antiques shops and art galleries. Come evening, you can either stay here for dinner or head to livelier Holland Village, where you'll find a host of decent restaurants as well as an often bustling strip of bars and cafes.

Local Life

→ **Jogging** If you've brought a pair of trainers with you on your travels, do as many Singapore residents do and work that city pollution out of your lungs with a brisk jog around the Botanic Gardens. Early morning is best, when the air is still cool; or else just before sunset.

→ **Shopping** If the glitzy high-rise shopping malls of nearby Orchard Rd get a bit too much for you, then shift down a gear or two and amble over to Dempsey Hill or Holland Village where you'll find plenty of small, independent shops and boutiques.

→ **Gourmet** It's not just the expats that lap up the Western-food offerings in Holland Village and Dempsey. Follow moneyed Singaporeans too through the doors of cute cafes and well-stocked delicatessens to get your fix of comfort food.

Getting There & Away

→ **MRT** The Botanic Gardens and Holland Village both have their own MRT stations. The Botanic Gardens one is just off our map, at the north entrance to the gardens.

→ **Bus** Dempsey Hill isn't connected to the MRT. You can walk here from Botanic Gardens, or else catch a bus (7, 77, 106, 123 or 174) from behind Orchard MRT, on Orchard Blvd. Get off two stops after the Botanic Gardens then walk up to your left. Bus 7 is one of many that links Holland Village with Dempsey Hill. It's not far to walk between the two, but the walk is an unpleasant one along busy Holland Rd.

Lonely Planet's Top Tip

Check the Botanic Gardens website (www.sbg.org.sg) for details of upcoming classical music concerts, which are staged for free by Symphony Lake. Also keep an eye out for free guided tours of the gardens. At the time of research they were being done on Saturday mornings, but this could change.

Best Places to Eat

→ Au Jardin (p105)
→ Jones the Grocer (p105)
→ Original Sin (p104)
→ Samy's Curry Restaurant (p105)
→ Holland Village Food Centre (p105)
→ Casa Verde (p106)

For reviews, see p104 →

Best Places to Drink

→ Baden (p106)
→ Wala Wala Cafe Bar (p106)
→ PS Café (p106)
→ 2am: Dessert Bar (p106)

For reviews, see p106 →

Best Places for Browsing

→ Dempsey Hill Antiques Shops (p108)
→ Holland Road Shopping Centre (p107)
→ Museum of Contemporary Arts (p104)

For reviews, see p107 →

SIGHTS

FREE MUSEUM OF CONTEMPORARY
ARTS (MOCA)   ART GALLERY
Map p216 (27A Loewen Rd; ⏰11am-7pm; Ⓜ️Orchard then 🚌7, 77, 106, 123 or 174) Devoted
entirely to showcasing contemporary art,
MOCA holds some eye-catching and reasonably cutting-edge exhibitions, providing an interesting contrast to the gallery's
whitewashed, colonial-era building and its
leafy Dempsey Hill surrounds.

SRI MUNEESWARAN
HINDU TEMPLE   HINDU TEMPLE
off Map p216 (3 Commonwealth Dr; Ⓜ️Commonwealth) This modern temple was relocated
here in 1998 after the area's Hindu community grew too large for the original hut-and-shrine set up that had been built by Indian
railway workers in 1932. Dedicated to the
deity Sri Muneeswaran, the temple's key
feature is the lack of central pillars in the
inner sanctum, which allows devotees to
have full view of rituals. This is believed to
be the largest shrine for Sri Muneeswaran
in Southeast Asia. Free **yoga classes** are

held here on Sundays (4–5pm and 6–7pm)
and Mondays (7–8pm).

✖️ EATING

**A favourite for expats, Holland Village is
home to a host of quiet, family-friendly
restaurants and cafes that do expensive,
but good quality, predominantly
Western food. The food offerings at
Dempsey Hill are of a similar vein, but
the location is less city-residential and
more colonial hill–station; this was once
an army barracks after all. Dempsey
isn't connected to the MRT system.
Most people take a taxi here, but plenty
of buses from Orchard MRT Station run
close. Get off two stops after the Botanic
Gardens then walk up to your left.**

✖️ Holland Village

ORIGINAL SIN   VEGETARIAN $$
Map p216 (📞6475 5605; www.originalsin.com.
sg; 43 Jln Merah Saga 01-62; mains $20-30;

◉ TOP SIGHTS
SINGAPORE BOTANIC GARDENS

More than 150 years old, Singapore's splendid Botanic
Gardens were originally used as a breeding ground for
agricultural projects, most notably rubber plantations,
while the gardens' now famous orchid breeding began
in the 1920s. Visitors can learn about this history at the
excellent National Orchid Garden (adult/student/child
$5/$1/free; ⏰8.30am-7pm).

The rest of the gardens are a wonderful 63 hectares
of trees, plants, flowers, lawns and lakes; perfect for
leisurely strolls, picnics, jogging or just mucking about
with the kids. Favourite spots of ours are the small Ginger Garden, the picturesque Swan Lake and the four-hectare patch of rainforest, a sample of the kind that
once covered all of Singapore.

If you can time your visit to coincide with the
volunteer-run free guided tours on Saturday mornings
(9am), you won't be disappointed. And if you're lucky
enough to be in town when an open-air classical music
concert is being held by Symphony Lake, go.

The Botanic Gardens MRT station should be open by
the time you read this. It's at the far north corner of the
gardens. Otherwise, walk or catch a bus (🚌7, 77, 123,
106 or 174) from behind Orchard MRT on Orchard Blvd.

DON'T MISS...

➡ National Orchid
Garden
➡ Rainforest
➡ Ginger Garden
➡ Free guided tours
on Saturday mornings

PRACTICALITIES

➡ Map p216
➡ 📞6471 7318
➡ www.sbg.org.sg
➡ 1 Cluny Rd
➡ Admission free
➡ ⏰5am-midnight
➡ Ⓜ️Botanic Gardens

⊗11.30am-2.30pm & 6-10pm; Ⓜ Holland Village) This is the most popular of a string of fine-dining options on this quiet residential street. And no wonder; it's friendly and relaxed, and the food is exceptional, ranging from towering ricotta cakes to melt-in-your-mouth moussaka and excellent risottos, not to mention an expansive Antipodean wine list. Book a mosaic-topped outdoor table if you can.

HOLLAND VILLAGE
FOOD CENTRE   HAWKER CENTRE $
Map p216 (Lorong Mambong; dishes from $3; ⊗6am-10pm; Ⓜ Holland Village) Avoid the raft of expats dining at the expensive restaurants across the street and join in-the-know locals for cheap Singapore grub. A small clutch of stalls sell chicken rice, prawn noodles and other hawker-centre classics. And, if you're new to the hawker-food scene, there's a handy signboard outside which gives the lowdown on the most popular dishes.

YEE CHEONG YUEN
NOODLE RESTAURANT   CHINESE $
Map p216 (31 Lorong Liput; mains $4-6; ⊗10am-10pm; Ⓜ Holland Village) More of a coffeeshop with air-con than a proper restaurant, this no-nonsense noodle joint, which also has some outdoor seating, has been dishing out *hor fun* (thick, flat, rice noodles) since the 1970s. If you don't fancy noodles, the chopped chicken is also pretty darn good.

DA PAOLO PIZZA BAR   ITALIAN $$
Map p216 (www.dapaolo.com.sg; 44 Jln Merah Saga; pizza $20-30; ⊗noon-2.30pm & 5.30-10.30pm Mon-Fri, 9am-10.30pm Sat & Sun; Ⓜ Holland Village) This very successful Italian chain has somewhat of a hold on this part of Holland Village, with three outlets on this street alone; a solid restaurant (attached), a fine deli (at No 43) and this very popular pizza place with terrace seating.

DAILY SCOOP   ICE CREAM $
Map p216 (www.thedailyscoop.com.sg; 43 Jln Merah Saga; ⊗11am-10pm Mon-Thu, 11am-10.30pm Fri & Sat, 2-10pm Sun; Ⓜ Holland Village) More than 40 flavours (ranging from honey vanilla to durian!) of hand-churned ice cream with which to fill a freshly made, thick-ridged cone. Want more? Get them to blend a different flavour into a thick milkshake for you. They also do waffles, brownies and very good coffee.

✗ Dempsey Hill

JONES THE GROCER   DELI, CAFE $$
Map p216 (www.jonesthegrocer.com; Block 9, Dempsey Rd; mains from $20; ⊗9am-11pm) Expat heaven, this beautiful gourmet deli stocks pretty much anything you could possibly be missing from home, but is also a lovely restaurant-cafe. The setting is urban-industrial, with high ceilings and exposed piping, but the atmosphere is wonderfully informal – you can sit and eat, or simply browse and drool. The highlight for most people is the magnificent cheese shop, almost worth the trip out here alone.

SAMY'S CURRY RESTAURANT   INDIAN $
Map p216 (www.samyscurry.com; Civil Service Club, Block 25, Dempsey Rd; mains $6-10; ⊗11am-3pm & 6-10pm, closed Tue) A Dempsey institution, Samy's opened in 1950 and has been on this particular spot since the 1980s. Its once charming location has slowly been eroded over the years – it's now hemmed in by two newer large restaurants – but the food is as outstanding as it always was, and this is one of the least pretentious restaurants in Dempsey.

BARRACKS CAFE   INTERNATIONAL $$
Map p216 (www.dempseyhouse.com; 8D Dempsey Rd; mains $22-32, pizza $18-25; ⊗noon-10.30pm Mon-Fri, 11am-10.30pm Sat & Sun) Housed in the tall green building called House, funky Barracks Cafe is a decent spot for a bite to eat. It's more restaurant than cafe, but still reasonably informal and has a pleasant wood-decked terrace out the back with a forest view. Food is mostly Western, although some dishes have an Asian twist – Vietnamese coconut poached chicken pizza, anyone?

✗ Botanic Gardens

TOP⟩ AU JARDIN
CHOICE   FRENCH $$$
Map p216 (☎6466 8812; www.lesamis.com.sg; EJH Corner House, Singapore Botanic Gardens, Cluny Rd; ⊗7-10.15pm Tue-Sun, noon-2pm Tue-Fri, 11.30am-2pm Sun; set menus $150-225; Ⓜ Botanic Gardens) Set in a beautifully renovated colonial-era black-and-white bungalow, and surrounded by the extravagant lushness of the Botanic Gardens, there can hardly be a more charming restaurant in Singapore. It

comes at a price, naturally, but in terms of the quality of the food and the whole dining experience, this place is hard to beat. Dress up, forget the bill and have a romantic stroll through the gardens afterwards.

CASA VERDE INTERNATIONAL $$

Map p216 (6476 7326; www.lesamis.com.sg; Singapore Botanic Gardens, 1 Cluny Rd; mains from $15; sandwiches from $12; coffee from $3.50; 7.30am-9.30pm; MBotanic Gardens) The most popular place to eat at the Botanic Gardens, family-friendly Casa Verde has a pleasant fan-cooled outdoor seating area and does decent Western grub – pasta, sandwiches, salads – plus very good wood-fired pizzas and a smattering of local dishes.

HALIA MODERN ASIAN $$

Map p216 (6476 6711; www.halia.com.sg; Singapore Botanic Gardens; mains $30-60; noon-3pm & 6-10pm; MBotanic Gardens) The outdoor deck makes this a great spot and it's surrounded by the Botanic Gardens' ginger plants, a feature which is built upon by including a number of unusual ginger-based dishes and drinks in the menu. Ideal for a light lunch if you want more privacy than Casa Verde, or a romantic dinner if you can't afford Au Jardin. As well as the daily lunch and dinner sittings, at weekends you can also come for brunch (10am-4pm) or English tea (3-5pm) with jam and scones among an array of other goodies.

🍷 DRINKING & NIGHTLIFE

Lorong Mambong in Holland Village is pedestrianised in the evenings and transforms from a quiet street into a lively drinking strip, packed with bars and restaurants, many of which have tables and chairs spilling out onto the road. Dempsey is more upmarket and much quieter, with most people coming here to eat rather than drink, but there are a few cafe-bar options if you fancy finishing off your meal with a quick tipple.

🍸 Holland Village

BADEN BAR

Map p216 (42 Lorong Mambong; 2pm-2am; MHolland Village) The friendliest and most laid back of the bars in Holland Village, this German bar-restaurant has street-side seating on lively Lorang Mambong, a selection of European beers (from $11) and some decent food ($16–36). The pork knuckle with potato and sauerkraut is particularly good.

WALA WALA CAFE BAR BAR

Map p216 (www.imaginings.com.sg; 31 Lorong Mambong; 3pm-1am Sun-Thu, 3pm-2am Fri & Sat; MHolland Village) Perennially packed at weekends (and on most evenings in fact), Wala Wala's main draw is its live music on the second floor. Downstairs it pulls in football fans with its large sports screens. Like most of the places here, tables spill out onto the street in the evenings. Beers go from $10, so it's decent value for this part of town.

2AM: DESSERT BAR BAR

Map p216 (www.2amdessertbar.com; 21a Lorong Liput; MHolland Village) Hip, sweet and terribly chic, 2am is a unique concept and one of Singapore's more unusual places to come for a drink (from $15). The desserts are special on their own, but to enhance your enjoyment of them each one has been given its own wine pairing on the menu; tiramisu and Shiraz, caramel mousse and Pinot Noir. Staff members are young and friendly and happy to give you their recommendations if you're not sure what works.

🍸 Dempsey Hill

PS CAFÉ CAFE

Map p216 (www.pscafe.sg; 28B Harding Rd; 11.30am-5pm & 6.30pm-10.30pm Mon-Thu, 11.30am-5pm & 6.30pm-1.30am Fri, 9.30am-5pm & 6.30pm-1am Sat, 9.30am-5pm & 6.30pm-10.30pm Sun) Like nearby Jones the Grocer, this is another expat haven on Dempsey, with solid western food (mains $20–30) and scrummy desserts. We like just coming here for a drink, though. Bag a table outside on the terrace, order a freshly ground coffee with a cheeky slice of cake and enjoy the leafy views.

SLIGHTLY OFF THE RAILS

If you fancy visiting some of Singapore's quirkier sights, hop on the MRT and track down some of this lot:

➡ **Commonwealth MRT Station** Head through the food court south of the station and walk 250m east down the first street you see. This takes you to a spiritual, architectural duo, the likes of which you'll only see in places like Singapore: rising like a gigantic crystalline outcropping, the near-cubist design of the **Catholic Church of the Blessed Sacrament** (off Map p216) offers a stark contrast to its closest neighbour, the traditionally designed Sri Muneeswaran Hindu Temple.

➡ **Chinese Garden MRT Station** Hop off the train and head south into the Chinese Garden (p114), a very much artificial park replete with pagodas, arches and traditional Chinese structures. Give the rather inhumane Live Turtle & Tortoise Museum a wide berth, though.

➡ **Yishun MRT Station** When you get off the train at Yishun, head west until you get to the **Darul Makmur Mosque** (Map p207). It's a large and modern-looking black-and-white mosque with a particularly fetching onion-dome tower, somewhat different from the more traditional mosques of the inner city. There are also a number of smaller temples in the neighbourhood worth checking out.

➡ **Ang Mo Kio MRT Station** An excellent example of the Singaporean fetish for landscaping perfection, **Ang Mo Kio Town Garden East** (Map p207), just across from the station, is one of those magnificently manicured neighbourhood parks in which every tree seems to have been planted equidistant from the last.

➡ **Eunos MRT Station** Though not as chock-a-block with temples, shrines and other random spiritual spots as Geylang, the blocks south of the Eunos MRT station offer some interesting surprises for those who care to wander. Especially beautiful are the Malay-style mosques in the area, and the very colourful **Mangala Vihara** (Shrine of Blessing; Map p85) on Jln Eunos, just one block south of the station.

TIPPLING CLUB BAR
Map p216 (www.tipplingclub.com; 8D Dempsey Rd; ☺6pm-late Mon-Fri, noon-3pm & 6pm-late Sat) Perch yourself on a seat at the long bar and tuck into the fine selection of whiskys (from $18) at this trendy urban-industrial bar. There are more than a dozen single malts on the menu. For something a bit quirkier try the 'smoky old bastard', a large whisky served in a glass tube filled with smoke made from dried orange powder and flavoured with maple syrup and banana.

RED DOT BREWHOUSE BAR
Map p216 (www.reddotbrewhouse.com.sg; Block 25A, 01-01 Dempsey Rd; beer from $11; ☺midday-midnight Mon-Thu, midday-2am Fri & Sat; 10am-midnight Sun) Nestled in a quiet spot in Dempsey Hill, Red Dot Brewhouse has been brewing and serving up microbrews since before it was trendy to do so. Forget the food (average) and work your way through the list of beers (great!). On tap there are seven beers (from $11) including the eye-catching GREEN pilsner. Its colour comes

from the spirulina in the brewing process. Grab a seat on the cozy deck outside and let the beers do the rest of the work.

 SHOPPING

HOLLAND ROAD SHOPPING CENTRE GIFTS
Map p216 (211 Holland Ave; ☺10am-8pm; Ⓜ Holland Village) A warren of independent stores and stalls with decor stuck in the 1980s, this old-fashioned shopping centre remains a magnet for expats and fashionable Singaporeans and is a great place for art, handicrafts, gifts, home ware and offbeat fashion. The highlight is **Lim's Arts & Living** (Shop 01, Level 2), with its carvings, home furnishings, cutesy gifts and stationery and Asian textiles. But there are dozens of fun shops worth having a nose around. On Level 3 there's a series of massage and reflexology shops to soothe shopping-weary limbs, while the top floor has a roof cafe.

DEMPSEY HILL ANTIQUES

Dempsey Hill has boomed in recent years as more and more of the former British Army barrack buildings have been turned into high-end restaurants and bars.

Happily, many of the art and antique shops that populated the area before the boom have survived, and during the daytime this is a peaceful, almost rustic area to wander around, perusing anything from Kashmiri carpets and teak furniture to landscaping ornaments and antiques.

Try **Shang Antiques** (Block 16, Dempsey Hill), which specialises in Southeast Asian antiques, some of them around 2000 years old, with price tags to match. **Pasardina Fine Living** (Block 13, Dempsey Hill) has just about everything decorative and Asian for the home, while **Asiatique** (Block 14, Dempsey Hill) stocks Indonesian furniture made from recycled wood.

There are more than a dozen other similar shops, with most open daily from around 10am to 6pm.

West & Southwest Singapore

Neighbourhood Top Five

1 Ride the spectacular **cable car** (p111) to the summit of Mt Faber or across the harbour to Sentosa Island.

2 Join true twitchers for a spot of birdwatching on the mangrove swamps of **Sungei Buloh Wetland Reserve** (p113).

3 Stretch your legs for a park-to-park walk along the **Southern Ridges** (p112) to Mt Faber.

4 Pull levers and twiddle knobs at kids' favourite, the **Singapore Science Centre** (p113), before catching an IMAX film at the enormous **Omni-Theatre** (p113) next door.

5 Step back in time and experience 1950s-style tourism at Singapore's most old-fashioned theme park: the wonderfully quirky **Haw Par Villa** (p111).

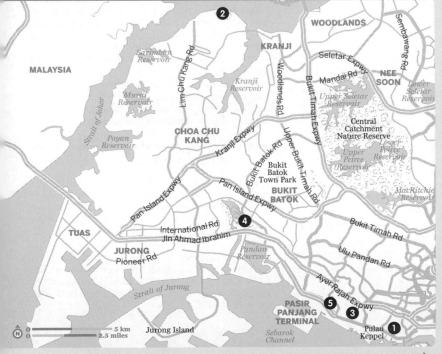

For more detail of this area, see Map p218 and p219 ➡

Lonely Planet's Top Tip

For a healthy way of taking in some of this area's less-visited attractions, don a hat, pack plenty of water and hike at least part of the 9km-long Southern Ridges walking trail (p112). It takes you from park to park, right across southwest Singapore, and eventually brings you to Mt Faber.

Best Places to Eat

➡ Eng Lock Koo (p115)

➡ Emerald Lodge (p115)

➡ Sky Dining (p115)

For reviews, see p115 ➡

Best Places for Walks

➡ Southern Ridges (p112)

➡ Mt Faber (p111)

➡ Sungei Buloh Wetland Reserve (p113)

➡ Labrador Nature Reserve (p112)

➡ Chinese Garden (p114)

For reviews, see p111 ➡

Best Places for Wildlife

➡ Sungei Buloh Wetland Reserve (p113)

➡ Jurong Bird Park (p113)

➡ Labrador Nature Reserve (p112)

For reviews, see p111 ➡

Explore West & Southwest Singapore

This vast area is packed with sights that together would take a number of days to see. But you don't need to see them all. None is an absolute top-draw, must-see sight; most are quirky or somewhat specialist, so pick and choose what best suits you so you can plan your foray into western Singapore without wasting too much travel time.

Bundling sights together into one trip makes sense. The Science Centre, Omni-Theatre and Snow City stand side by side, while a number of sights in the northwest are accessed via Kranji MRT station.

Consider timing your visit to Mt Faber to coincide with sunset, so as the sun goes down you can either be on the cable car or at a restaurant or bar on the summit. It's then easy to get back to your hotel via HarbourFront MRT station.

Local Life

➡ **Deals** Don't forget to look into the combined ticket deals for the Science Centre, the Omni-Theatre and Snow City. Likewise, Jurong Bird Park is part of a possible three-in-one ticket deal with Singapore Zoo and the Night Safari. You can also get various Sentosa Island deals if you're travelling there by cable car.

➡ **Bus it** As with northern and central Singapore, the area covered in this chapter is vast so the temptation is to visit the sights by taxi. No need. Every place we cover here can be reached by MRT, or by MRT followed by a short bus ride. The exception is Mt Faber, but there's a cable car for that!

➡ **Sun-kissed** The west and southwest is full of parks, hills and natures reserves. They're wonderful places for strolling around, but don't underestimate the strength of the Singapore sunshine. Come prepared.

Getting There & Away

➡ **MRT** This vast area is actually served pretty well by the MRT. Some attractions have their namesake stations. Otherwise, HarbourFront, Jurong East, Boon Lay and Kranji are all useful stations, which are either walking distance to sights or have bus connections to them.

➡ **Bus** For the more out-of-the-way sights you'll need to combine MRT trips with a bus ride. We list all the options with each review. The Kranji Express (p114) is a handy minibus service you can use to visit the farms in the northwest.

◉ SIGHTS

◉ Southwest Singapore

MT FABER & THE CABLE CAR   PARK

Map p218 (MHarbourFront) Standing proud (if not tall) at 116m on the southern fringe of the city and overlooking Sentosa Island, Mt Faber forms the centrepiece of Mt Faber Park, one of the oldest parks in Singapore.

From the summit the strange splendour of Singapore rolls away to the horizon in all directions. To the south are scenes of Keppel Wharves and industrial Pasir Panjang. Turn your gaze north and Singapore's highrise buildings are set in a perfect panorama.

To get to the top, ride the spectacular **cable car** (www.mountfaber.com.sg; adult one-way/return $24/26, child one-way/return $14/15; ⊙8.30am-9.30pm) from the HarbourFront Centre, take bus 409 (weekends only, midday to 9pm) or walk. It's a short but steep climb through secondary rainforest, dotted with strategically placed benches, pavilions and lookout posts as well as some splendid colonial-era black-and-white bungalows.

The summit is also the climax to the bracing, 4km-long walk along the Southern Ridges (p112).

There are plenty of eating options at the summit, but you'd still be wise to bring your own water if you're hiking up here.

Note, the cable car stretches from Mt Faber down to the HarbourFront Centre and on to Sentosa Island. The tickets prices are the same wherever you get off.

FREE HAW PAR VILLA   MUSEUM

Map p218 (262 Pasir Panjang Rd; ⊙9am-7pm; MHaw Par Villa) Originally known as the Tiger Balm Gardens, this wonderfully weird, unquestionably tacky and very old-fashioned theme park was the brainchild of Aw Boon Haw, the creator of the medicinal salve Tiger Balm. He built a villa here, now demolished, in 1937 for his beloved brother and business partner Aw Boon Par and together they gradually built a Chinese mythology theme park within the grounds as a way of reminding the local Chinese population of their roots and to show visitors the merits of Chinese values. Thousands of statues and dioramas were constructed over the years, and are still being added to today, to create one of Singapore's quirkiest attractions.

The result is a visual barrage of folklore and fable, with scenes from the Romance of the Three Kingdoms, Journey to the West, Confucianism, and – everybody's favourite – the **Ten Courts of Hell**, a walk-through exhibit depicting the myriad gruesome torments that await sinners in the underworld.

Also within the grounds is the **Hua Song Museum** (adult/child $4/2.50; ⊙9am-5pm), a well laid out and engaging museum offering a glimpse into the lives, enterprises and adventures of Chinese migrants around the world.

REFLECTIONS AT BUKIT CHANDU   MUSEUM

Map p218 (www.s1942.org.sg; 31K Pepys Rd; admission $2; ⊙9am-5.30pm Tue-Sun; MPasir Panjang) Atop Bukit Chandu (Opium Hill) and housed in a renovated colonial-era villa, this absorbing WWII interpretive centre, telling the tale of the fall of Singapore, makes a worthwhile stop en route to Kent Ridge Park. The focus is on the 1st and 2nd Battalions of the Malay Regiment who bravely but unsuccessfully attempted to defend the hill in the Battle of Pasir Panjang when the Japanese invaded in 1942.

High-tech displays, using films from the period and audio effects to transport you to the scene of the battle, are all quite evocative.

To get to the museum, go to Pasir Panjang MRT Station then cross the main road and walk uphill along Pepys Rd for about 15 minutes.

FREE NUS MUSEUMS   MUSEUMS

off Map p218 (www.nus.edu.sg/museum; University Cultural Centre; 50 Kent Ridge Cres; ⊙9am-5pm Mon-Sat; MBuona Vista, then 🚌95) On the campus of the National University of Singapore (NUS), these three small but interesting art museums all hold fine collections. On the ground floor is the **Lee Kong Chian Art Museum**, with an excellent collection of ancient Chinese ceramics and bronzes, plus broken porcelain and other artefacts recovered from shipwrecks.

One floor down is the **South & Southeast Asian Gallery**, showing a mixture of art from across the region, including textiles and sculptures.

On the top floor is the **Ng Eng Teng Gallery**, displaying paintings, drawings and sculptures by Ng Eng Teng (1934–2001), one of Singapore's foremost artists specialising in imaginative, sometimes surreal, depictions of the body.

WALKING THE SOUTHERN RIDGES

Mt Faber is connected to West Coast Park via a series of parks and hills known as the Southern Ridges. It's a wonderfully accessible area to walk in, and much less testing than the hikes around Bukit Timah or MacRitchie Reservoir. The whole route stretches for 9km, but we recommend the shorter 4km-stretch from Kent Ridge Park to Mt Faber. Although the walking itself isn't tough, Singapore's hot, humid weather makes it important to still pack plenty of water.

Start at **Kent Ridge Park** (Map p218), which is located a short walk beyond the excellent museum known as Reflections at Bukit Chandu. Once you reach the lovely shaded park follow signs for the **lookout point**, for views over the port and the southern islands, and for **canopy walk**, a short treetop boardwalk, before strolling downhill to HortPark, also signposted.

HortPark (Map p218) is more exposed but has more for the kids to do, with a small children's playground in **Fantasy Garden** and cute herb and flower gardens with winding pathways and stepping stones crossing trickling streams. The prototype **glasshouses** filled with all manner of flora are unfortunately not open to the public.

From HortPark cross Alexandra Rd over the leaf-like bridge and gently ascending walkways known as **Alexandra Link**. These walkways eventually lead you to **Telok Blangah Hill Park** (Map p218) with its flower-filled **Terrace Garden**, great city views and the cool, curvy bridge known as **Henderson Waves**, an undulating sculptural pedestrian walkway, suspended 36m above the ground.

The final 500m to the summit of Mt Faber is a short but reasonably steep climb that's rewarded with more fine views, a choice of restaurants and the option of a cable car ride back down the hill. It is also easy to walk down to HarbourFront MRT Station from here, on a pathway that descends the forested hillside and which passes some attractive colonial-era black-and-white bungalows.

To get to Kent Ridge Park, either take the MRT to Kent Ridge, where you can pick up the far western end of the park by walking along Science Park Drive, or take the MRT to Pasir Panjang, cross the main road then walk about 15 minutes up Pepys Rd to Reflections at Bukit Chandu. The park is just behind this museum. If you go this way, you can grab a bite to eat at Eng Lock Koo on the corner of Pepys Rd.

On the same campus, but in a different block, is the **Raffles Museum of Biodiversity Research** (http://rmbr.nus.edu.sg; Block S6, Level 3, NUS Faculty of Science, Science Dr 2, Lower Kent Ridge Rd; ⊙9am-5pm Mon-Fri), an old-fashioned museum with exhibits on flora and fauna, including stuffed and preserved examples of some rare and locally extinct creatures.

Once Bus 95 enters the university campus wait until the stop after the sports fields then keep walking straight and the Cultural Centre housing the museums will be on your right. You can then take the free campus bus to get back to the Faculty of Science for the biodiversity research museum.

LABRADOR NATURE RESERVE   PARK

Map p218 (www.nparks.gov.sg/labrador; Labrador Villa Rd; ⓂLabrador Park) This thickly forested park overlooking Keppel Harbour and the northwest tip of Sentosa Island is home to a variety of plants, flowers and birdlife, but the main reason to come here is to visit the **war relics** that scatter the park and which, astonishingly, were only rediscovered in the 1980s when now-abandoned plans to turn the area into a theme park were begun.

You'll find a few old gun emplacements mounted on moss-covered concrete casements as well as the remains of the entrance to the old fort that stood guard on this hill. The undoubted highlight always used to be the **Labrador Secret Tunnels** (adult/child $8.60/5.35; ⊙9am-5pm Tue-Sun), a fascinating series of storage and armament bunkers that could be explored, but they were closed at the time of research and there was no word on when, or if, they might reopen. Check the website before you come if you specifically want to see the tunnels.

The small coastal section of the park, at the bottom of the hill, has been cleared, but the rest is lush, overgrown forest, so come armed with mosquito repellent if you plan spending some time here exploring.

West Singapore

SUNGEI BULOH WETLAND RESERVE
NATURE RESERVE

Map p219 (www.sbwr.org.sg; 301 Neo Tiew Cres; admission free Mon-Fri, adult/child $1/0.50 Sat & Sun; ⊙7.30am-7pm Mon-Sat, 7am-7pm Sun; Ⓜ Kranji, then 🚌 925) One of the few remaining mangrove areas in Singapore, this 87-hectare wetland nature reserve of mudflats, ponds and secondary forest is a twitcher's paradise, with migratory birds such as egrets, sandpipers and plovers joining resident favourites like herons, bitterns, sunbirds, coucals and kingfishers. This is also the best place to see monitor lizards.

There are three main walking trails (one to five hours return), each dotted with bird-viewing huts and lookouts. The landscape is raw, muddy swamp, but if you're into bird-spotting this is just the place. But if you really can't bear being bitten by mosquitoes, maybe give this reserve a miss.

A free **guided tour** runs every Saturday at 9.30am. The 10-minute **video** about the reserve (9am, 11am, 1pm, 3pm, 5pm Monday to Saturday, 9am to 5pm hourly Sunday) is free too. There's a pleasant **cafe-restaurant** in the visitors centre, overlooking the monitor-lizard-filled ponds. On Sundays bus 925 drops you at the reserve. Otherwise it's a 15 minute walk away.

SINGAPORE SCIENCE CENTRE
MUSEUM

Map p219 (www.sci-ctr.edu.sg; 15 Science Centre Rd; adult/child $9/5; ⊙10am-6pm Tue-Sun; Ⓜ Jurong East) Endearingly geeky, this science museum is packed with the type of push-pull-twist-and-turn gadgets that kids can spend hours playing with. Covering subjects like the human body, aviation, optical illusions, ecosystems, the universe and robotics, it's educational as well as absorbing.

Come out of Jurong East MRT station, turn left along the covered walkway, cross the road and continue past a covered row of stalls before crossing Jurong Town Hall Rd.

OMNI-THEATRE
CINEMA

Map p219 (www.omnitheatre.com.sg; ⊙10am-6pm Mon-Fri, 10am-8pm Sat & Sun; adult/child $10/7; 21 Jurong Town Hall Rd; Ⓜ Jurong East) This IMAX cinema next door to the Science Centre and Snow City contains Asia's largest seamless dome screen and shows stunning 45-minute documentary films – on the hour every hour.

JURONG BIRD PARK
ZOO

Map p219 (www.birdpark.com.sg; 2 Jurong Hill; adult/child $18/12; ⊙8.30am-6pm; Ⓜ Boon Lay, then 🚌 194 or 251) Run by the same company that runs the excellent Singapore Zoo and Night Safari, Jurong Bird Park is a bit more neglected than its higher profile siblings. True twitchers will flock to Sungei Buloh Wetland Reserve, but this place is set up better for young kids and is an easy way to see a selection of around 600 species of birds. Be aware, though, that many of the enclosures are caged, and ageing somewhat.

A **monorail** (adult/child $5/3) can transport you around it all if you're feeling lazy.

TIGER BREWERY
BREWERY

Map p219 (✆6860 3005; www.apb.com.sg/brewery-tour.html; 459 Jln Ahmad Ibrahim; admission $16; ⊙10am, 11am, 1pm, 2pm, 4pm & 5pm Mon-Fri; Ⓜ Boon Lay, then 🚌 182) Well, you've been drinking their beers all holiday, so you might as well see how they make them.

Tours of the Tiger Brewery last for about 90 minutes, including 45 minutes of free-flow beer drinking. You'll be taken through the brew house and the packaging hall and be shown some back-in-the-day Tiger-beer paraphernalia and old beer-making equipment before being led to the highlight of the tour: the Tiger Tavern, a very smart pub with pool table, sports screens and free beer!

Tours must be booked in advance, either through the website or by phone.

SINGAPORE TURF CLUB
HORSE RACING

Map p219 (www.turfclub.com.sg; 1 Turf Club Ave; Ⓜ Kranji) Not quite as manic as a day at the races in Hong Kong, a trip to Singapore Turf Club is nevertheless a hugely popular day out. There is a four-level grandstand with a seating capacity of up to 35,000. Seating options range from bargain non-air-conditioned seats to the exclusive Hibiscus lounge. Dress code is enforced – smart casual in one section and suits and ties in another – and foreigners should bring their passports to get in.

Races take place mostly on Fridays (6.20–10.50pm) and Sundays (12.50pm–6.30pm), but check the website before you go.

Come out of Kranji MRT, turn left and the Woodlands Rd entrance is on your left.

FREE KRANJI WAR MEMORIAL
CEMETERY

Map p219 (9 Woodlands Rd; ⊙8am-6.30pm; Ⓜ Kranji) The austere white structures and rolling hillside of the Kranji War Memorial

WORTH A DETOUR

VISITING SINGAPORE'S FARMS

Few visitors to Singapore realise that there's a small but thriving farming industry alive and well in northwest Singapore. We're not talking rolling fields of grazing cows here; in Singapore, limited space calls for the type of farm that specialises in organic vegetables, goat's milk, or plants, flowers and herbs. But they can be fun places to visit – a pleasant escape from the city centre.

The **Kranji Countryside Association** (www.kranjicountryside.com) is a farm collective helping to promote the industry. It runs a daily minibus service, the **Kranji Express** (adult/child $3/1; duration 90mins; ☺9am, 10.30am, midday, 1.30pm, 3pm & 4.30pm) that does a loop from the Kranji MRT Station, visiting many of the best farms en route.

Farms you'll visit include ones where you can buy goat's milk, sample frog meat, see fish, grab a coffee, have lunch or even spend the night.

You can hop off the bus whenever you see a farm you like the look of, then hop back on again when the bus next comes around, about 90 minutes later. The scheduled stops change from time to time, but usually include the following:

➡ **Sungei Buloh Wetland Reserve** (p113)

➡ **GardenAsia** (www.gardenasia.com) A large, well-stocked garden centre with a lovely cafe called Petals & Leaves.

➡ **Max Koi Farm** Fish farm with a cafe.

➡ **D'Kranji Farm Resort** (www.dkranji.com.sg) Smart villa-style accommodation, plus restaurant and beer garden.

➡ **Bollywood** (admission $2; www.bollywoodveggies.com) A very popular place to stop; has a bistro, large herb gardens and garden stalls.

➡ **Hay Dairies** A goat farm where you can buy fresh goat's milk and other snacks.

➡ **Jurong Frog Farm** A bit run down, but visitors can sample frog meat here.

➡ **FireFlies Health Farm** (www.fireflies.sg) Organic farm selling fruit, veg and herbs.

The bus loop usually includes a second stop at Sungei Buloh, GardenAsia and Max Koi Farm before heading back to the MRT station.

contain the WWII graves of thousands of Allied troops. Headstones, many of which are inscribed simply with the words: 'a soldier of the 1939–1945 war', are lined in neat rows across manicured lawns. Walls are inscribed with the names of 24,346 men and women who lost their lives in Southeast Asia, and registers, stored inside unlocked weatherproof stands, are available for inspection.

It's about 10 minutes' walk from Kranji MRT station. Turn left (west) along Woodlands Rd, cross straight over the main junction then take the first left.

SNOW CITY
SKI CENTRE

Map p219 (www.snowcity.com.sg; 21 Jurong Town Hall Rd; adult/child per hr $14/11.50; ☺9.45am-5.15pm Tue-Sun; ⓜJurong East) A hangar-sized deep freeze chilled to a numbing –5°C, Snow City features a slope three-storeys high and 70m long, accessed via a silvery Star Trek–style airlock. Each session gives you an hour to throw yourself at high speed down the slope on a black inner tube. Ski and snowboarding lessons also available.

All visitors must be wearing long trousers (which can be rented) and socks (which can be bought). Visitors are provided with a ski jacket and warm boots.

CHINESE GARDEN
PARK

Map p219 (1 Chinese Garden Rd; ☺6am-11pm Chinese Garden; ⓜChinese Garden) This spacious garden, which occupies 13.5 hectares in the vicinity of Jurong Lake, is pleasant place for an afternoon stroll, though by itself is not worth the trek from the city.

The garden is actually an island containing a number of Chinese-style pavilions and a seven-storey pagoda providing a great view. Apart from the pavilions, there is an extensive and impressive display of *penjing* (Chinese bonsai; open 9am to 5pm), and an extremely rundown turtle and tortoise museum, which is worth avoiding.

The garden is a five-minute walk from Chinese Garden MRT station.

EATING

As well as the restaurants listed here, remember that some of the bigger attractions in this part of Singapore have their own dining facilities. The big transport-hub MRT stations, such as Jurong East, have large food courts. Kranji station also has some restaurants.

ENG LOCK KOO
HAWKER CENTRE **$**

Map p218 (114 Pasir Panjang Rd, cnr Pepys Rd; mains from $3; ⊘5am-3pm; Ⓜ Pasir Panjang) Perfect for breakfast or lunch if you're on your way to either Reflections at Bukit Chandu or Kent Ridge Park for the Southern Ridges walk, this small collection of stalls inside a corner-shop premises does tea and coffee, all the usual of the hawker-centre favourites – chicken rice, *nasi goreng* (fried rice) – and has an airy open-sided seating area. A real locals' favourite.

EMERALD LODGE
INTERNATIONAL **$$**

Map p218 (www.mountfaber.com.sg; Upper Terrace, Mt Faber Rd; mains $13-15; ⊘9am-1am; Ⓜ HarbourFront) The most affordable option at the summit of Mt Faber, Emerald Lodge has a friendly, informal atmosphere, shaded terrace seating and reasonable pastas and salads as well as beer and coffee. On weekends bus 409 runs up here from HarbourFront MRT Station (midday–9pm). At other times you'll have to take a taxi, ride the cable car or climb up yourself. It's about 100m up the hill from the Jewel Box.

JEWEL BOX
INTERNATIONAL **$$$**

Map p218 (✆6377 9688; www.mountfaber.com.sg; 109 Mt Faber Rd; mains from $25; Ⓜ HarbourFront) This dining complex, run by the same management that runs Emerald Lodge, is where the Mt Faber cable car terminates and has a collection of high-end restaurants, all with fabulous harbour views. Sleek and trendy **Black Opal** (⊘9am-11pm) does mostly European food; **Sapphire** (⊘11am-11pm Sun-Thu, 11am-1am Fri & Sat) has an international menu and open-air seating, while **Empress Jade** (⊘midday-3pm & 6-11pm) serves Chinese cuisine. **Moonstone** (⊘4pm-12.30am Sun-Thu, 4pm-2am Fri & Sat) is the rooftop bar.

SKY DINING
INTERNATIONAL **$$$**

(✆6377 9688; www.mountfaber.com.sg; per couple $115-198; ⊘6.30-8.30pm) Impress the pants off the object of your desires with Sky Dining in the Mt Faber cable car – a romantic three-course dinner with plummeting 60m-high views. Must book online.

SHOPPING

VIVOCITY
MALL

Map p218 (www.vivocity.com.sg; Ⓜ HarbourFront) Singapore's largest shopping mall was unveiled in 2006 in an attempt to lure shoppers away from the madness of Orchard Rd. Orchard Rd is still retail king, but there's no denying Vivocity is a pleasant place to shop, with lots of open space, an outdoor kids' playground on level 2, a rooftop 'skypark' where the little ones can splash about in free-to-use paddling pools and a large Golden Village cineplex. Once you're done shopping there's a range of restaurants and bars with outdoor seating where you can sit and soak up the sea breeze.

PARTY AT THE ST JAMES POWER STATION

The posterboy of Singapore's night scene, **St James Power Station** (Map p218; www.stjamespowerstation.com; 3 Sentosa Gateway) is a 1920s coal-fired power station ingeniously converted into an entertainment complex. All the bars and clubs are interconnected, so one cover charge (men $12, women $10, Wednesdays men $30) gets access to all of them. Some bars – **Gallery Bar**, **Lobby Bar** and **Peppermint Park** – have no cover charge at all. Minimum age is 18 for women and 23 for men at all except Powerhouse, where the age is 18 for both.

There's **Dragonfly** (⊘6pm-6am), a Mandopop and Cantopop club; **Movida** (⊘6pm-3am), a Latin live-band dance club; **Powerhouse** (⊘8pm-4am Wed, Fri & Sat), a large dance club aimed at the younger crowd; and the **Boiler Room** (⊘8.45pm-3am Mon-Sat), a mainstream rock club featuring live bands. There's also French bordello–inspired **Mono** (⊘6pm-6am), a karaoke bar for those inclined towards belting out their own tunes. Stumble outside into **Street Bar** (⊘6pm-5am) for a post-party feed.

Sentosa & Other Islands

Sentosa Island p117

Essentially one giant theme park, Sentosa is a firm favourite with families. Expect activities galore, rides-a-go-go and three pretty decent beaches on which to dine, drink or just chill.

Pulau Ubin p121

An unkempt jungle of an island, Ubin offers a forest full of weird and wonderful creatures, bundles of village-life charm and, best of all, the chance to explore it all by bicycle.

Southern Islands p122

Perfect for a picnic by the sea, or just a nice excuse for a boat trip, these three small islands make up one of Singapore's quieter getaway options.

Sentosa Island

Explore

Epitomised by its star attraction, Universal Studios, Sentosa is essentially one giant theme park. And as such, kids love it. Packed with rides, activities and shows, most of which cost extra, it's very easy for a family to rack up a huge bill in one day spent here. And that's not counting visits to the casino. The beaches, of course, are completely free and very popular with locals and tourists alike.

You need at least a full day to experience everything Sentosa has to offer (and a very large wallet), but it's quite possible to just come here for a morning or afternoon on the beach. In fact, some people just come here for a drink in the evening. There are certainly worse ways to watch the sunset than at a beach bar on Sentosa, gin and tonic in hand.

The Best...

➡ **Sight** Universal Studios (p117)

➡ **Place to Eat** Cafe del Mar (p119)

➡ **Activity** Swimming on Palawan Beach (p119)

Top Tip

Be sure to pick up a Sentosa Island map leaflet, available at booths as you enter the island. The map on it is much larger and more detailed than the one in this guidebook.

Getting There & Away

Cable car Ride the cable car from Mt Faber or the HarbourFront Centre.

Monorail The Sentosa Express (7am–midnight) goes from VivoCity to three stations on Sentosa: Waterfront, Imbiah and Beach.

Walk Simply walk across the Sentosa Boardwalk from VivoCity.

⊙ SIGHTS

UNIVERSAL STUDIOS AMUSEMENT PARK

Map p220 (www.rwsentosa.com; Resorts World; adult/child/senior $72/52/36; ⊙10am-7pm) Universal Studios is the top-draw attraction in Resorts World. Shops, shows, restaurants, rides and roller coasters are all neatly packaged into fantasy-world themes based on your favourite Hollywood films. One of the highlights is the pair of 'duelling roller coasters' in Sci-fi City, said to be the tallest of their kind in the world. Sometimes during peak or summer months Universal Studios is open until 9pm. Check the website for the latest info.

FORT SILOSO MUSEUM

Map p220 (Siloso Point; adult/child $8/5; ⊙10am-6pm) Dating from the 1880s, when Sentosa was called Pulau Blakang Mati (Malay for 'the island which lies death'), Fort Siloso was built to protect Britain's valuable colonial port. Ultimately it failed.

Designed to repel a maritime assault from the south, Siloso's heavy guns had to be turned around when the Japanese invaded from the Malaya mainland in WWII. The British surrender soon followed, and later the fort was used by the Japanese as a prisoner-of-war camp.

Well-laid-out **exhibits** – photos, wax models, videos, audio recordings – talk visitors through the fort's history. There are **old gun emplacements** that can be viewed and the **underground tunnels** are fun to explore.

UNDERWATER WORLD AQUARIUM

Map p220 (✆6275 0030; www.underwater world.com.sg; behind Siloso Beach; adult/child $25.90/17.60; ⊙9am-9pm) Leafy sea dragons and wobbling medusa jellyfish are mesmeric, while stingrays and 10ft sharks cruise inches from your face as the travelator transports you through the Ocean Colony's submerged glass tubes. Watch divers feeding the fish or muster some nerve for the 30-minute **Dive with the Sharks** experience ($120 per person, bookings essential). The lights are turned off after 7pm and the aquarium takes on an eerie torchlit atmosphere.

Entry includes admission to next-door **Dolphin Lagoon**, where Indo-Pacific humpbacked dolphins (aka pink dolphins) dutifully perform with seals at 11am, 2pm, 4pm and 5.45pm. A 7pm show can also be seen

SENTOSA & OTHER ISLANDS SENTOSA ISLAND

on Saturdays and school-holiday Sundays. For $170 you can **swim with the dolphins**. Call or book through the Underwater World website.

IMAGES OF SINGAPORE — MUSEUM

Map p220 (Imbiah Lookout; adult/child $10/7; ⏰9am-7pm) This diverting historical and cultural museum kicks off with Singapore as a Malay sultanate and takes you through its consolidation as a port and trading centre, WWII, and the subsequent Japanese surrender. Scenes are recreated using lifelike wax dummies, film footage and dramatic light-and-sound effects. Re-creations of local customs and tradition are particularly interesting.

BUTTERFLY PARK & INSECT
KINGDOM — INSECT PARK

Map p220 (Imbiah Lookout; adult/child $16/10; ⏰9.30am-7pm) A tropical rainforest in miniature, the Butterfly Park has more than 50 species of butterflies, many of which are endangered and nearly all of which have been bred in the park itself. The Insect Kingdom houses thousands of mounted butterflies, rhino beetles, Hercules beetles (the world's largest) and scorpions. Children stare wide-eyed, while adults feign disinterest.

RESORTS WORLD
SENTOSA — INTEGRATED RESORT

Map p220 (www.rwsentosa.com; Resorts World) Resorts World is a huge but largely disappointing pedestrianised zone that stretches from the Maritime Xperiential Museum and up towards the Merlion statue. It's crammed with shops, restaurants, cafes and a couple of hotels, many of which are uninspiring, although L'Atelier de Joël Robuchon (p119) is a notable exception. Uni-

versal Studios is undoubtedly a bright spot that shines from all the dross. Underneath it all lurks **Resorts World Casino** (Basement Level, Resorts World; admission locals/foreigners $100/free; ⏰24hr).

MARITIME EXPERIENTIAL MUSEUM — MUSEUM

Map p220 (www.rwsentosa.com; Resorts World; admission $5, theatre show $6; ⏰9am-7pm, theatre shows 10am-6pm) Still hadn't been completed at the time of research, but should be open by the time you read this (hopefully they'll have thought of a better name for it by then). Promises to give you scale models of historic ships, nautical-based galleries and exhibitions, and the world's first 4D multisensory typhoon theatre! No, we haven't got a clue what that is, either. But it sounds cool.

EATING

As well as the places reviewed below, don't forget that the beach bars we list in our Drinking section all do food as well as drinks. And there are dozens of restaurants and cafes in Resorts World. Most attractions have at least a snack stall by the entrance, if not a full-blown cafe-restaurant.

KOUFU FOODCOURT — FOOD COURT $

Map p220 (Palawan Beach; mains from $5, beer from $4) Small air-con-cooled beachside food court with the usual range of rice and noodle dishes. Slightly more expensive than food courts elsewhere in Singapore, but still probably the cheapest place to eat a decent meal on Sentosa.

SENTOSA & OTHER ISLANDS SENTOSA ISLAND

ℹ SENTOSA ENTRANCE FEE & TRANSPORT

There is a small entrance fee to enter Sentosa Island, but it changes price depending on which form of transport you take. If you walk across from VivoCity, the fee is $1. If you ride the Sentosa Express monorail, it's $3. If you ride the cable car, you don't have to pay any extra because the entrance fee is included in the price of your cable car ticket.

Once you're on the island, it's easy to get around, either by walking, taking the Sentosa Express (7am–midnight), riding the 'beach tram' (an electric bus that shuttles the length of all three beaches, 9am–11pm) or by using the three colour-coded bus routes that link the main attractions (7am–midnight). All transport on the island is free. You'll have to pay, though, if you want to rent bicycles, Segways and the like.

SAMUNDAR INDIAN $$

Map p220 (85 Palawan Beach; mains $8-15; ⊙11am-9pm) Boasts one of those vast menus that can drive you mad with indecision, but stick with the tandoor and you won't go wrong (unless you're vegetarian – but even then you have 15 choices). Also does good-value set meals for similar prices to the mains.

CHINATOWN COFFEE SHOP COFFEESHOP $

Map p220 (Costa Sands Resort, behind Siloso Beach; mains $4.50-8; ⊙8am-10pm) A restaurant set-up with a food court menu, this no-nonsense place inside the grounds of Sentosa's only budget digs, Costa Sands Resort, does set breakfasts, dim sum and rice dishes as well as *kopi* (coffee) and *teh* (tea).

CLIFF SEAFOOD $$$

Map p220 (Sentosa Resort, 2 Bukit Manis Rd; mains $75; ⊙6.30-10pm) Perched high above Palawan Beach (although tree cover obscures some of the view), the Cliff is located by the lovely swimming-pool area of the luxury hotel Sentosa Resort. Has great service and wonderful seafood. Take the pain out of ordering and go for the four-course set menu ($128), then sit back as plate after plate of marine masterpiece files past you.

The long **bar** (⊙10.30am-midnight) that sits to one side of the restaurant is perfect for a refined drink with a view.

L'ATELIER DE JOËL ROBUCHON INTERNATIONAL $$$

Map p220 (☑6577 8888; Hotel Michael Level 1, 101-103 & 104-105, Resorts World; meals from $200; ⊙5.30-10.30pm) World-renowned chef Joël Roubuchon's latest Singapore offering is this fancy affair inside Hotel Michael in Resorts World. Service is excellent and the menu is worthy of the name Robuchon. Dishes to look out for include the suckling pig, the hamburgers with foie gras and the steak tartare.

 DRINKING & NIGHTLIFE

WAVE HOUSE BAR

Map p220 (Siloso Beach; ⊙11am-11pm weekdays, 11am-2am weekends) Surfer-friendly beach bar with its own ordinary pool as well as two 'flowriders': wave pools that you can

pay to surf in (see p120). As at Cafe del Mar, you can get beers here for $10.

COASTES BAR

Map p220 (Siloso Beach; ⊙9am-11pm weekdays, 9am-1am weekends) A bit more grown up than its neighbours, Coastes has more tables and chairs than sofas and loungers, but still has a very relaxed beachside vibe. A nicer place to eat than the other bars, although all their menus are similar burger-pasta-pizza affairs.

TANJONG BEACH CLUB BAR

Map p220 (Tanjong Beach; www.tanjongbeachclub. com; ⊙11am-11pm Tue-Fri, 10am-midnight Sat & Sun) The beautiful people flock here to sip cocktails and stretch out on deck chairs. If you don't fancy swimming at the beach, there's also a pool for dip. The secluded location makes it an ideal getaway from the sometimes-madding Sentosa crowds.

 ENTERTAINMENT

SONGS OF THE SEA SHOW

Map p220 (Siloso Beach; admission $10; ⊙7.40pm & 8.40pm, plus 9.40pm on Sat) Set out on *kelongs* (offshore fishing huts), this popular show combines musical gushings with a spectacular $4-million sound, light and laser extravaganza – worth hanging around for.

CINEBLAST, 4D MAGIX & DESPERADOS CINEMA

Map p220 (Imbiah Lookout; adult/child $18/11; ⊙10am-9pm) Three attractions offering slightly different variations of the same theme – 4-D virtual-reality thrill rides and interactive shows – the fourth dimension being the water they spray at you (how rude!).

 ACTIVITIES

SWIMMING SWIMMING

Sentosa has three beaches where you can swim. All are artificial, family-friendly and safe, as long as you stick to the designated swimming zones. **Siloso Beach** is the most popular by some distance and is jam-packed with beach activities. You can also rent sunbeds ($15). **Palawan Beach**, with its small children's play area and free-to-use paddling pools, is great for younger kids. **Tanjong Beach** is the quietest of the three.

A couple of the bars on Siloso Beach also have small swimming pools for their customers, while non-guests can also pay to use the swimming pool at Shangri-La's Rasa Sentosa Resort (adult/child $30/15, at weekends $50/25).

CABLE CAR
CABLE CAR

Map p220 (www.mountfaber.com.sg; adult one-way/return $24/26, child one-way/return $14/15; ☺8.30am-9.30pm) The most spectacular way to get to Sentosa, the cable car ride is an attraction in itself. It leaves from either the summit of Mt Faber (p111) or from next to the HarbourFront MRT.

IFLY
SKYDIVING

Map p220 (www.iflysingapore.com; Beach Station; adult/child $69/59; ☺10am-9pm) Indoor skydiving in a vertical wind chamber, and exceptionally popular. The price includes an hour's instruction then two short skydives. They say the time you spend on one skydive here is like free-falling from 12,000ft to 3,000ft. Gulp!

LUGE & SKYRIDE
TOBOGGANING

Map p220 (admission $12; ☺10am-9.30pm) Take the skyride (a ski-resort-type chairlift) from Siloso Beach up to Imbiah Lookout, then hop onto your toboggan on wheels and luge your way back down the hill. Young kids love this.

WAVE HOUSE
SURFING

Map p220 (www.wavehousesentosa.com; Siloso Beach; admission from $15; ☺10am-midnight Sun-Thu, 10am-1am Fri & Sat) Specially designed wave pools allowing surf dudes and dudettes to practise their gashes and their cutbacks. The pools are part of a bar-restaurant area, which is one of Siloso's coolest hangouts for youngsters.

MEGAZIP
ZIPLINE

Map p220 (Siloso Beach; admission $29; ☺2-7pm Mon-Fri, 11am-7pm Sat & Sun) A 450m-long, 75m-tall zipline from Imbiah Lookout to a tiny island off Siloso Beach. An electric cart is on hand to shuttle riders up from the beach to the start point, where there is also a small adventure park with a climbing wall ($24) and other activities.

GOGREEN SEGWAY ECO ADVENTURE
SEGWAYS

Map p220 (www.segway-sentosa.com; Beach Station; 1 circuit $12, 30-minute guided ride $36; ☺10am-9.30pm) Get perpendicular on these two-wheeled vehicles and scoot around a 10-minute circuit, or opt for the longer guided trip along the beachfront. You can also rent electric bikes (per hour $12) from here.

CYCLING, PEDAL BOATS & KAYAKS
BIKE RENTAL

Map p220 (Siloso Beach; bicycles per hr $12, kayaks per 30 min $8, pedal boats per 30 min $21; ☺9am-6pm) If Segways and electric bikes don't float your boat and you fancy a good old-fashioned cycle, then head to this beach kiosk just outside the grounds of the Shangri-La swimming pool, where you can rent bicycles as well as kayaks and pedal boats.

NATURE WALK
WALKING

Map p220 (Imbiah Lookout; ☺9am-6pm) Starts at the disappointing **Sentosa Nature Discovery** centre, but then opens out into 1.8km of forest trails, some of which follow part of the route once taken by the now-defunct monorail, which used to snake its way around this part of the island before it was shut down in 2005.

FLYING TRAPEZE
TRAPEZE

Map p220 (Siloso Beach; per swing $10, 3 swings $20; ☺2.30-6pm Mon-Fri, 2.30-7pm Sat & Sun) Set up on the beach, this small area is for adults and children over the age of four to learn the basics of trapeze swinging. Guaranteed to cure or create a lifelong fear of heights.

SPA BOTANICA
SPA

Map p220 (☎6371 1318; www.spabotanica.com; Allanbrooke Rd; massage treatments from $85; ☺10am-10pm) Singapore's original indoor and outdoor spa. The signature treatment here is the galaxy steam bath, a 45-minute wallow in medicinal chakra mud in a specially designed steam room. It also has a mud pool outside as well as landscaped grounds and pools. Go on, treat yourself. You can get a free shuttle bus here from VivoCity or from Paragon Shopping Centre on Orchard Rd.

SENTOSA GOLF CLUB
GOLF

Map p220 (☎6275 0022; www.sentosagolf.com; 27 Bukit Manis Rd, green fees per round $280-400, club rental per set $80, shoe rental $10) Luxury golf club with two of the best championship courses in Asia.

Pulau Ubin

Explore

It may be just a 10-minute bumboat ride from Changi Village, but Ubin seems worlds apart from mainland Singapore, and is the perfect city getaway for those who love the outdoors; particularly cycling.

Singaporeans like to wax nostalgic about Ubin's *kampong* (village) atmosphere, and it remains a rural, unkempt expanse of jungle full of fast-moving lizards, strange shrines and cacophonic birdlife. Tin-roofed buildings bake in the sun, chickens squawk and panting dogs slump in the dust, while in the forest, families of wild pigs run for cover as visitors pedal past on squeaky rented bicycles. Set aside a full day if you can. It takes a couple of hours just to get here and, once you arrive, you won't want to be rushed.

The Best...

➡ **Sight** Chek Jawa Wetlands (p121)
➡ **Place to Eat** Pulau Ubin Village (p122)
➡ **Activity** Cycling (p122)

Top Tip

To help reduce litter, maps are no longer given out on Pulau Ubin. However, you will find maps of the island drawn on wooden signboards that you can photograph for later navigation.

Getting There & Away

Boat Getting to Pulau Ubin is half the fun. First catch bus 2 from Tanah Merah MRT Station (30 minutes) to the terminus bus stop at Changi Point Ferry Terminal. From there it's a 10-minute chug-along bumboat ride to Ubin (one-way $2.50, bicycle surcharge $2; 5.30am–9pm). The small wooden boats seat 12 passengers, and only leave when full, but you rarely have to wait long. No tickets are issued. You just pay the boathand once you're on board.

◉ SIGHTS

FREE CHEK JAWA WETLANDS NATURE RESERVE
Map p223 (⊘8.30am-6pm) If you only have time to go to one part of the island, make it this part. Chek Jawa Wetlands, in the island's east, has a 1km **coastal boardwalk**, which takes you out over the sea before looping back through protected mangrove swamp to the 20m-high **Jejawi Tower**, a lookout tower offering stunning views of the area.

You can't bring your bikes into the reserve so make sure the one you've rented comes with a bike lock so you can lock it securely to the bike stands at the entrance.

GERMAN GIRL SHRINE TAOIST TEMPLE
Map p223 Definitely one of Ubin's quirkier sights. Legend has it that the young German daughter of a coffee plantation manager was running away from British troops who had come to arrest her parents during WWI and fell to her death into the quarry behind her house. Discovered a day later, she was initially covered with sand, though Chinese labourers eventually gave her a proper burial. Her ghost supposedly haunts the area to this day.

Somewhere along the way, however, this daughter of a Roman Catholic family became a Taoist deity, whose help some Chinese believers seek for good health and, particularly, good fortune. The shrine is now filled with all manner of charms, offerings, folded lottery tickets, a medium's red table and chair, burning candles and joss paper, and it's housed in a bright yellow shack next to an Assam tree.

WEI TUO FA GONG TEMPLE BUDDHIST TEMPLE
Map p223 This 80-year-old temple sits on small hillock overlooking a pond filled with carp and turtles and contains a number of shrines surrounded by a huge variety of statuettes and iconography. They don't get too many visitors out this way, so chances are you'll be invited to stay for a cup of tea.

PULAU UBIN VILLAGE VILLAGE
Map p223 Although not really a tourist sight, the island's only village of note is a ramshackle time capsule of Singapore's past and an interesting place to wander round. Fish traps and the skeletal remains of abandoned jetties poke out of the muddy water, stray cats prowl for birds, and docile dogs flop unmolested on the sleepy streets.

The boat will drop you here, it's where everyone rents bikes and, apart from Celestial Resort, it's the only place with any restaurants. So, like it or not, you'll spend at least some of your time here.

EATING & DRINKING

There's a beach restaurant and bar with a slightly shanty vibe at Celestial Resort (Map p223; p152), but apart from that the only place to have a meal is in **Pulau Ubin Village**. Get off the boat and turn left. There are half a dozen or so places here, most housed in *kampong* huts with tin roofs. They all serve similar fare, with noodles and rice dishes featuring alongside lots of seafood (naturally). Chilli crab is a favourite – expect to pay between $20 and $40. Wash it down with a Tiger beer – what else?

There are a couple of **drinks stalls** along Jln Endul Senin, where you can also buy snacks.

ACTIVITIES

KETAM MOUNTAIN BIKE PARK   CYCLING
Map p223 A series of trails of varying difficulty leads around Ketam Quarry and through some of the surrounding area. While it's not the most hardcore bike park on the planet, you really need to be more than just a beginner to deal with the steep slopes, sharp corners and relatively poor traction at vari-

ous points on most of the trails. There's also a small bike-skills zone off to your left as you enter the area. This is also where you'll find the German Girl Shrine.

SWIMMING & KAYAKING   WATER SPORTS
Map p223 (www.celestialresort.com; Celestial Resort, Jln Endul Senin; swimming $5, kayaking per hr $10, fishing half-day $30, snorkelling 30 mins $10)
It's possible to swim in the sea at the small beaches on Ubin, but the water's pretty grim so most people don't dare. You can, however, swim in the (slightly) cleaner lake that's inside the grounds of Celestial Resort. Even if you don't actually swim here, the small artificial beach is more pleasant to lie on than the ones on the coast of the island.

You can also rent kayaks here, do fishing and go snorkelling. And there's a small restaurant and a bar.

Southern Islands

Explore

Three other islands popular for local escapes are St John's, Lazarus and Kusu. On weekends they can be mildly crowded, but during the week they are almost deserted – unless your visit coincides with a school camp. They can be great for fishing, swimming, a picnic and guzzling six-packs.

CYCLING AROUND UBIN

Apart from walking (which isn't a bad option at all) cycling is the only way to get around Ubin. Those heading for the Ketam Mountain Bike Park tend to bring their own better-quality bikes with them, but for the rest of us there are plenty of places in Pulau Ubin Village that rent perfectly adequate bikes for the day, from around $5–$10, and $2 for children's bikes. The bikes are pretty much identical, whichever place you rent from. They should throw in a basket, a bike lock and a helmet if you ask, and many have kids bikes too.

You can't get maps of the island, but there are maps on signboards dotted around the place, so you can follow them. Because of the large swamp area in the central northern region of the island, you can't do a complete loop so if you want to explore the east and the west (note: the far west is off limits) you'll have to do a bit of backtracking, but distances here are small so it hardly matters.

Although it looks like you can on the signboard maps, you can't in fact cross Sungai Mamam swamp for a shortcut between Noordin Campsite and Mamam Campsite. You have to go back via the main road.

Facilities are almost non-existent: You can stay the night on St John's, and there are toilets on St John's and Kusu, but there is nowhere to buy food or drink on any of the islands, so come prepared.

The Best...

➡ **Sight** Kusu Kramats (p123)

➡ **Place for a picnic** Kusu Island (p123)

➡ **Activity** Paddling on Kusu's shallow beach (p123)

Top Tip

Be aware that there are no changing facilities at any of the beaches on these three islands. They're fine for a quick dip or a paddle, but if you want a typical day at the beach, you're better off heading to Sentosa.

Getting There & Away

Ferry The Southern Islands ferry from Marina South Pier (www.islandcruise.com.sg; 31 Marina Coastal Dr; adult/child return $15/12; ☉10am & 2pm Mon-Fri, 9am, midday & 3pm Sat, 9am, 11am, 1pm, 3pm & 5pm Sun) stops first at St John's (45 minutes), hangs around for about an hour, then goes on to Kusu (15 minutes). You can hop off one and catch the next with your return ticket. But there aren't that many boats; two, three or five, depending on what day it is. Coming back, the last ferry leaves Kusu at 4pm Monday to Friday, at 4.30pm on Saturdays and at 6.15pm on Sundays. This schedule could change, though, so check the website before making your plans. To get to Marina South Pier, take the MRT to Marina Bay then take bus 402.

◎ SIGHTS

KUSU ISLAND   ISLAND

By far the smallest of the three islands, Kusu is also the most pleasant. It's been nicely landscaped, has a decent beach and there's even a bit of history and culture to enjoy.

The boat drops you in an area of landscaped gardens – perfect for picnics – where there's also a small **turtle sanctuary** (awww!) and **Tua Pek Kong Temple**, a Chinese Taoist temple with some colourful dragon artwork. Further on is the **beach**; a decent strip of sand with lovely shallow water in a protected cove: ideal for young kids.

All of this, though, is on reclaimed flat land, which surrounds the original piece of the island – a huge forest-covered rock, at the top of which sits the **Kusu Kramats**, three Malay shrines that devotees have been visiting since the 19th century. You can visit the shrines, all painted a bright canary yellow, by climbing the 152 steps up through the trees to the top.

ST JOHN'S ISLAND   ISLAND

Strangely spooky, St John's has a chequered past: it was a quarantine for immigrants in the 1930s before being turned first into a political prison and then later into a rehabilitation centre for opium addicts. There is still a strange prisonlike feel to the place, with huge fences topped with barbed wire separating some areas from others and a few watchtowers remaining. But visitors are allowed to come and go as they please these days (although there's a marine research centre that's out of bounds) and the island makes for a quirky half-day trip.

There's a small **beach** where some people picnic and a tiny **mosque** with a tin roof that's used by workers who help to maintain the island, but mostly people come here for a quiet spot of **fishing**.

Huge dorm rooms of 60-plus beds are booked out by schools for summer camps (you can't book per bed; you have to book the whole dorm). There is also one self-contained, three-bedroom bungalow (see p152), which you can rent for the night. Camping is not allowed, although people occasionally do it.

LAZARUS ISLAND   ISLAND

Connected to St John's via a concrete walkway, Lazarus is almost entirely undeveloped, with little more than a bit of jungle and a **beach**. If you thought St John's was quiet, wait till you come here! The beach is a lovely long sweeping affair – and posh yachts sometimes park up beside it for the afternoon – but it's littered with rubbish that's been swept up by the tides, and no one is here to clean it up. Part of the coastline that faces Singapore (the beach faces the other way) had been cleared when we were last here, and there were signs that perhaps a resort of some sort might be on its way, but it was very early stages. But for now at least, the island is little more than a place to walk to from St John's.

Day Trips from Singapore

Pulau Bintan p125

Expats and moneyed Singaporeans lap up the all-inclusive resorts in the north, but exploring Bintan's cultural heartland around its capital, Pinang, is a far more rewarding experience.

Johor Bahru p128

Just under an hour away by bus from Singapore, the Malaysian city of Johor Bahru, or JB, is a place for cheap food and cheap-ish shopping, though it also plays host to some charming attractions.

Melaka p134

A former colonial outpost in Malaysia, Melaka is Unesco-listed for its wealth of old-world architectural features, and popular for its fantastic food culture.

Pulau Tioman p132

It's a 35-minute flight to this low-key Malaysian paradise of an island. From diving packages to just chilling on white-sand beaches, Tioman is well worth visiting for a beach getaway.

Pulau Bintan

◉ SIGHTS

◉ Pinang

Explore

Skip the pricey, all-inclusive beach resorts in the north and explore Bintan's cultural heart in the area further south, around this Indonesian island's largest town, Pinang.

A world away from ultraclean Singapore, the noisy, dusty, potholed streets here are very Indonesian. Dodge mopeds and rickshaws as you fight through the busy backalleys to a local coffeeshop, giving yourself the chance to get your bearings and read the map you picked up at the tourist office.

Rested and refreshed, head to the small jetties where you can board bumboats to either Senggarang (to see a Chinatown on stilts!) or Penyengat, a small island with royal tombs, palaces, a beautiful mosque and a wonderfully rural atmosphere.

The Best...

⇒ **Sight** Masjid Raya Sultan Riao (p126)

⇒ **Dish** *Ikan bakar* at Penyengat (p128)

⇒ **Place to Eat** Ocean Corner (p127)

Top Tip

It's cheaper and far less hassle to change money at moneychangers than in a bank. There are loads on Jln Merdeka (turn left out of the ferry terminal).

Getting There & Away

Boat Ferries leave for Pinang (two hours) from Singapore's Tanah Merah Ferry Terminal (bus 35 from Bedok MRT Station) and are run by Wave Master, Penguin and Falcon. See p126 for schedules and prices. A 30-day, single-entry tourist visa for Indonesia ($40 or US$25, cash only) can be bought on arrival at Pinang. The 13,000Rp departure tax must be paid in local currency when you leave.

Need to Know

⇒ **Area Code** ☑+62 771

⇒ **Location** 60km from Singapore.

⇒ **Tourist Office in Pinang** ☑25373; Jln H Agus Salim; turn left out of the ferry terminal and it's on your left after 50m; ◎8am-4pm.

Bintan's capital is an historic port town and trade centre with a still-thriving market culture and plenty of hustle and bustle. Touts swarm all over you as you get off the ferry. Ignore them all, and head straight to the very helpful tourist office (turn left as you leave the ferry terminal complex, and it's on your left after 50 metres) where you can pick up some handy advice and a street map.

CETIYA BODHI SASANA   BUDDHIST TEMPLE

(Jln Plantar 2) This small Chinese temple down by the docks can actually be seen from the water as you leave on boats to Senggarang. There's a small open-air stage in front of it, where Chinese opera performances are sometimes held. Frenetic dragon boat races start here every year during Dragon Boat Festival (fifth day of the fifth lunar month). To get here, turn left out of the ferry terminal, walk about 500m down the main road then turn left (opposite Vihara Bhatra Sasana temple) down Jln Plantar 2. Just before you reach the water, turn left to the temple. The area here is a fascinating maze of alleyways and market stalls.

VIHARA BHATRA SASANA   BUDDHIST TEMPLE

(Jln Merdeka) Dragons adorn the beautifully painted upturned eaves on the roof of this Chinese temple. A statue of Kuan Yin (Guanyin), the goddess of mercy, stands at the central altar. Turn left out of the ferry terminal and keep walking to the end of the road. The temple is on your right, on the corner with Jln Ketapang.

SULTAN SULAIMAN BADRAL ALAMSYAH   MUSEUM

(Jln Ketapang; ◎9am-3pm Mon-Fri, 9am-4.30pm Sat & Sun) Housed in an attractive building built by the Dutch in 1918, this small museum is full of mostly Chinese artefacts – coins, pottery, musical instruments, clothing, jewellery – but lacks English captions. Look out for the old *caping,* a type of chastity belt. To get here, turn right at Vihara Bhatra Sasana and it's soon on your left.

FERRIES TO BINTAN'S CAPITAL, PINANG

Ferries leave for Pinang (two hours) from Singapore's Tanah Merah Ferry Terminal.

Ferry Companies

Falcon (☑9147 1068; Tanah Merah Ferry Terminal; one-way/return $40/50)

Penguin (☑6542 7105; Tanah Merah Ferry Terminal; adult/child one-way $28/23, return $50/40)

Wave Master (☑6786 9959; Tanah Merah Ferry Terminal; one-way/return $40/50)

Singapore to Pinang (Singapore time)

Monday to Friday 8.50am (Falcon), 9.20am (Wave Master), 12.30pm (Penguin), 3pm (Falcon), 3.30pm (Wave Master), 6.20pm (Penguin)

Saturday and Sunday 8.50am (Falcon), 9.20am (Wave Master), 10.20am (Penguin), 1.10pm (Falcon), 3.30pm (Wave Master), 5.10pm (Falcon), 5.30pm (Wave Master), 6.20pm (Penguin)

Pinang to Singapore (Indonesian time)

Monday to Friday 7am (Penguin), 10.10am (Falcon), 10.30am (Wave Master), 2pm (Penguin), 4pm (Falcon), 4.30pm (Wave Master)

Saturday and Sunday 7am (Penguin), 10am (Falcon), 10.25am (Wave Master), 1.30pm (Penguin), 2pm (Falcon), 2.25pm (Wave Master), 6pm (Falcon), 6.30pm (Wave Master)

Indonesia is one hour behind Singapore.

◉ Penyengat

Once the heart of the Riao-Johor sultanate and the cultural hub of the Malay empire, the tiny island of Penyengat grew in the 16th century when the Malay sultanate fled here after being defeated by the Portuguese in Malacca. It's now home to Indo-Malaysians and Hakka Chinese immigrants who live either in stilt houses on the coastline or in brightly painted bungalows in the island's lush interior.

It's a 15-minute boat ride from Pinang (per person one-way 5000Rp). The 15-man boats only leave when full so you sometimes have to wait a while. To get to the jetty, turn left out of the main ferry terminal, left at the first crossroads and then walk straight down the alleyway in front of you, which leads to the jetty.

MASJID RAYA SULTAN RIAO   MOSQUE

This beautiful fairytale castle of a mosque was built in 1832 and is painted in pastels of yellow and green. Its minarets are topped with tall conical spires and are almost Gothic Revival in style. This is an active mosque and although visitors are welcomed, they should be wearing appropriate clothing; cover yourself up, or else admire the building from afar.

TOMBS AND PALACES   HISTORICAL SITE

Penyengat was the royal capital of the Riao-Johor sultanate, and the island is dotted with the ruins of the palaces and tombs of these Malay rulers. Ones to look out for on your wanders include the ruined palace **Astana Kantor**, straight on from the mosque, and the **tomb of Raja Hamidah**, off to the left of the mosque. There are many others that you'll stumble across as you walk around the island.

FORT   HISTORICAL SITE

At the far west of the island are the ruins of an impressive stone fort, built by the sultan Raja Haji in the 18th century to fend off Dutch attacks. Ironically, the **cannons** you see here are Dutch made. Raja Haji, incidentally, was the author of the first Malay grammar book, a reminder that this island was once a hotbed of intellectual and religious minds, and at one time was home to more than 9,000 people.

BECAK RIDES TOURS

Penyengat is small enough to walk around, but a fun alternative is to take a tour in a *becak* (pronounced 'beerchuk'), a motorcycle rickshaw with a sidecar. The standard tour lasts for one hour and costs around 25,000Rp.

◉ Senggarang

This predominantly Chinese village on the other side of the bay from Pinang is reached by small wooden boats (per person one-way 5000Rp, 10 minutes), which are taken from the jetty called Plantar 1. To get to Plantar 1, continue past the alleyway that leads down to the jetty for boats to Penyengat and take the next left.

CHINATOWN STILT HOUSING

Unless you ask specifically to be dropped at the temples, your boat will drop you at the jetties that are used to access Senggarang's so-called Chinatown. Far removed from the Chinatown you will have seen in Singapore, this one is residential rather than commercial, but is interesting because all the homes – and there are hundreds – are built on wooden stilts and so are suspended above the sea water, rather than on dry land. Residents are mostly Teochew Chinese and the community is believed to have been here since the 18th century. Many of the homes have private shrines in their entranceways.

VIHARA DHARMA SASANA BUDDHIST TEMPLES

This well-maintained temple complex, looking out to sea, is accessed through a beautifully decorative Chinese archway and contains three main temples. The oldest two, and the first ones you approach after walking through the archway, are side by side and facing the sea, and are thought to be between 200 and 300 years old, although they have been repainted and repaired many times. Their roof carvings are particularly ornate. Behind them is a more modern temple and two huge and very colourful Buddha statues.

To get to the temples, either tell your boatman to take you directly to the temple jetty (6000Rp to 8000Rp) or go to the usual Senggarang jetty and walk straight along it before taking the first left. Continue all the way to the end of this boardwalk then turn right and keep walking until you hit dry land. From there you'll see the archway entrance to the complex.

BANYAN TREE TEMPLE BUDDHIST TEMPLE

If you walk out of the Vihara Dharma Sasana temple complex and keep going straight, you'll soon reach a small village where you'll find a particularly unusual temple, housed in a building thought to date from 1811. Originally the house of a wealthy Chinese man, who is believed to be buried here, the building has, over the years, been swallowed up by the roots of a large banyan tree. It's only in recent decades that the site has become a shrine, as locals and devotees from further afield began to come here to give offerings and ask for blessings from what is now believed to be a sacred spot.

You can get back to the jetty from here without returning to the temple complex by taking the first left on your way back.

EATING

If you're planning to catch an early morning ferry from Singapore, it's worth knowing that the Tanah Merah Ferry Terminal has a branch of the excellent coffeeshop chain Killiney Kopitiam, where you can enjoy a sea view out on the verandah while you eat a Singaporean breakfast of *kaya* toast, runny eggs and *kopi*. They do plenty of main dishes too and, if you don't like *kopi*, they also do fresh Western-style coffee.

✗ Pinang

Turn left out of the ferry terminal and you'll soon find a few *kedai kopi* (locals coffeeshops), where you can grab a drink, a snack or a bowl of *goreng* (noodles).

Come evening, head out to the ocean road (turn right out of the ferry terminal) and you'll have a choice of dozens of food stalls from which to eat and drink at. The first collection of stalls you'll come across (100 metres from the ferry terminal) will be at the small square known as **Ocean Corner**. Here you'll find plenty of rice and noodle dishes (*nasi goreng, mee goreng*), satay and a peanut-flavoured rice-noodle dish called *ketoprak*. Further on from Ocean

Corner is a larger square with similar stalls. Stalls on the ocean road tend to open from 5pm to midnight.

Other delicacies to look out for are *gong gong,* snails eaten with a toothpick (expect to pay around 20,000Rp for a small portion), and *otak otak,* small fishcakes barbecued in strips of banana leaves (around 500Rp each).

✗ Penyengat

The jetty you walk along as you arrive on the island has a few small restaurants with outdoor seating. Look out for *ikan bakar,* a delicious barbecued fish dish eaten with a side salad, a sweet-chilli dip and plain rice. Expect to pay around 35,000Rp for one serving. Do as the locals do, and eat it with your fingers. The silver teapots on the table are filled with water for washing your hands with.

✗ Senggarang

A couple of locals open up the front of their stilt houses as small restaurants. Expect only the most basic of dishes, and little choice. Otherwise, you can grab snacks at small shops in the village near the Banyan Tree Temple.

Johor Bahru

Explore

Easy to visit in a day from Singapore, JB (no one calls it Johor Bahru) has some attractive architecture but isn't really a sightseeing spot. The main reason to visit is to experience a city with a more laid-back atmosphere than fast-paced Singapore.

Once you get off your bus or train, head to a coffeeshop in the old colonial district for a leisurely meal before wandering the pleasant lanes and shophouses nearby. See a couple of the area's temples before getting a cab or walking to the Royal Abu Bakar Museum, housed in the former royal palace and JB's only must-see sight.

After a stroll in the gardens next door, head back to the colonial district for a bite and a drink in a funky back-alley bar before making your way back across the border.

The Best...

➡ **Sight** Royal Abu Bakar Museum (p130)
➡ **Place to Eat** Kedai Kopi Dan Makanan Kin Wah (p130)
➡ **Place to Drink** Roost Juice Bar (p131)

Top Tip

Immigration at the Woodlands checkpoint, for people coming back into Singapore, can be hellishly busy on a Sunday evening. Try to avoid coming back at this time if you can.

SLEEPING IN PINANG

Prices are cheaper than in Singapore, and rooms are often larger, but standards are generally lower.

➡ **Hotel Melia** (☑21898; 29 Jln Pasar Ikan; r from $40; 🕾) Friendly modern midrange hotel with huge clean rooms, decent attached bathrooms, free wi-fi and free breakfast. Turn left out of the ferry terminal, take the first left at the small crossroads, bear round to the right and the hotel is on your left.

➡ **Hotel Tanjung Pinang Jaya** (☑21236; 692 Jln Pasar Ikan; r from $22) This large hotel located on a bend in the road is brightly painted but a bit shabbier and more old-fashioned than the others. Rooms are large, but a bit rundown. Staff are friendly, but don't speak much English. No internet. Just past Melia as the road bears round to the left.

➡ **Lesmina Hotel** (☑315000; 29 Jln Pasar Ikan; r from 128,000Rp) Smallest rooms of the three hotels reviewed here, but still reasonably sized doubles and clean, if not sparkling, bathrooms. Staff are friendly and some speak a little bit of English. Continue past Hotel Melia, follow the road round the staggered corner, and Lesmina is on your right.

Johor Bahru

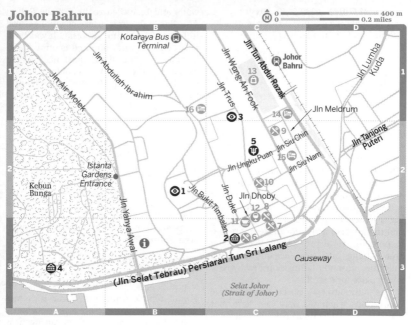

Johor Bahru

Getting There & Away

Bus There are three ways of getting to JB by bus, and it takes about an hour. The easiest way is to catch the direct 'Singapore–Johor Express' bus ($2.50, one hour, 6.30am–11pm), which leaves every 15 minutes from Queen St Bus Terminal in Little India. The cheapest way is to catch a local bus to the border – bus 170 ($1.70), for example, which also leaves from Queen St Bus Terminal – and then catch a local bus (RM1) from the other side, or even just walk to JB from immigration. The quickest way is to catch the MRT to Kranji then take bus 160 from there to the border. Coming back, board your bus from Kotaraya Bus Terminal in JB, from where you have a similar choice with buses running from around 5am to midnight.

Taxi A taxi from central Singapore to JB will cost you around $40. You can also pay for a seat in a shared taxi from Queen St Bus Terminal for $12 per person. Shared taxis leave when full.

Need to Know
➡ **Area Code** ☎+60 7
➡ **Location** 1.4km from Singapore.

➡ **Tourist Office** ☎222 3590; www.
tourismmalaysia.gov.my; 2 Jln Ayer Molek;
⊘8am-1pm & 2-5pm Mon-Fri

 **SIGHTS**

ROYAL ABU BAKAR MUSEUM   MUSEUM

Map p129 (Jln Ibrahim; adult/child US$7/3;
⊘9am-5pm Sat-Thu) The former Istana Besar (main palace) of the Johor royal family was built in Victorian style on a small
hill overlooking the Johor Strait by the
Anglophile sultan Abu Bakar in 1866. The
palace is now a museum chock-full of the
sultan's possessions, furniture and hunting trophies. There are some superb pieces,
making it worth a visit for those interested
in perusing royal bric-a-brac. Even if you
aren't going into the museum, the surrounding grounds (admission free) are a
lovely place for a stroll.

The museum was closed for extensive
renovations when we were last here, but
was due to open again in 2012.

JOHOR OLD CHINESE
TEMPLE   TAOIST TEMPLE

Map p129 (Jln Trus; ⊘7.30am-5.30pm) Once the
centre of JB's Chinese immigrant community, and used by five different ethnic groups
to worship five different Chinese gods, this
small but atmospheric temple is more than
130 years old. Little remains of its original
masonry after major renovations in 1995,
but it does house some genuine antiques. A
large bronze bell, in a room off to the right,
has engravings that date it to 1875, while
in a small hallway behind that room are
wooden tablets whose Chinese inscriptions
also date the original temple to the 1870s.

SULTAN ABU BAKAR MOSQUE   MOSQUE

Map p129 (Jln Gertak Merah) A real good-looker
of a mosque, the stunning whitewashed
walls and blue-tiled roofing of the Sultan
Abu Bakar features a mix of architectural
influences, including Victorian. It was built
between 1892 and 1900 and is quite rightly hailed as one of the most magnificent
mosques in the area. It can hold up to 2000
people. Sadly, non-Muslims cannot enter
the building itself, but can only admire it
from the outside.

CHINESE HERITAGE MUSEUM   MUSEUM

Map p129 (Jln Tan Hiok Nee; admission RM5;
⊘9am-5pm Tue-Sun) Well laid-out exhibits
chronicling the history of Chinese immigrants in this part of the Malay peninsula.
Learn how the Cantonese brought their car-
pentry skills here, while the Hakkas traded
in Chinese medicines and the Hainanese
kickstarted a trend in coffeeshops, which
lasts to this day.

SRI RAJA MARIAMMAN
DEVASTHANAM   HINDU TEMPLE

Map p129 (4 Jln Ungku Puan) This beautiful
Hindu temple with ornate carvings and
devotional artwork, and a tall, brightly
painted *gopuram* (tower) entranceway is
the heart of JB's Hindu community.

BANGUNAN SULTAN
IBRAHIM   NOTABLE BUILDING

Map p129 (Bukit Timbalan) The former state
secretariat building was built by the British
in 1940 and casts an imposing figure over
this part of town. It used to house the Johor State Legislative Assembly, and during
WWII the Japanese used it as a fortress, but
it now lies largely unoccupied, with plans to
perhaps turn it into a museum. You can see
inside the entrance, but can't fully explore
the building.

 EATING & DRINKING

KEDAI KOPI DAN MAKANAN
KIN WAH   COFFEESHOP $

Map p129 (Jln Tan Hiok Nee; dishes from RM3;
⊘7am-5pm) Hugely popular, this no-
nonsense coffeeshop has a point-and-
choose buffet-style set-up with simple but
tasty local dishes and, of course, *kopi* (coffee). Tables and plastic stools spill out into
the five-foot way and onto the pavement
during the lunchtime rush.

 MALAYSIAN VISAS

Most foreigners do not need a Malaysian visa for short-term stays,
but check before you leave. Border
formalities are fairly straightforward,
although weekends can get busy.
Don't forget your passport!

DAY TRIPS FROM SINGAPORE JOHOR BAHRU

RESTORAN HUAMUI   COFFEESHOP $

Map p129 (131 Jln Trus; mains RM5-7; ⊙8am-6pm) This airy, fan-cooled coffeeshop with delightful mosaic-tiled flooring is also very popular with locals. The menu is a mix of Malay, Indonesian and Chinese. We loved the *kampong* fried rice. Also does *kaya*-toast set breakfasts.

NIGHT MARKET   MALAY $

Map p129 (off Jln Siu Chin; dishes from $4; ⊙3.30pm-midnight) Open-air stalls selling all manner of local dishes line the T-shaped alleyway here, which links Jln Siu Chin, Jln Meldrum and Jln Wong Ah Fook, and which heaves with customers come early evening. Many of the stalls are Muslim-run, so don't expect to be able to sink a beer with your meal. Wash it down instead with a fresh coconut. There are all sorts of noodle and rice dishes to be found, but our favourite here is the *sup kambing,* a slightly spicy mutton soup, which you mop up with chunks of French bread.

IT ROO CAFE   CAFE $$

Map p129 (17 Jln Dhoby; mains RM6-14, coffee from RM3; ⊙midday-10pm) A tourist-friendly cafe with a mix of Southeast Asian and Western dishes, friendly It Roo has been going since 1961. It originally opened as a bar before switching to its current, more refined guise. The specialty dish is the *chicken chop,* golden-fried chicken breast with a black pepper or mushroom sauce. Cool off under the air-con, or sit outside on the patio.

HIAP JOO BAKERY & BISCUIT FACTORY   BAKERY $

Map p129 (13 Jln Tan Hiok Nee; rolls & cakes RM1-4; ⊙6am-7pm) Despite the rather grand name, Hiap Joo is a tiny bakery that uses a traditional coal-fired stone oven to bake delicious buns, cakes and biscuits. It's been in business since 1930 and specialises in fresh bread rolls and banana cake. The bread rolls are ready by 12.30pm, and sold out by 3pm. The banana cake is baked all day, with the last batch done by about 2.30pm.

ANNALAKSHMI   SOUTH INDIAN VEGETARIAN $

Map p129 (www.annalakshmi.com.sg; 39 Jln Ibrahim; meals by donation; ⊙11am-3pm) An eat-as-much-as-you-like, pay-as-much-as-you-want buffet with good-quality Indian vegetarian food. Also has branches in Singapore (p60), India and Australia. The restaurant chain is part of the Temple of Fine Arts (www.templeoffinearts.org/sg), a Hindu organisation dedicated to promoting art and culture.

ROOST JUICE BAR   BAR

Map p129 (9 Jln Dhoby; ⊙10am-4pm & 6pm-midnight) A trendy back-alley bar with retro furniture and laidback staff, this is the coolest hangout in the colonial district. Beer is half the price you'd pay in Singapore, and the fresh-fruit smoothies (served in mini seaside buckets!) are delicious.

🔒 SHOPPING

Recent price rises mean shopping in JB as opposed to Singapore is no longer the bargain it once was. Prices are still slightly cheaper, but quality is poorer.

JOHOR BAHRU CITY SQUARE   MALL

Map p129 (108 Jln Wong Ah Fook) If you do fancy a browse, or just a few minutes of air conditioning, this large shopping mall is worth a visit.

DAY TRIPS FROM SINGAPORE JOHOR BAHRU

Pulau Tioman

Explore

The largest and most spectacular of Malaysia's east coast islands, Tioman has some lovely beaches, clear water, good snorkelling and some excellent dive sites. It's a welcome change from the overcrowded beaches in Thailand, though hardcore partygoers should be forewarned: no raves to be found here. It takes a while to get here and people usually stay at least two nights or more.

The Best...

⇒ **Sights** Tekek to Juara Hike (p133)
⇒ **Place to Eat** Hijau Restaurant (p134)
⇒ **Place to Drink** Sunset Beach Bar (p134)

Top Tip

Come on a weekday to avoid the weekend crush. You'll find it hard to get booze outside of meal times so if you like a drink, stock up on alcohol and check that your room has a small fridge.

Getting There & Away

Air Berjaya Air (☑6227 3688; www.berjaya-air.com; 67 Tanjong Pagar Rd) operates daily flights ($305) direct to Tioman's airport from Singapore's Changi Airport. The flight takes 35 minutes.

Bus/boat Early birds can catch the Five Star Tours (☑6392 7011) bus to Mersing ($31 one way; 6.30am; 4hr) at Golden Mile Complex, except during the monsoon season between October and February. Alternatively, hop on the Transnasional (☑6294 7034; $16.50) bus, which leaves the Lavender St Bus Terminal (Map p204)

Pulau Tioman

at 9am and 10am. You can also take a Causeway Link Express ($2.40, every 15 min) from the Queen St Bus Terminal (Map p204) to Larkin in Johor Bahru where you can get a taxi (RM160 per taxi, maximum four passengers; 2hr) to Mersing. When you arrive at Mersing, you have two options. The speedboats (RM45 one way) are quickest, taking a bit more than an hour, but many people find them unpleasantly fast. The normal ferries (RM35 one way) leave around five times a day and take up to three hours, stopping off at the various beaches in a south-to-north direction. Departures are dependent on tide, conditions and number of passengers.

Need to Know

➡ **Area Code** ☑60 9
➡ **Distance from Singapore** 178km
➡ **Tourist Office** Get information from the ferry terminal at Mersing.

⊙ SIGHTS & ACTIVITIES

Tioman is all about beaches, snorkelling and diving (not necessarily in that order). The ferry will take you south to north through **Kampung Genting**, **Paya**, **Tekek**, **Air Batang** (aka ABC) and **Salang**. Each one of these has a strip of beach, some better than others.

Genting is forgettable except as a transit point to the quiet beach of **Nipah**, where in-the-know visitors flock to. The main beach on Tekek is forgettable and most people who get off here are inevitably package tourists who are heading to Berjaya Resort. It's also the main town: the airstrip, post office, ATM and duty-free stores (stock up on booze) are all there.

Tekek is also the starting point for a fabulous **hike** through the rainforest interior of Tioman. It's a 7km, sweaty bash through a jungle trail so take plenty of water. Towards the end, watch out for an unmarked trail leading to a **waterfall** where you can take a well-deserved dip. You'll exit at arguably the best beach on the island, **Juara**. This gorgeous stretch of beach is quiet and most of the chalets open up onto the white sand. For those not inclined to hike across, you can get a 4WD ride across for RM30 one way.

ABC reminds one fellow Lonely Planet author of Tahiti. It's true as there's a certain laid-back charm to the place, even though the beaches aren't particularly attractive. **Salang** is the most popular, with the highest number of beach chalet operations, diving operations, and the best nightlife on the island, and proximity to the **Monkey**

SLEEPING IN PULAU TIOMAN

There's a huge range of accommodation on Tioman, the majority of it identical, basic wooden beach chalets, typically with a bed, fan and bathroom. Most of them offer food, with varying degrees of skill. Expect to pay RM40–160 for a chalet, depending on size, proximity to beach and whether it's got a fan or air-con. There are also upmarket resorts all with their own private beach, and inhouse bars and restaurants.

➡ **Nazri's Place** (☑419 1329; Air Batang; chalets from RM100) Longstanding favourite, with two separate locations on ABC. Reasonable chalets in a garden setting. Friendly owner.

➡ **Ella's Place** (☑419 5005; Salang; chalets RM35-60) The best of the Salang cheapies, with friendly owners, decent food and a great stretch of beach.

➡ **Bushman's** (☑419 3109; Juara; chalets RM80-120) Wooden chalets sit on a perfect spot right on the Juara beach. Lovely little cafe too.

➡ **Japamala Resort** (☑03 2161 0769; www.japamalaresorts.com; chalets RM400-200) The ultraswish boutique resort (book in advance) is the best on Tioman and is located on the quiet southwest corner of the island. A jungle lodge is set to open in 2012.

➡ **Berjaya Tioman Beach Resort** (☑419 1000; chalets RM275-385) This is the largest and fanciest resort on Tioman, although it's slightly rough around the edges. It offers a huge range of activities.

Bay and **Pulau Tulai** snorkelling and diving sites.

You can rent snorkelling gear from RM20 at most the accommodation places. Most accommodation owners can point you in the right direction for diving trips including ones where you can get PADI certification.

 EATING & DRINKING

Most of the chalets will have their own kitchen and dining room serving up a range of Malay dishes, and a sprinkling of Chinese and Western dishes. Look out for grilled seafood and satay too. As Malaysians are predominantly Muslim, alcohol isn't readily available all day. You can get cheap cans of beer (from RM5) during lunch and dinner times. Each beach has one or two beachside bars: wander round till you find a place that's buzzing. If you're into late nights and dancing, Salang is the place to decamp.

HIJAU RESTAURANT   INTERNATIONAL **$$**
(Air Batang; dishes from RM10) This hillside terrace restaurant at the northern end of ABC beach dishes up a huge variety of Indian and Malay favourites, all cooked to high standards. Bottles of wine or ice-cold beer help ease the spicy burn.

SUNSET CORNER   PIZZA **$$**
(Air Batang; drinks from RM 5, pizzas from RM18) Don't judge this beach shack by its appearance. Its serves up cheap beers and cocktails to accompany some wicked thin-crust pizza. Pull up a deck chair on the beach and watch the stars overhead. Just ahead of Nazri's Place, on the southern end of the beach.

Melaka

Explore
Outlined to the west by sandy coastline and filled inland with waves of jungle-carpeted hills, the sultry city-state of Melaka is the cradle of modern Malaysia. Melaka is a medium-sized town that's easy to navigate and compact enough to explore on foot or trishaw. The colonial areas of Melaka are mainly on the eastern side of the river, focused around Town Sq (also known as Dutch Sq) and Christ Church. Bukit St Paul (St Paul's Hill), the site of the original Portuguese fort of A'Famosa, rises above Town Sq. Located further north is Melaka's tiny Little India. Bustling, scenic Chinatown is to the west. Here is where most visitors stay and spend their time poking around shops and dining at restaurants that line the streets.

THE KTM TRAIN SERVICE
The Malaysian-run **KTM train service** out of Singapore to Kuala Lumpur in Malaysia offers ample opportunities for some less-than-obvious but nonethless interesting day trips. There's a certain romance in taking a slow-moving train that meanders through the Malaysian countryside. Along the way, passengers (if they haven't been lulled to sleep) can catch glimpses of palm tree, rubber and various other fruit plantations. Curious locals wave to passing trains, and the country air just smells fresher and greener.

Get yourself to the **Woodlands Train Checkpoint Station** (☑6767 5885; 11 Woodlands Crossing; 🚌170, Causeway Link from Queen St). There's no point taking the train into Johor Bahru as it's less than a 10-minute ride across from Woodlands. To make a day of it all, get a cheap ticket to either Kluang (two hours, from $30 return) or Segamat (3½ hours, from $45 return). These are the two larger towns en route to Kuala Lumpur. In Kluang, wander the old streets of Jln Stesen or Jln Ismail or hike Gunung Lambak. In Segamat, it's all about food. Get a coffee and *kaya* toast from Nanyang Kopitiam and look out for the famous namesake durians along the roadside. It takes over five hours to get to Kuala Lumpur for those who really want to go all the way (though you'd be hard pressed to return in the same day).

The posh **Eastern & Oriental Express** also travels up towards Thailand from Woodlands in Singapore. See p180.

The Best...

⇨ **Sight** Baba-Nonya Heritage Museum (p137)

⇨ **Place to Eat** Nancy's Kitchen (p138)

⇨ **Place to Drink** Geographér Cafe (p139)

Top Tip

Get 20% off many local attractions by picking up coupons at the Tourism Melaka office across from the Stadthuys.

Getting There & Away

Bus The easiest way (apart from driving your own car) is to get a long-distance bus service from the Golden Mile Complex ($20-33; 4hr; ⊘several daily). You could also catch a bus to Larkin bus station in Johor Bahru from where you can catch a Melaka-bound bus (from RM15).

Need to Know

⇨ **Area Code** ✆60 6

⇨ **Location** 250km from Singapore.

⇨ **Tourist Office** ✆281 4803; www.melak. gov.my; Jln Kota; ⊘ 9am-1pm & 2-5.30pm) Diagonally across the square from Christ Church. The more useful Tourism Malaysia office is at the Menara Taming Sari tower (✆283 6220; ⊘9am-10pm).

SIGHTS

HISTORIC TOWN CENTRE   MUSEUMS

Melaka has a ridiculous number of museums clustered along Jln Kota. The best ones include the dusty **Islamic Museum** (Map p136; Jln Kota; admission RM1; ⊘9am-5.30pm Wed-Sun) and the small but worthwhile **Architecture Museum** (Map p136; Jln Kota; admission RM2; ⊘9.30am-5pm Tue-Sun) that focuses on local housing design. If you've only got time to visit one museum, however, make it the **Muzium Rakyat** (People's Museum; Map p136; Jln Kota; admission RM2; ⊘9am-5:30pm Wed-Mon) for its creepy yet compelling 'Beauty Museum' on the 3rd floor, which explores how different cultures mutilate themselves in order to look good (Western plastic surgery hasn't made it in yet).

ST PAUL'S CHURCH   HISTORIC BUILDING

This church is a wonderfully breezy sanctuary reached after a steep and sweaty climb up a flight of stairs on Jln Kota. Originally built by a Portuguese captain in 1521 as the small Our Lady of the Hill chapel, St Paul's Church is a sublime testament to Catholicism in East Asia and offers bright views over Melaka from the summit of Bukit St Paul. St Francis Xavier was temporarily interred here, and visitors can now look into his ancient tomb in the centre of the church. A marble statue of the saint gazes wistfully over his beloved city. It has been in ruins for more than 150 years.

PORTA DE SANTIAGO (A'FAMOSA)   HISTORIC BUILDING

Map p136 (Jln Kota) A quick photo stop, but a must for anyone visiting Melaka, Porta de Santiago was built by the Portuguese as a fortress in 1511. The Dutch were busy destroying the bulk of the fort when forward-thinking Sir Stamford Raffles came by in 1810 and saved what remains today. Look for the 'VOC' inscription of the Dutch East India Company on the arch; this part of the fort was used by the Dutch after their takeover in 1670.

STADTHUYS   HISTORIC BUILDING

Map p136 (Town Sq; admission adult/child RM5/2; ⊘9am-5.30pm Sat-Thu, 9am-12.15pm & 2.45-5.30pm Fri) Melaka's most unmistakable landmark and favourite trishaw pick-up spot is the Stadthuys, the imposing salmon-pink town hall and governor's residence. It's believed to be the oldest Dutch building in Asia, built shortly after Melaka was captured by the Dutch in 1641, and is a reproduction of the former Stadhuis (town hall) of the Frisian town of Hoorn in the Netherlands. With substantial solid doors and louvred windows, it is typical of Dutch colonial architecture. There are several museum displays within.

BOOKING A BUS ONLINE

With myriad bus companies offering tickets to various parts of Malaysia, it can get confusing. A great website to book tickets is **Bus Online Ticket** (www.busonlineticket.com).

Melaka

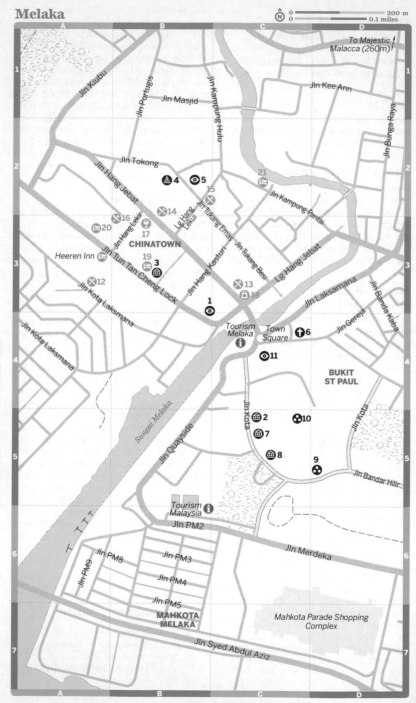

Melaka

CHRIST CHURCH
CHURCH

Map p136 (Jln Gereja) Constructed from pink laterite bricks brought from Zeeland in Holland, there are still Dutch and Armenian tombstones in the floor of the church's interior, while the massive 15 metre-long ceiling beams overhead were each cut from a single tree.

CHINATOWN
HISTORIC AREA

Map p136 This is Melaka's most vibrant area, where you could easily entertain yourself for a few days simply by strolling through the teeter-tottering lanes. Jln Tokong, Hang Jebat and Tun Cheng Lock form the main streets in Chinatown. Surreptitiously peer into small shops where you might see a painter at work, an old man fabricating bicycle parts with a blow-torch or a stout woman plucking chickens for the restaurant next door. When your feet get sore, pop in for a half-hour of foot reflexology or a massage.

BABA-NONYA HERITAGE MUSEUM
MUSEUM

Map p136 (48-50 Jln Tun Tan Cheng Lock; adult/child RM10/5; ⊙10am-12.30pm & 2-4.30pm Wed-Mon) The captivating museum is arranged to look like a typical 19th-century Baba-Nonya residence. Furniture consists of Chinese hardwoods fashioned in a mixture of Chinese, Victorian and Dutch designs with mother-of-pearl inlay. Displays of 'Nonya ware', multicoloured ceramic designs from Jiāngxī and Guǎngdōng provinces in China and made for Straits Chinese, add to the presentation. The highlight is the tour guides, who tell tales of the past with a distinctly Peranakan sense of humour. The admission price includes a tour if there are enough people.

FREE 8 HEEREN STREET
HISTORIC BUILDING

Map p136 (8 Jln Tun Tan Cheng Lock; ⊙11am-4pm Tue-Sat) Run by the Heritage Trust of Malaysia, this 18th century Dutch period residential house was restored as a model conservation project. The friendly host will show you around and describe what era each style of the building came from and what life would have been like inside its walls over the centuries. You can also pick up a copy of *Endangered Trades: A Walking Tour of Malacca's Living Heritage* (RM5) for an excellent self-guided tour of the city centre.

CHENG HOON TENG TEMPLE
BUDDHIST TEMPLE

(25 Jln Tokong; ⊙7am-7pm) Malaysia's oldest traditional Chinese temple (dating from 1646 and also known as Qing Yun Temple or Green Clouds Temple) remains a central

---

PAINTING THE TOWN RED

The red-pink paint found slathered over the Stadthuys can be attributed to the British, who brightened it up from a sombre Dutch white in 1911. The most likely reason is that the red laterite stone used to build the Stadthuys showed through the whitewashed plastering, and/or heavy tropical rain splashed red soil up the white walls – the thrifty Brits decided to paint it all red to save on maintenance costs. The vivid colour theme extends to the other buildings around Town Sq and the old clock tower.

DAY TRIPS FROM SINGAPORE MELAKA

SLEEPING IN MELAKA

⇒ **Cafe 1511 Guest House** (Map p136; ☎286 0150; www.cafe1511.com; 52 Jln Tun Tan Cheng Lock; s/d incl breakfast RM90/100; 🖥@) With only five rooms in this well-restored Peranakan house next to the Baba-Nonya museum, you should book ahead. Central location and great breakfast.

⇒ **Hotel Puri** (Map p136; ☎282 5588; www.hotelpuri.com; 118 Jln Tun Tan Cheng Lock; r incl breakfast RM120-500; 🖥) Hotel Puri is an elegant creation in a superb old renovated Peranakan manor house. Rooms are simply decorated and there's free wi-fi in the lovely courtyard garden.

⇒ **River View Guesthouse** (Map p136; ☎012 327 7746; riverviewguesthouse@yahoo. com; 94-96 Jln Kampung Pantai; r RM45-60; 🖥@) Bordering the riverfront promenade, this immaculate guesthouse is housed in a large heritage building. Basic rooms reflect the low price. The owners are friendly and offer advice, a map and home-made cake.

⇒ **Majestic Malacca** (Map p136; ☎289 8000; www.majesticmalacca.com; 188 Jln Bunga Raya; r from US$335; @🖥🏊) A 1920s colonial Chinese building with tasteful modern rooms, on-site spa and chi-chi restaurant. It's pricy but it's boutique in the true sense of the word.

place of worship for the Buddhist community in Melaka. Notable for its carved woodwork, the temple is dedicated to Kuan Yin, the goddess of mercy. In 2002 the structure won a Unesco award for outstanding architectural restoration. Across the street from the main temple is a traditional opera theatre.

 EATING & DRINKING

Melaka is studded with restaurants and watering holes, and for a day trip you'll probably spend the most time in the Chinatown area. This place is your best and easiest bet for restaurants and bars. Whatever you do, you have to try *cendol* **(a dessert of shaved ice and jelly with coconut milk and palm sugar syrup).**

LOW YONG MOW
DIM SUM $

Map p136 (Jln Tokong; dim sum RM1-8; ☺5am-noon, closed Tue) Famous for large and delectably well-stuffed *pao* (steamed pork buns), this place is Chinatown's biggest breakfast treat. With high ceilings, plenty of fans and a view of Masjid Kampung Kling, the atmosphere oozes all the charms of Chinatown. Take your pick from the endless variety of dumplings, sticky rice dishes and mysterious treats that are wheeled to your table. It's great for early-bus-departure breakfasts and is usually packed with talkative, newspaper-reading locals by around 7am.

NANCY'S KITCHEN
NONYA $$

Map p136 (15 Jln Hang Lekir; dishes from RM10; ☺11am-5.30pm, closed Tue) Long-running Nancy's is the go-to spot for Nonya cuisine. Your patience when waiting for a seat and food service will be rewarded. Try the house speciality, chicken candlenut or *ayam buah keluak* (chicken cooked with a local nut). Don't forget to take away some Nonya *kuih* (sweets) or *bak chang* (stuffed rice dumplings).

DONALD & LILY'S
NONYA $

Map p136 (snacks from RM3; ☺9.30am-4pm, closed Tue) Just finding this place is an adventure. Take the alleyway on your left that runs behind Heeren Inn from Jln Hang Kasturi. You'll see a little stairway behind 31 Jln Tun Tan Cheng Lock leading to hidden but very popular Donald & Lily's. Why bother looking? This is the locals' favourite place for regional-style laksa and Nonya *cendol*. The setting is like being in someone's living room, and the service is beaming.

HOE KEE CHICKEN RICE
COFFEESHOP $$

Map p136 (4 Jln Hang Jebat; meals RM15; ☺8.30am-3pm, closed last Wed of month) Melaka's busiest restaurant, with the local speciality chicken rice ball and *asam* fish head (fish heads in a spicy tamarind gravy). You'll need to arrive here off-hours or expect to wait, especially on weekends. The ambience, with wooden ceilings and tables, is undeniably charming (in a faux Chinese coffee-house way).

JONKER 88 HERITAGE DESSERT $

Map p136 (88 Jln Hang Jebat; ⊘11am-10pm Tue-Thu, till 11pm Fri &Sat, till 9pm Sun) You'll find Melaka's best and arguably most famous dessert, *cendol,* at many stalls along Jonker St, but this one is particularly good. There are many variations on the theme, including a durian version.

GEOGRAPHÉR CAFÉ BAR

(www.geographer.com.my; 83 Jln Hang Jebat; ⊘10am-1am Wed-Sun) This ventilated, breezy bar with outside seating and late hours in a prewar corner shophouse is a godsend. Seat yourself with a beer amid the throngs and watch the world go by.

SHOPPING

Jln Hang Jebat (Jonker's Walk or 'Junk Street') and Jln Tun Tan Cheng Lock were once famous for their antiques, but there is only a handful of 'junk' shops left now. Browse other shops for funky Southeast Asian and Indian clothing, shoulder bags, incense, handmade tiles, charms, cheap jewellery and more. Peek into an array of silent artists' studios where you might see a painter busy at work.

JONKER'S WALK NIGHT MARKET MARKET

Map p136 (Jln Hang Jebat; ⊘6-11pm Fri-Sun) Melaka's weekly shopping extravaganza keeps the shops along Jln Hang Jebat open late while trinket, food hawkers and the occasional fortune teller close the street to traffic. It's gotten far more commercial and clogged with Singaporean tourists over the years, but is an undeniably colourful way to spend an evening shopping and grazing.

Sleeping

Staying in Singapore is expensive. Period. Budget travellers have it best, as hostel rooms can be had for $20 a night. Most midrange hotels are more about location than quality. However, if you're willing to spend, luxury digs will make you never want to leave.

Hostels

While there may be a slew of hostels in Singapore, most of them aren't anything more than small rooms jam-packed with double-decker beds. Private rooms all have shared bathrooms. Note that hostels tend to get booked up on weekends, especially the (limited) private rooms, so book in advance. Little India is the place with the most budget beds. Service quality also varies dramatically, from 'can't be bothered' to 'friendly and helpful'. Free wi-fi at most hostels.

Hotels

From top-notch places like the Raffles Hotel and the Capella in Sentosa to cool boutique options like Naumi, Wanderlust and the New Majestic, good hotels are plentiful in Singapore. Standards are high, but then so are the prices – check web offers for the occasional bargain. Most of the midrange and high-end options are expensive identikit international chain hotels. Midrange cheapie chains (Hotel 81, Fragrance) that sometimes rent by the hour offer alternative no-frills accommodation in decent locations.

Serviced Apartments

For medium- to long-term stays, Singapore has a number of serviced apartments. It is also possible to rent rooms in private flats (check the classified pages of the *Straits Times* for listings). Rents are high, regardless of how near or far from the city centre you are.

Probably the best place to start looking for long-term rental in Singapore is **Singapore Expats** (www.singaporeexpats.com), which has detailed information on the different districts, outlines the whole rental procedure and carries an apartment search engine. The Singapore section of www.craigslist.org is also a good place to look for long-term stays.

Note: Actual Prices May Vary

In Singapore's midrange and top-end hotels, room rates are about supply and demand, fluctuating daily. Travellers planning a trip to Singapore need to keep this in mind, especially if you're planning to come here during a major event. For example, room prices TRIPLE during the Formula One night race.

Be aware that top hotels usually add a 'plus plus' (++) after the rate they quote you. Ignore this at your peril. The two plusses are service charge and GST, which together amounts to a breezy 17% on top of your bill. All prices quoted in our listings are from the day of our visit inclusive of the ++ tax; your own price may vary.

Accommodation Websites

Apart from booking directly on the hotel's website listed in our reviews, you can also book rooms on these websites.

Lonely Planet (hotels.lonelyplanet.com)

Wotif (www.wotif.com)

Tripadvisor (www.tripadvisor.com)

Agoda (www.agoda.com)

Asiarooms (www.asiarooms.com)

Lonely Planet's Top Choices

Capella (p151) Luxe gorgeous rooms and villas set in Sentosa.

Raffles Hotel (p143) This colonial legend offers a top-notch, posh experience.

Wanderlust (p147) Brand-new boutique digs in the heart of Little India.

New Majestic Hotel (p145) Long-standing boutique hotel with unique, kitschy rooms.

Best by Budget

$

InnCrowd (p147)
Fernloft (p145)
Hive (p147)

$$

Gallery Hotel (p143)
YMCA International House (p144)
Perak Hotel (p147)

$$$

Naumi (p143)
Fullerton Hotel (p143)
Marina Bay Sands Hotel (p143)

Best for a Splurge

Goodwood Park Hotel (p149)
St Regis (p149)
Four Seasons Hotel (p149)

Best for Contemporary Cool

Naumi (p143)
Fort Canning Hotel (p143)
Quincy (p149)

Best for Kids

Costa Sands Resort (p151)
Marina Bay Sands (p143)
Shangri-La's Rasa Sentosa Resort (p152)

Best Views

Marina Bay Sands (p143)
Fullerton Hotel (p143)
Swissôtel the Stamford (p143)

NEED TO KNOW

SLEEPING

Price Ranges
$$$ over $250 a night
$$ $100–250 a night
$ under $100 a night

Reservations
Book way in advance during peak periods (ie Formula One race). Even average hostels tend to be booked up over the weekends.

Tipping
Tipping isn't expected in hostels. It's good form to tip hotel porters and cleaning staff a dollar or two.

Checking In & Out
Check-in time is usually 2pm and check out at 11am. If the hotel isn't at full occupancy, you can usually extend these hours out by an hour or two if you ask politely.

Breakfast
Hostels usually include a simple breakfast (toast with spreads and coffee/tea). Midrange and top-end hotels don't usually include breakfast unless it's a special deal. It never hurts to ask when booking.

Air-conditioning
All listings have air-conditioning, unless otherwise stated.

Where to Stay

Neighbourhood	For	Against
Colonial District, Marina Bay & the Quays	Located in the heart of Singapore, with good transport options. Variety of accommodation, from the cheapest of the cheap no-frills hostels to the priciest luxury hotels.	Cheap accommodation in the area is generally of poor to average quality, usually located where it's noisy.
Chinatown & the CBD	A stone's throw from some of the best places to eat. Great nightlife, bags of culture, good transport links and an excellent range of accommodation, many in restored shophouses.	Too touristy for some. Budget accommodation prices are higher here than in Singapore's main backpacker haunt, Little India.
Little India & Kampong Glam	Backpacker Central, with the largest choice of cheap accommodation in Singapore. Has some lovely higher-end boutique hotels. Also has a unique atmosphere that is unlike any other district of Singapore. Fabulous food and good transport links.	Too grotty for some. Streets can get very noisy in the evenings, especially at weekends. Not much in the way of quality, international-standard hotels.
Orchard Road	On the doorstep of shopping heaven! Fine choice of quality hotels, including a number of top-name international chains.	Slim pickings for budget travellers.
Eastern Singapore	Quiet (a relative concept in Singapore), close to the cooling breeze of East Coast Park, close to the airport.	The MRT service doesn't run to this area; sights in the east are quite spread out so there's no real central location to stay in.
Sentosa & Other Islands	Hotels on Sentosa are all either on or close to the beach, and located in an area with sporting activities galore. Ideal for families. Quieter options can be found on St John's Island and Pulau Ubin.	Sentosa is largely synthetic so lacks character. From Sentosa, it's a slight hassle to get into the centre of Singapore; this becomes more of an issue from the other islands.

🛏 Colonial District, Marina Bay & the Quays

TOP CHOICE RAFFLES HOTEL   HOTEL $$$

Map p208 (☑6337 1886; www.raffleshotel.com; 1 Beach Rd; ste from $750; @☒; MCity Hall) The grand old dame of Singapore's Colonial District has had many facelifts in her 121 years and is looking as spritely as ever. She's seen many a famous visitor in her time, from Somerset Maugham to Michael Jackson, and it's easy to see what the fuss is about (cost be damned). Rooms are all class – expect a spacious parlour, rattan furniture, verandahs, lazily swirling ceiling fans and a Singapore sling from the Long Bar. Be advised: dress code is in effect, and Raffles' turbaned doorman will not allow those in sleeveless shirts, sandals or grubby backpacker attire to enter.

TOP CHOICE NAUMI   BOUTIQUE HOTEL $$$

Map p208 (☑6403 6000; www.naumihotel.com; 41 Seah St; r from $400; @☎☒) Lying in the shadow of the Raffles Hotel, Naumi is dressed so sharply in glass and steel you could get cut just by looking. It balances cool looks with lots of silk and leather and fluffy pillows. The small rooftop infinity pool offers jaw-dropping views across to Raffles Hotel and the Swissôtel.

FORT CANNING HOTEL   BOUTIQUE HOTEL $$$

Map p208 (☑6559 6770; www.hfcsingapore.com; 11 Canning Walk; r $400-500; MDhoby Ghaut; @☒) Absolutely drop-dead gorgeous refit of a colonial complex at the top of Fort Canning Park. Rooms here are the epitome of modern chic, though the open bathroom in some means you'll need to be more than 'just friends' when sharing a room. Deluxe garden rooms have a small but cosy outdoor deck for lounging, cigar in hand.

FULLERTON HOTEL   HOTEL $$$

Map p210 (☑6733 8388; www.fullertonhotel.com; 1 Fullerton Sq; r from $400; MRaffles Place; @☒) The Fullerton has the distinction of being both one of Singapore's most magnificent pieces of colonial architecture and the only hotel we've ever heard of that's also a restored post office. The heritage principles involved in the restoration mean some of the Armani-beige rooms overlook the inner atrium. Spend a bit extra to gain access to the hotel's private Straits Club and upgrade to river- or marina-view rooms, all of which are stunning. The **Fullerton Bay Hotel** (☑6333 8388; www.fullertonbayhotel.com; 80 Collyer Quay) is the modern sister property up the road with flashy, bay-facing rooms at similar rates.

SWISSÔTEL THE STAMFORD   HOTEL $$$

Map p208 (☑6338 8585; www.swissotel.com/singapore-stamford; 2 Stamford Rd; d from $450; @☒) Everyone raves about IM Pei's iconic Swissôtel, the tallest hotel in Southeast Asia. It boasts one of Singapore's hippest dining complexes (Equinox), the views are sublime, and service standards are as elevated as the building. Rooms are predictably decked out in corporate-friendly hues and patterns. Yep, lots of cream and brown.

RITZ-CARLTON   HOTEL $$$

Map p208 (☑6337 8888; www.ritzcarlton.com; 7 Raffles Ave; r from $550; @☒) No expense was spared, no feng shui geomancer went unconsulted and no animals were harmed in the building of this 'six star' establishment. Guests will be torn between taking a romantic soak in the bath (oh, the unimpaired views!) or taking a self-guided audio tour to view the in-house art collection (oh, the Hockney, Warhol, Stella and Chihuly pieces!).

GALLERY HOTEL   HOTEL $$

(☑6849 8686; www.galleryhotel.com.sg; 1 Nanson Rd; d incl breakfast from $320; @☒; MClarke Quay) With its grey fascia studded with primary-coloured window boxes, the Gallery remains one of Singapore's truly boutique hotels. Sure, guests have to switch elevators on the 4th floor to get to the rooms but knock-down online deals bring you top-end rooms at midrange prices. Rooms feature retro furnishings, steel beams and frosted-glass bathroom walls. The glass rooftop pool and free internet access are bonuses.

MARINA BAY SANDS   HOTEL $$$

Map p210 (☑6688 8897; www.marinabaysands.com; 10 Bayfront Ave; r from $400; @☒; MPromenade) Located in the slightly inaccessible Marina Bay area (the closest train station is a 10-minute walk away), the Sands hotel is famed for its amazing rooftop pool. The infinity pool straddles across the roofs of the three hotel buildings – which is probably where you'll spend the most time seeing as the rest of the hotel is a cavernous, busy, cold and decidedly average 'painted in hues of cream' type place. Deals available online.

YMCA INTERNATIONAL HOUSE
HOSTEL, HOTEL $$

Map p208 (📞6336 6000; www.ymcaih.com.sg; 1 Orchard Rd; dm/d/f incl breakfast $47/210/250; @🛜🏊; MDhoby Ghaut) Has a fantastic location at the start of Orchard Rd. Rooms have been upgraded with LCD TVs, birch-coloured walls, and carpets the colour of streaky bacon. Roomy four-bed dorms have an attached bathroom. It has a restaurant, a fitness centre, a rooftop pool, squash and badminton courts and a billiard room. Staff attitudes have markedly improved since we last visited. Deals available online.

VICTORIA HOTEL
HOTEL $$

Map p208 (📞6622 0909; www.victoriahotelsingapore.com; 87 Victoria St; s/d $140/160, deluxe r $210; @🛜; MBugis) Thanks to its central location and midrange price, the Victoria is popular with businesspeople and casual travellers alike. The hotel offers comfortable rooms furnished with bed, TV, desk and chair. Single rooms are a bit on the cramped side, but the deluxe rooms feature queen-sized beds and bathrooms with bathtubs. Free wi-fi in the cafe downstairs.

HOTEL BENCOOLEN
HOTEL $$

Map p208 (📞6336 0822; www.hotelbencoolen.com; 47 Bencoolen St; s/d incl breakfast $148/178; @🏊; MDhoby Ghaut) Rooms at the 'Uncoolen' are far from stylish, but they've been renovated and decked out in uninspired shades of green and cream. The single rooms are tiny, with a shower to match. Larger double rooms will get you an LCD TV and a bathtub. The outdoor spa pool is almost big enough for a soak.

PARK VIEW HOTEL
HOTEL $$

Map p208 (📞6338 8558; www.parkview.com.sg; 81 Beach Rd; r $140-200; @; MBugis) Not a bad little midrange hotel, Park View is centrally located to the Bugis shopping area (though where the park is we can't say). Though all rooms have bathtubs, some of the cheaper rooms are windowless. Don't expect anything beyond dull shades of white and brown in the rooms here, but you get a lot of value for its central location.

BEACH HOTEL
HOTEL $$

Map p208 (📞6336 7712; www.beachhotel.com.sg; 95 Beach Rd, s/d $130/150, deluxe r $170; @; MBugis) Just down the block from the Park View (which views no park) is the Beach Hotel (which has no beach). Rooms, prices and amenities are much the same here as there, though rack-rate at the Beach is a few dollars less.

BACKPACKER COZY CORNER GUESTHOUSE
HOSTEL $

Map p208 (📞6339 6128; www.cozycornerguest.com; 490 North Bridge Rd; dm incl breakfast $15-20, d incl breakfast $50-55; @; MBugis) Yes, we'll say it – this place can get a little too cosy when it's busy (and it usually is). The location is a huge plus, though rooms are dark and a little cramped. Ask for a dorm facing away from North Bridge Rd unless you like the noise of heavy traffic and merrymakers from the street. Expect to wait for internet access.

AH CHEW HOTEL
HOSTEL $

Map p208 (📞6837 0356; 496 North Bridge Rd; dm from $15, r from $30; MBugis) Above the Tong Seng Coffee Shop, with its frontage facing the restaurant-bar strip on Liang Seah St, this dusty old flophouse has a certain dingy charm (think 1970s *Southeast Asia on a Shoestring*) and the cheapest, noisiest beds in Singapore.

BOOKING ON THE FLY

If you arrive in Singapore without a hotel booking, don't despair. The efficient **Singapore Hotel Association** (www.stayinsingapore.com.sg) has desks at Changi airport, one at each of the terminal's arrival halls.

There are dozens of hotels on its lists, ranging from $37 a night right up to Raffles Hotel. There's no charge for the service, and promotional or discounted rates, when available, are passed on to you. You can also book the hotels over the internet on the association's website.

If you've made it as far as Orchard Rd and still don't have a hotel room (and don't fancy sleeping in the park), **Singapore Visitors Centre@Orchard** (📞1800 736 2000; cnr Cairnhill & Orchard Rds; ⏰9.30am-9.30pm) works with hotels in the local area and can help visitors get the best available rates.

HISTORIC HOTELS

It's not just the Raffles that has an illustrious past. Goodwood Park Hotel (p149), dating from 1900 and designed to resemble a Rhine castle, served as the base for the Teutonia Club, a social club for Singapore's German community, until 1914 when it was seized by the government as part of 'enemy property'. In 1918 the building was auctioned off and renamed Club Goodwood Hall, before it morphed again into the Goodwood Park Hotel in 1929, fast becoming one of the finest hotels in Asia.

During WWII it accommodated the Japanese high command, some of whom returned here at the war's end to be tried for war crimes in a tent erected in the hotel grounds. By 1947 the hotel was back in business with a $2.5 million renovation program bringing it back to its former glory by the early 1960s. Further improvements in the 1970s have left the hotel as it is today.

The Fullerton Hotel (p143) occupies the magnificent colonnaded Fullerton Building, named after Robert Fullerton, the first governor of the Straits Settlements. When the hotel opened in 1928, the $4 million building was the largest in Singapore. The General Post Office, which occupied three floors, was said to have the longest counter (100m) in the world at the time. Above the GPO was the exclusive Singapore Club, in which Governor Sir Shenton Thomas and General Percival discussed surrendering Singapore to the Japanese.

In 1958 a revolving lighthouse beacon was added to the roof; its beams could be seen up to 29km away. By 1996 the GPO had moved out and the entire building underwent a multimillion-dollar renovation and reopened in 2001 to general acclaim, receiving the prestigious Urban Redevelopment Authority Architectural Award the same year.

SOMERSET BENCOOLEN
SERVICED APARTMENT $$$

Map p208 (⌨6849 4688; www.somerset.com; 51 Bencoolen St; 1-bedroom apt per week from $2590; @☒; ⓂDhoby Ghaut) If you're going to live large in Singapore, the Somerset Bencoolen might be the place to do it. The fully furnished serviced apartments are big and beautiful, with floor-to-ceiling windows offering spectacular views. The rooftop pool is an especially nice touch, as are the guided floorlights in the lobby, presumably to get you to your room when you come home drunk. Book in advance or get waitlisted.

🛏 Chinatown & the CBD

Riding the shophouse restoration wave, Chinatown has some particularly fine mid- to top-range boutique hotels. There's also a growing band of good-value, centrally located hostels.

TOP CHOICE NEW MAJESTIC
HOTEL
BOUTIQUE HOTEL $$$

Map p201 (⌨6511 4700; www.newmajestichotel.com; 31-37 Bukit Pasoh Rd; r from $400; @☎☒; ⓂOutram Park) Has some stiff competition from Chinatown's burgeoning boutique hotel market, but still arguably the best of the lot, offering occupants 30 unique rooms done up in a mix of vintage and designer furniture. Among the highlights are the private garden suite, attic rooms with loft beds and 6m-high ceilings, and the fabulous aquarium room with a glass-encased bathtub as its central feature. Rooms are also fitted with high-end gadgetry and coffee makers, and discounts can bring rates down to less than $300.

TOP CHOICE FERNLOFT
HOSTEL $

Map p201 (⌨6323 3221; www.fernloft.com; 2nd fl, 5 Banda St 02-92; dm $22 r from $65; @☎; ⓂChinatown) Located in a housing block overlooking the Buddha Tooth Relic Temple, this compact branch of the excellent Fernloft chain of hostels is run by the wonderful Auntie Aini. There are only two private rooms, but they are large and decked out in decent furniture for a hostel. The dorm room has comfortable wooden-framed beds, rather than the cheapo metal-tube variety found elsewhere in Singapore. As with so many hostels in Singapore none of the rooms has a window, but everything is kept clean and tidy and the corner-terrace seating overlooking the green is a lovely spot to hang out.

PILLOWS & TOAST
HOSTEL $

Map p201 (☎6220 4653; www.pillowsntoast.com; 40 Mosque St; dm $26 33; @🛜; Ⓜ Chinatown) It's dorm beds only in this super friendly, centrally located hostel, but the rooms are bright and clean and come with comfortable wood-framed bunk beds. Common areas are small but well looked after.

CLUB
BOUTIQUE HOTEL $$$

Map p201 (☎6808 2188; www.theclub.com.sg; 28 Ann Siang Rd; r $400-450; Ⓜ Outram Park; @🛜) Black and white everything – as seems to be the trend in many of Singapore's boutique hotels – but much more spacious than most, and right in the heart of Chinatown's most chic drinking area. Rooms are bright and airy with lots of glass, mirrors and natural light. Rack rates are obscene, so it's a good job the discounts are so good (often 40%). The rooftop bar, Ying Yang, is cool as cats, but most punters seem to prefer nearby Screening Room (p63).

BEARY GOOD HOSTEL
HOSTEL $

Map p201 (☎6222 4955; www.abearygoodhostel. com; 66 Pagoda St; dm $26; @🛜; Ⓜ Chinatown) Like Pillows & Toast, Beary Good Hostel only has dorms, but that doesn't put the punters off. In fact, this place is so popular it's opened another branch, called Beary Nice Hostel, a stone's throw away in Smith St. Both are fun, brightly painted affairs and have separate bathrooms for boys and girls – a beary nice touch.

BERJAYA HOTEL SINGAPORE
HOTEL $$$

Map p201 (☎6227 7678; www.berjayahotel. com; 83 Duxton Rd; r from $250, ste $450; @🛜; Ⓜ Tanjong Pagar) More class than its trendier boutique-hotel neighbours, Berjaya has elegantly furnished, spacious rooms and tiptop service. Plenty of old-world charm, but loses points for charging $25 per day for internet use! Discounts bring standard rooms down to less than $200.

SAFF
BOUTIQUE HOTEL $$

Map p201 (☎6221 8388; 55 Keong Saik Rd; s/d from $230/250; @🛜; Ⓜ Outram Park) Three old shophouses, beautifully renovated, combine to create one of the more affordable boutique hotels in this area. Rooms share the brightly coloured paintwork of the hotel's facade and come in various themes – southeast Asian, Moroccan, Indian – although some lack natural light. Discounts see rooms drop to less than $150.

SERVICE WORLD
BACKPACKERS HOSTEL
HOSTEL $

Map p201 (☎6226 3886; www.serviceworld.com. sg; 2nd fl, 5 Banda St 02-82; dm from $20, r from $60; @🛜; Ⓜ Chinatown) If Fernloft is full, walk along the 2nd-floor of this housing block to No 82 where you'll find this small family-owned hostel offering little in the way of frills but much in the way of friendliness. Andrew Yip, who runs the place with his wife, is an author and photographer who is passionate about Singapore's traditional culture and art. Like Fernloft, rooms here are windowless, but they are much smaller than Fernloft's and come with cheaper furniture. No matter; there's plenty of space on the shared terrace to sit and chat with Mr Yip so you probably won't spend much time in your room.

HOTEL 1929
BOUTIQUE HOTEL $$

Map p201 (☎6347 1929; www.hotel1929.com; 50 Keong Saik Rd; s/d from $210/250; @; Ⓜ Outram Park) Owned by the same people behind nearby New Majestic, 1929 is also pretty slick, although not in the same class as its big brother. Rooms are tight, but good use is made of limited space, and interiors are cheerily festooned with vintage designer furniture (look out for reproduction Eames and Jacobson) and technicolour mosaics. Rooftop suites have private terraces, and discounts mean you can snag some rooms for less than $200.

SCARLET
BOUTIQUE HOTEL $$$

Map p201 (☎6511 3333; www.thescarlethotel. com; 33 Erskine Rd; r from $320; @🛜; Ⓜ Outram Park) Markets itself as Singapore's sexy boutique hotel, but the rooms are actually pretty homely – think cottage chic – decorated with lovely wooden furniture, thick drapes and tasteful artwork. Many of them are windowless, but the interiors are far from gloomy thanks to the cheerful decor. The wi-fi in the lobby only reaches some rooms. Discounts of 30% are common.

G HOTEL
HOTEL $$

Map p201 (☎6225 6696; www.ghotel.com.sg; 22 Teck Lim Rd; s/d from $100/160; @🛜; Ⓜ Outram Park) Small but tidy no-nonsense rooms, some with cute wooden shutters on the windows, come with friendly service but no internet (there's internet access and wi-fi in the lobby, though). You can normally shave $20 or $30 off the rack rates if you smile sweetly.

CHINATOWN HOTEL
HOTEL $$

Map p201 (☑6225 5166; www.chinatownhotel.com; 12-16 Teck Lim Rd; s/d from $155/175; @☏; ⓂOutram Park) Very friendly old-school Asian hotel with lots of beige upholstery and light-brown furniture. Rooms are simple, and haven't been refurbished for a while (cigarette burns on carpets hark back to a smokier age in Singapore) and some have no windows, but there's absolutely no pretentiousness here. Wi-fi is chargeable ($5 per hour). You should be able to grab a single for $100 if it's quiet; a double for about $130.

🛌 Little India & Kampong Glam

Unless stated, all rates in Little India & Kampong Glam include free breakfast, although it's usually just tea and toast.

TOP CHOICE INNCROWD
HOSTEL $

Map p204 (☑6296 9169; www.the-inncrowd.com; 73 Dunlop St; dm/d/tr $20/48/68; @☏; ⓂLittle India) Wildly popular, the InnCrowd is ground zero for Singapore's backpackers. Located right in the heart of Little India, this funkily painted hostel has helpful staff and all the facilities you'd expect of a decent hostel (travel advice, free internet, wi-fi, DVDs, laundry), plus a few you might not expect (a Wii console and pushalong-scooter tours!). Bookings are pretty much essential.

TOP CHOICE WANDERLUST
BOUTIQUE HOTEL $$$

Map p204 (☑6396 3322; www.wanderlusthotel.com; 2 Dickson Rd; r $300-650; ☏; ⓂLittle India, Bugis) A true boutique hotel, rooms at wonderful Wanderlust are all designed individually with a number of unusual themes – the 'mono' rooms are like sleeping in a comic book, while one of the 'whimsical' rooms will leave spaceship-loving kids starry-eyed. Service is excellent, as are the discounts (normally around 40%), and the lobby houses a slick, urban bar and a fine French restaurant.

HIVE
HOSTEL $

(☑6341 5041; www.thehivebackpackers.com; 269A Lavender St, at junction with Serangoon Rd; dm/s/d/tr from $20/35/50/85; @☏; ⓂBoon Keng) The Hive's friendliness and cleanliness go a long way towards making up for

a slightly inconvenient location. Dorms are fairly standard, lacking in natural light, but otherwise fine. The bright, colourful private rooms, though, are excellent value, and there's a comfortable lounge/dining area where guests can take their free breakfast. Five minutes' walk south from Boon Keng MRT Station.

PERAK HOTEL
HOTEL $$

Map p204 (☑6299 7733; www.peraklodge.net; 12 Perak Rd; r from $180; ⓂLittle India; @☏) A long-time favourite, the Perak Hotel (formerly called Perak Lodge), located on a quiet side street in the heart of Little India, mixes a classy colonial exterior with an oriental interior complete with Buddha statues and quaint sitting and meditation spaces. Rooms are comfortable and well furnished, staff members are welcoming and very helpful and the rates include free wi-fi.

ALBERT COURT VILLAGE HOTEL
HOTEL $$

Map p204 (☑6339 3939; www.stayvillage.com; 180 Albert St; r from $200; @☏; ⓂLittle India) A short walk south of Little India, this is a splendid, colonial-era hotel in a shophouse redevelopment that now shoots up eight storeys. All rooms have the usual mod cons, and include a choice of fan or air-con. Service is top-notch and there's wi-fi throughout, although it's chargeable (per day $15). The promotional rates go as low as $150, with the best deals to be had online.

SLEEPY SAM'S
HOSTEL $

Map p204 (☑9277 4988; www.sleepysams.com; 55 Bussorah St; dm/s/d/tr $28/59/89/99; @☏; ⓂBugis) Let down only by its unfriendly staff, Sleepy Sam's – located in the heart of Kampong Glam – continues to hover near the top of Singapore's best-hostel rankings thanks to its laidback ambience, pier-and-beam ceilings, beautiful book-filled common-area cafe and well-furnished dorm rooms. It's usually fully booked so call ahead.

PRINCE OF WALES
HOSTEL $

Map p204 (☑6299 0130; www.pow.com.sg; 101 Dunlop St; dm/d $20/60; @☏; ⓂLittle India) Australian-style pub and hostel, featuring a spit-and-sawdust live-music pub downstairs and clean, brightly painted dorms and private rooms upstairs. The noise won't suit everyone, but it's a fun place to stay, is very well run and is deservedly popular.

LITTLE INDIA'S BEST DORM-ONLY HOSTELS

Footprints (Map p204; ☑6295 5134; www.footprintshostel.com.sg; 25A Perak Rd; dm from $21-28; @♠; ⓜLittle India) Well run, with comfortable communal areas for lounging, eating and laptopping. Shared bathrooms are huge. Female-only dorms available.

Checkers Inn (Map p204; ☑6392 0693; www.checkersinn.com.sg; 46-50 Campbell Lane; dm $30; @♠; ⓜLittle India) Bright, spacious and fabulously funky. Female-only dorms also available.

28Dunlop (Map p204; ☑6291 0332; www.singaporebackpacker.com.sg; 28 Dunlop St; dm $28; @♠; ⓜLittle India) Clean, good-sized dorms come with attached private bathrooms.

The free breakfast includes fresh coffee and fruit as well as the usual buttered toast.

HANGOUT@MT.EMILY
BOUTIQUE HOSTEL **$$**

Map p204 (☑6438 5588; www.hangouthotels.com; 10A Upper Wilkie Rd; dm/d $41/117; @♠; ⓜLittle India, Dhoby Ghaut) The poshest dorms in Singapore are located slightly out of the way atop leafy Mount Emily, making this a quiet retreat rather than a handy hangout. Done out in vibrant colours, with murals by local art students, the unisex and mixed dorms and private rooms are immaculate, as are the bathrooms. It also has a lovely rooftop terrace, a cafe, free internet and cosy lounging areas. Note that we've listed the website rates. Walk-in rates are much higher so be sure to book online.

IBIS SINGAPORE ON BENCOOLEN
HOTEL **$$**

Map p204 (☑6593 2888; www.ibishotel.com; 170 Bencoolen St; r fr $200; @♠; ⓜBugis) With clean rooms decked out in pine and orangey hues, and with LCD TVs, comfy beds and great city views, the Ibis group probably hopes visitors extend their stay to match the length of the hotel's name.

ZENOBIA HOTEL
HOTEL **$**

Map p204 (☑6296 3882; www.zenobia.com.sg; 40-43 Upper Weld Rd; dm/s/d/tr $25/63/75/95; @♠; ⓜLittle India) Family-run no-frills hotel with small but clean and tidy rooms, all with private bathroom. Slightly smarter than nearby Haising Hotel. Rates include wi-fi.

HAISING HOTEL
HOTEL **$**

Map p204 (☑6298 1223; www.haising.com.sg; 37 Jln Besar; s/d/$50/60; weekends $60/70; @; ⓜBugis) One of the best-value nonhostel budget options in Little India, this basic Chinese-run hotel is friendly and clean enough. Rooms are poky and some come

without a window, but all have private bathrooms, TV and kettle. No breakfast.

MAYO INN
HOTEL **$$**

Map p204 (☑6295 6631; www.mayoinn.com; 9 Jln Besar; r $110-150; @♠; ⓜLittle India, Bugis) New, spotlessly clean midrange hotel with good-sized, IKEA-fitted rooms and sparkling bathrooms. More expensive rooms come with their own small roof terrace.

HOTEL 81
HOTEL **$**

Map p204 (☑6392 8181; www.hotel81.com.sg; 3 Dickson Rd; r from $89, weekends $99; @♠; ⓜLittle India, Bugis) A very well located branch of the popular Hotel 81 chain, this lower-end midrange hotel offers rooms that lack character but which are smart, spotless and come with decent-sized bathrooms. Strangely, wi-fi is only free if you book online, but you'll get the best room rates that way in any case.

SUPERB HOSTEL
HOSTEL **$**

Map p204 (☑8228 9869; superbhub@yahoo.com.sg; 2 Jln Pinang; s/d $50/70; ♠; ⓜBugis) Weird to say the least, Superb Hostel in Kampong Glam is a strange cross between a hostel dorm and an anonymous motel. Each floor contains a shared bathroom and one huge room that is partitioned off to create a number of tiny individual 'rooms', all with their own small desk, air-con unit and fan, but sharing the same ceiling. It's well run, though, and is in a nice quiet location close to the heart of Kampong Glam so the lack of communal chill-out space doesn't need to be an issue.

🛏 Orchard Road

TOP CHOICE GOODWOOD PARK HOTEL   HOTEL $$$
Map p212 (📞6737 7411; www.goodwoodparkhotel.
com; 22 Scotts Rd; r from $385; @🛜🏊; MOr-
chard) This historic hotel, dating from 1900,
has an old-fashioned feel but bags of class,
from its two beautiful swimming pools to
the hotel's pet cat roaming the lobby. Nice
touches in the rooms include arty black-
and-white photos of Singapore, Persian
rugs and neatly hidden TVs and minibars.
Loses points, though, for its $30 wi-fi fee.

LLOYD'S INN   HOTEL $
Map p212 (📞6737 7309; www.lloydinn.com; 2
Lloyd Rd; r from $90; 🛜; MSomerset) A quick
walk south of the Orchard Rd hubbub
is where you'll find this spread-out, cool
California-motel-style hotel on a quiet
street surrounded by old villas. Rooms are
clean, tidy and fairly spacious, and some
have lovely views of the interior courtyard
bamboo garden. Wireless internet and lo-
cal calls are free. Bookings are essential.
This is pretty much the cheapest hotel in
Orchard Rd, so it fills up fast.

FOUR SEASONS HOTEL   HOTEL $$$
Map p212 (📞6734 1110; www.fourseasons.com/
singapore; 190 Orchard Blvd; s/d from $435/475;
@🛜🏊; MOrchard) In a quiet, tree-lined
street just off Orchard Rd, the Four Seasons has an elegance few top-end hotels
round here can match. Rooms are stylish
with antique-looking furniture and tasteful decor throughout, and the service is exceptionally good. Among its many five-star
facilities are two air-conditioned indoor
tennis courts!

QUINCY   BOUTIQUE HOTEL $$$
Map p212 (📞6738 5888; www.quincy.com.sg;
22 Mount Elizabeth; s/d from $295/355; @🛜;
MOrchard) Very swish, ultramodern rooms
come with large double beds and plenty of
space. Everything here is included in the
price – wi-fi, use of the gym and the glass-
enclosed balcony pool, happy-hour drinks
and even a slightly gimmicky three meals a
day. (In food-crazy Singapore, who wants to
eat three meals a day in a hotel?)

ST REGIS   HOTEL $$$
Map p212 (📞6506 6888; www.stregis.com; 29
Tanglin Rd; r from $440; @🛜🏊; MOrchard) One
of the newest additions to Orchard Rd's

five-star hotel scene, St Regis doesn't dis-
appoint, from its funky facade to its classic
interior and impeccable service. Rooms are
enormous, with soft sink-into carpets and
tasteful artwork. And each comes with 24-
hour butler service. Surprisingly, they've
followed the rather dated policy of charging
for wi-fi; $20 a day for the privilege of using
your own laptop!

SHANGRI-LA HOTEL   HOTEL $$$
Map p212 (📞6737 3644; www.shangri-la.com/
singapore; 22 Orange Grove Rd; r from $360;
@🛜🏊; MOrchard) Announced by the grand-
est of grand lobbies, this vast, opulent hotel,
set in the leafy lanes surrounding the west
end of Orchard, boasts a luxurious interior
featuring a 15-acre tropical garden and
large rooms done out in rich, butterscotch
tones with the odd Asian touch. The Gar-
den Wing is slightly old-fashioned, almost
like staying on a resort, but rooms in the
other two wings are as modern and luxuri-
ous as you'd expect from a Shangri-La.

SINGAPORE MARRIOTT   HOTEL $$$
Map p212 (📞6735 5800; www.marriott.com/
sindt; 320 Orchard Rd; r from $400; @🛜🏊; MOr-
chard) Smaller rooms than its rivals, but
this is still a classy establishment, with a
fabulously central location. Service is first
class, facilities are as you'd expect (free wi-
fi, gym, pool, top restaurants), and there
are some poolside rooms, which offer more
space and a resort-type feel.

MANDARIN ORCHARD   HOTEL $$$
Map p212 (📞6737 4411; www.meritushotels.com;
333 Orchard Rd; r from $360; @🛜🏊; MSom-
erset) An elegant yet informal place. The
cheapest rooms are in the south tower,
while those in the main tower (capped by
the revolving bar Top of the M), are deco-
rated in warm tones with oriental-themed
furniture and fresh orchids in the bath-
rooms. Discounts are decent, meaning you
can sometimes stay here for less than $300.

HOTEL SUPREME   HOTEL $$
Map p212 (📞6737 8333; www.supremeh.com.
sg; 15 Kramat Rd; r from $180; @🛜🏊; MDhoby
Ghaut) One of the few inexpensive options
available around Orchard Rd, you can usually grab a room for $150 here. Decor is old-
fashioned – lots of browns and beiges – but
rooms are clean and large for this price. Try
Lloyd's Inn first, though, as it's much better value.

SLEEPING EASTERN SINGAPORE

Eastern Singapore

Far from the madding crowds, eastern Singapore is a great place to stay for those seeking a different perspective of the Lion City. An exceptionally pleasant part of town, one of the main attractions of a stay out here would be the chance to bookend every day among the cooling breezes of East Coast Park. The neighbourhood eastern Singapore covers a large part of the island of Singapore, everything east of the Kallang MRT station.

GRAND MERCURE ROXY
HOTEL $$

Map p214 (☑6344 8000; www.mercure.com; 50 East Coast Rd; s/d incl breakfast $200/250; @❄; ⌨36) This popular hotel (the entrance is on Marine Parade Rd) has a great location close to both Katong and the East Coast Park and is a mere 9km from the airport. The contemporary Asian design of the rooms is appealing and it has plenty of facilities. Bonus! Free airport shuttle.

GATEWAY HOTEL
BOUTIQUE HOTEL $

Map p214 (☑6342 0988; www.gatewayhotel.com. sg; 60 Joo Chiat Rd, Katong; r $88-208; ⓂPaya Lebar) The Gateway is one of the few boutique hotels in the area. Housed in a vaguely fort-like building with sloping tiled roofs, it offers modern rooms with louvred shutters, though the TV bolted to the ceiling adds an unintended hospital-ward effect. Ask for a room with a window, even though Joo Chiat Rd can get a little noisy.

BETEL BOX
HOSTEL $

Map p214 (☑6247 7340; www.betelbox.com; 200 Joo Chiat Rd; dm $20-23, d $60; @❄; ⓂPaya Lebar) This somewhat cramped hostel is encased by a riot of some of the best local eateries in Joo Chiat and is reasonably near to East Coast Park. Betel Box boasts a cosy air-conditioned communal area with free wi-fi, cheap beer, TV, DVDs, video games, computers and even a pool table (all of which are notorious for keeping guests in the hostel for too long). It's also equipped with tons of travel guides and a book-exchange corner. A traveller's cafe at the ground floor is in the pipeline. Betel Box also hosts some fantastic cycling and eating tours.

CHANGI VILLAGE HOTEL
HOTEL $$

(☑6379 7111; www.changivillage.com.sg; 1 Netheravon Rd; r $180-200; @❄) Formerly known as Le Meridian Changi, this plush and stylish hotel is a prime candidate for 'most remote' hotel in Singapore. The hotel is nestled among some gorgeous gardens, offering superb views (especially at night) across to Malaysia and Pulau Ubin from its rooftop wooden deck, just steps away from its rooftop pool. Close to the Changi Golf Course, the sailing club, beach park, airport and the gentle pace of Changi Village. Free airport shuttle. To get to the hotel, take bus 2 from Tanah Merah MRT.

GOLDKIST BEACH RESORT
CHALET $$

Map p214 (☑6448 4747; www.goldkist.sg; 1110 East Coast Parkway; chalets $228-288; ❄) Smack on the beach at East Coast Park, this is a popular spot for Singaporeans to 'escape' for the weekend, offering an attractive, peaceful (except at weekends!) alternative to the usual city-centre accommodation, especially for travellers with kids.

FANCY A CHEAP ROOM?

If you don't mind living in the heartlands of Singapore, you can find short-term rooms in local Housing Development Board (HDB) flats for an average of $35/night. Just search for rooms to rent on **Gumtree Singapore** (http://singapore.gumtree.sg). These offer great value as you get a room, some with attached bathroom, for less than the cost of some dorm beds. Find one walking distance to an MRT station and you've saved money for shopping and beer and other fun things.

STUCK AT THE AIRPORT?

If you're only in Singapore for a short time or have an endless wait between connections, try the **Ambassador Transit Hotel** (www.airport-hotel.com.sg; s/d $68/76; Terminal 1 ✆6542 5538; ✉; Terminal 2 ✆6542 8122; Terminal 3 ✆6507 9788). Rates quoted are for the first six hours and each additional hour block thereafter is $15; rooms don't have windows and there are budget singles ($41) with shared bathrooms. The Terminal 1 branch has a sauna, gym and outdoor pool.

The only swish option at Changi Airport is Terminal 3's **Crowne Plaza Hotel** (✆6823 5300; www.cpchangiairport.com; r from $250; @✉). The business-oriented focus shows through its sleek lines, geometric-patterned carpets and (over)use of wood panels.

The chalets are comfortable and clean, and there are plenty of facilities, from swimming to bike riding and fishing, plus the popular East Coast restaurants and pubs. Transport hassles into the city are the only downside. Online discounts.

COSTA SANDS RESORT (DOWNTOWN EAST)
RESORT $$

(✆6582 3322; www.costasands.com.sg; 1 Pasir Ris Close; r $90-200; ✉☎; Ⓜ Pasir Ris) A family-friendly resort located on the end of the eastern MRT line, with a host of amenities in the attached Downtown East facility to keep one busy for days. The family suites are plush with a large-screen TV, living area and separate bedroom. Check the website for details on the cheaper, larger but more remote chalets in nearby Pasir Ris Park.

LE PERANAKAN HOTEL
BOUTIQUE HOTEL $$

Map p214 (✆6665 5511; www.radiancegrp.com/leperanakan; 400 East Coast Rd; r $160-250; ☎; ☐10, 12, 14, 32) There's absolutely nothing French about 'Le' Peranakan, but, hey, it's a boutique hotel so anything goes. Rooms are on the poky side, though the Peranakan-inspired motifs on the carpet, curtains and furniture are a nice touch. Slightly far from the best bits of Katong, but the bus stop is right outside.

FERNLOFT
HOSTEL $

Map p214 (✆6449 9066; www.fernloft.com; 693 East Coast Rd; dm $20-25, d $65; @☎; ☐36) It'd be nice if the rooms had loftier ceilings, but the in-house Balinese-inspired bar soon makes one forget about the ordinary if tidy rooms at this hostel. Patrons are offered a free welcome drink and 30% off meals and drinks at the bar. The cool bar, free wi-fi, airport transfer and free breakfast help seal the deal.

FRAGRANCE HOTEL
HOTEL $$

Map p214 (✆6344 9888; www.fragrancehotel.com; 219 Joo Chiat Rd, Katong; s/d $154/188; Ⓜ Paya Lebar) Fragrance has sniffed out a niche in the 'quickie' hourly hotel market and now has 20 (!) branches, many of them in Geylang, with gaudy names like Pearl and Crystal. The hotels, including this original branch, are attractive and clean enough, and worth a shot if you snag rooms at promotional rates (we've seen rooms knocked down to $83).

HOTEL 81 JOO CHIAT
HOTEL $$

Map p214 (✆6348 8181; www.hotel81.com.sg; 305 Joo Chiat Rd, Katong; r $120-150; Ⓜ Paya Lebar) One of the burgeoning chain of no-nonsense business (and funny business) hotels sprouting up in central Singapore, this one, strung out behind a row of restored Peranakan shophouses, is among the best looking, though all branches are identikit inside. It offers specially fitted rooms for the disabled. Check the website for 24 other locations. Online rates run from $79 to $119.

🛏 Sentosa & Other Islands

As well as the places listed below, it's perhaps worth knowing that the garish Resorts World complex (www.rwsentosa.com) on Sentosa Island has six hotels to choose from. Handy to fall back on if the others we've listed are full.

TOP CHOICE CAPELLA
HOTEL $$$

Map p220 (✆6591 5000; www.capellasingapore.com; 1 The Knolls; r from $700; @☎✉) The best hotel on Sentosa, if not in Singapore, Capella is pure class with outrageously luxurious rooms and a magical location, perched high above everything else around it. The lobby and the Chinese restaurant are housed in a beautifully renovated, whitewashed colonial-era building, dating from the 1880s. The rooms, other restaurants, bar, fitness centre, long-stay apartments and serene three-level swimming pool are dotted around lush, landscaped gardens in arty rectangular blocks. And, as you'd expect from Sentosa's star stay, service is stellar.

COSTA SANDS RESORT HOTEL $

Map p220 (☑6275 1034; www.costasands.com. sg; 30 Imbiah Walk; huts peak/off-peak $119/79, r peak/off-peak $259/199; @🛜🏊) Sentosa's only budget sleeping option, Costa Sands has tidy (but nothing special) midrange rooms in the main block surrounding the central pool area, as well as 15 cute but basic *kampong* (village) huts off to one side. The hotel rooms have all the usual facilities, including wi-fi and en suite bathroom. The huts are air-conditioned, but much more basic; no running water (there's a separate shared shower room), no TV and no internet access. And it's bunk beds only, with each hut able to sleep four people (making this a bargain if friends are happy to share). The huts are very popular, so bookings are highly recommended. 'Peak' time at Costa Sands is defined as every Friday and Saturday, plus public holidays and school holidays.

SHANGRI-LA'S RASA SENTOSA RESORT RESORT $$$

Map p220 (☑6275 0100; www.shangri-la.com; 101 Siloso Rd; r from $400; @🛜🏊) Singapore's only true beachfront resort is ideal for a short family break. Rooms are very smart – brightly decorated and extremely comfortable – service is top-notch, and the huge kid-friendly pool area, which has children's water slides and leads down towards Siloso Beach, is extremely inviting. Dining options include Chinese, Italian and even Moroccan.

CELESTIAL RESORT RESORT $$

Map p223 (☑6542 6681; www.celestialresort. com; Jln Endul Senin; r $118-268 weekdays, $138-288 weekends; @) Clean, tidy and very pretty rows of brightly painted rooms, all with en suite, are accessed via palm-shaded boardwalks that run the length of this small resort on Pulau Ubin. There's an artificial beach area beside a lake, where you can swim, fish, kayak or just sunbathe. Also has a beachside restaurant and bar.

MAMAM BEACH CAMPING $

Map p223 You can camp for free at two small beaches on Pulau Ubin; Noordin Beach and Mamam Beach. Neither is particularly idyllic (especially as your sea view includes the national border fence, pile-driven into the seabed, just off the coast), but Mamam is the nicer of the two, and does at least have toilets and washing facilities, although no showers. You should register at the police post (to your right as you step off the boat) if you intend to camp on Ubin.

ST JOHN'S HOLIDAY BUNGALOW CHALET $

(St John's Island; bungalow $53.50 Tue-Fri, $107 Sat & Sun) This three-bedroom bungalow on St John's Island can easily sleep six people (one double bed, four singles) and comes with a basic kitchen and cooking utensils. You can only book it by going in person to the **Sentosa Information Centre** (◷9am-8pm) on the 3rd floor of VivoCity (p115) and it's often booked quite far in advance. Rates double during the school holidays.

Understand
Singapore

Singapore Today

With a GDP growth rate of 14.5% in 2010 (number three in the world) and cash reserves of over $100 billion, it seems like Singapore doesn't have anything to worry about. Or does it? The soaring cost of living, and social issues with regards to immigration, population and gambling are just some of the things modern Singapore is grappling with.

Best on Film

12 Storeys (Eric Khoo, 1997) A dark comedy about the lives of separate individuals living in the same public housing apartment block.
881 (Royston Tan, 2007) Musical comedy about the *getai* (stage singing) aspirations of two friends. Colourful, campy, and touches on a fading Singapore artform.
I Not Stupid (Jack Neo, 2002) Chinese-language comedy that focuses on the pressures of the education system in Singapore.

Best in Print

Singapore Story (Lee Kuan Yew, 1999) To get the official story on the Singapore Miracle, go straight to the source – the man who masterminded the whole thing.
Singapore: A Biography (Mark Ravinder Frost & Yu-Mei Balamsingchow, 2010) Staid title aside, this is a well-written and handsomely illustrated history of Singapore across 450 riveting pages.
Little Ironies: Short Stories of Singapore (Catherine Lim, 1978) The doyenne of Singapore fiction has published numerous short-story collections and novels, one of which was made into a film. This is her first collection.

Singaporean Concerns

Singaporeans will tell you they love to complain and in some cases, they have every right to. House prices are soaring: in June 2011, a public-built flat fetched $880,000. Throw in a hike in the price of public transport and there's plenty of cause for coffeeshop grumbling. Overcrowding is a concern: Singapore's population has more than doubled from 2.4 million in 1980 to 5.1 million in 2010. Plus there's construction everywhere. It's a city that is constantly being tinkered with. The Colonial buildings along the Padang are being renovated into the National Art Gallery, the MRT circle line is set to be completed in 2012 with three new lines set to progressively open from 2013 to 2020. Of course, these are things to be happy about...when construction is actually completed.

New condominiums everywhere. New botanic gardens on the bay. Biomedical research hubs. LucasArts setting up shop. Hang on, we were here six months ago, where did that building come from? And where did our favourite pub go? It was here last week. Welcome to Singapore.

One Election to Rule them All?

In 2006, though the ruling People's Action Party (PAP) won the expected majority in a landslide victory, claiming 82 of the 84 seats in parliament, their actual votes fell by 8.69%. More than a third of the eligible electorate voted against the incumbent. The tone for the next election had been set.

With the election of 2011, the political landscape did indeed reflect the expected appetite for change. This election had the highest proportion of contested seats (94.3%) since Singapore achieved its independence in 1965. Local media, often accused of being mouthpieces of the government, appeared to give more even coverage to the PAP and opposition parties. Social media, once banned in campaigning, played a huge part in dissemination of information. Even Prime Minister Lee Hsien Loong participated in an online chat (his first). Attendance at opposition rallies were off the charts.

The results of the election were telling. The PAP lost a further 6.46% of the electorate, gaining 60.14% of the votes and 81 out of 87 seats. The biggest gains went to the Worker's Party (WP), with their political agenda that focuses on the everyday concerns of Singaporeans (wages, cost of living and healthcare, public transport, affordability of housing, disproportionately high salaries of ministers).

Post-election, it seems as though the PAP have realised that their position had gone from unshakable to 'Oh, we might need to do something about this'. A review of ministerial salaries was immediately mooted, and Senior Minister Goh Chok Tong and Minister Mentor Lee Kuan Yew both tendered their resignations.

Hey Big Spender

Despite initial opposition, the Singapore government's decision to allow the building of two casinos, Marina Bay Sands and Resorts World, has paid off, at least on paper. Less than a year into operation, both casinos have announced record profits set to tip $1 billion. The financial success led industry experts to declare Singapore's casinos the second-most profitable after Macau, overtaking Vegas (gasp!). All in one year.

In defending the government's decision to go ahead with the casinos, then Senior Minister Goh Chok Tong explained that while, 'from the moral standpoint, the Government and most people in Singapore are against gaming', the choice was ultimately based on the difficulty in relying on manufacturing to generate growth, Singapore's lack of natural tourist attractions and a need to create jobs.

But while there have been an estimated 35,000 jobs created, there is a darker side to the story. According to H2 Gambling Capital, the average gambling losses per adult resident jumped 53% from $924 to $1413 last year and this figure is estimated to hit $1849 by the end of 2011. Credit Counselling Singapore reported more gamblers seeking help. The government's decision to levy $100 casino entry fees for locals as a deterrent to gambling might not be as effective as originally envisaged. The jury's still out, but the long-term effects of the casinos on Singaporean society may well outweigh the economic benefits the casinos have brought in.

if Singapore were 100 people

74 are Chinese
14 are Malay
9 are Indian
3 are Others (Eurasians, Westerners etc.)

broadband access
(% of population)

people with
broadband

people without
broadband

population per sq km

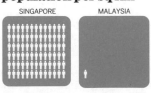

SINGAPORE   MALAYSIA

≈ 87 people

History

For a speck on the map, Singapore has always punched above its weight. It only really came into its own after Lee Kuan Yew spearheaded its independence in 1965. In a short span of time, Singapore was transformed into a stable, safe and properous country – thanks to visionary city planning, export, shipping and manufacturing.

PRE-COLONIAL SINGAPORE

Pretty much every museum you'll see in Singapore is devoted to post-colonial history, simply because there is not a great deal of undisputed precolonial history. It is known that the island waxed and waned in importance as empires to the north and south rose and fell – and archaeological digs have demonstrated there were substantial settlements there in the past – but there is little in the way of concrete historical material owing to a lack of written records.

Malay legend has it that long ago a Sumatran prince visiting the island of Temasek saw a strange animal he believed to be a lion. The good omen prompted the prince to found a city on the spot of the sighting. He called it Singapura (Lion City).

The island waxed and waned in importance as empires to the north and south rose and fell

Chinese traders en route to India had plied the waters around what is now Singapore from at least the 5th century AD, though the records of Chinese sailors as early as the 3rd century refer to an island called Pu Luo Chung, which may have been Singapore, while others claim there was a settlement in the 2nd century.

Between the 7th and 10th centuries, Srivijaya, a seafaring Buddhist kingdom centred at Palembang in Sumatra, held sway over the Strait of Malacca (now Melaka). Raids by rival kingdoms and the arrival of Islam spelled the eclipse of Srivijaya by the 13th century. Based mainly on the thriving pirate trade, the sultanate of Melaka quickly acquired the commercial power that was once wielded by Srivijaya.

TIMELINE	300	1200s	1390s
	Chinese seafarers mark the island on maps, labelling it Pu Luo Chung, believed to have come from the Malay name Pulau Ujong, meaning 'island at the end'.	Prince of Sumatran Srivijayan dynasty founds a settlement on the island and calls it Singapura (Lion City), having reputedly seen a lion there. Later named Temasek (Sea Town).	Srivijayan prince Parameswara flees Sumatra to Temasek after being deposed. He later founds the Sultanate of Malacca, under which Temasek is an important trading post.

The Portuguese took Melaka in 1511, sparking off a wave of colonialism. The equally ambitious Dutch founded Batavia (now Jakarta) to undermine Melaka's position, finally wresting the city from their European competitors in 1641. In the late 18th century, the British began looking for a harbour in the Strait of Melaka to secure lines of trade between China, the Malay world and their interests in India. Renewed war in Europe led, in 1795, to the French annexation of Holland, which prompted the British to seize Dutch possessions in Southeast Asia, including Melaka.

After the end of the Napoleonic Wars, the British agreed to restore Dutch possessions in 1818, but there were those who were bitterly disappointed at the failure of the dream of British imperial expansion in Southeast Asia. One such figure was Stamford Raffles, lieutenant-governor of Java.

THE RAFFLES ERA

For someone who spent a limited amount of time in Singapore, Sir Stamford Raffles had an extraordinary influence on its development. His name appears everywhere in the modern city – Raffles Place in the CBD, Stamford Rd, Raffles Hotel, the Raffles City shopping mall, the prestigious Raffles Institution (where Lee Kuan Yew went to school) – but his impact extends far beyond civic commemoration.

The streets you walk along in the city centre still largely follow the original plans Raffles drew. The ethnic districts still evident today, particularly in the case of Little India, were demarcated by him. Even the classic shophouse design – built of brick, with a continuous covered verandah known as a 'five-foot way' and a central courtyard for light, ventilation and water collection – has been attributed to him. More importantly, Singapore's very existence as one of the world's great ports is a direct consequence of Raffles' vision of creating a British-controlled entrepôt to counter Dutch power in the region.

When Raffles landed at Singapore in early 1819, the empire of Johor was divided. When the old sultan had died in 1812, his younger son's accession to power had been engineered while an elder son, Hussein, was away. The Dutch had a treaty with the young sultan, but Raffles threw his support behind Hussein, proclaiming him sultan and installing him in residence in Singapore.

In Raffles' plans the sultan wielded no actual power but he did serve to legitimise British claims on the island. Raffles also signed a treaty with the more eminent *temenggong* (senior judge) of Johor and set him up with an estate on the Singapore River. Thus, Raffles acquired the

1613	1819
Portuguese attack the town on the island and burn it to the ground. Singapura never regains its former importance while the Portuguese rule Malacca, and it slides into obscurity.	Sir Stamford Raffles, seeking a site for a new port to cement British interests in the Malacca Strait, lands on Singapura and decides it's the ideal spot.

RICHARD I'ANSON / LONELY PLANET IMAGES ©

Statue of Sir Stamford Raffles at Raffles Landing (Map p210)

use of Singapore in exchange for modest annual allowances to Sultan Hussein and the *temenggong*. This exchange ended with a cash buyout of the pair in 1824 and the transfer of Singapore's ownership to Britain's East India Company.

Along with Penang and Melaka, Singapore formed a triumvirate of powerful trading stations known as the Straits Settlements, which were controlled by the East India Company in Calcutta but administered from Singapore.

Raffles had hit upon the brilliant idea of turning a sparsely populated, tiger-infested malarial swamp with few natural resources into an economic powerhouse by luring in the ambitious and allowing them to unleash their entrepreneurial zeal. While it was to be many decades before Singapore's somewhat anarchic social conditions were brought under control, the essential Rafflesian spirit still underpins the city's tireless drive to succeed.

COLONISATION & OCCUPATION

Singapore Under the British

Raffles' first and second visits to Singapore in 1819 were brief, and he left instructions and operational authority with Colonel William Farquhar, former Resident (the chief British representative) in Melaka. When Raffles returned three years later, he found the colony thriving but displeasingly chaotic.

It was then that he drew out his town plan that remains today, levelling one hill to form a new commercial district (now Raffles Place) and erecting government buildings around another prominence called Forbidden Hill (now called Fort Canning Hill).

His plan also embraced the colonial practice, still in evidence, of administering the population according to neat racial categories. The city's trades, races and dialect groups were divided into zones: Europeans were granted land to the northeast of the government offices (today's Colonial District), though many soon moved out to sequestered garden estates in the western suburbs. The Chinese, including Hokkien, Hakka, Cantonese, Teochew and Straits-born, predominated around the mouth and the southwest of the Singapore River, though many Indians lived there too (hence the large Hindu temple on South Bridge Rd). Hindu Indians were, and still are, largely centred in Kampong Kapor and Serangoon Rd; Gujarati and other Muslim merchants were housed in the Arab St area; Tamil Muslim traders and small businesses operated in the Market St area; and the Malay population mainly lived on the

WILLIAM FARQUHAR

Colonel William Farquhar was a keen naturalist. He commissioned local Chinese artists to paint a series of 477 startlingly vibrant images of local flora and fauna.

1823	1824	1826	1867
Raffles signs treaty with the Sultan and Temenggong of Johor, who hand control over most of the island to the British. Raffles returns to Britain and never sees Singapore again.	Anglo-Dutch Treaty carves up the region into different spheres of influence, effectively removing any lingering threat to the island and cementing British sovereignty over Singapore.	Penang, Melaka and Singapore combined to form the Straits Settlements. Large waves of immigration wash over Singapore's free ports as merchants seek to avoid Dutch tariffs.	Social problems and discontent at ineffectual administration persuades the British to declare the Straits Settlements a separate Crown Colony, no longer run from India.

swampy northern fringes of the city. In time, of course, these zones became less well defined, as people decanted into other parts of the island.

While the British ran the colony, they needed the cooperation of their subjects, particularly the Chinese, for whom the British echoed the admiration other European powers had for the Chinese communities under their rule.

Just as the infamously harsh Dutch East Indies governor-general Jan Pieterszoon Coen described the Chinese residents of Batavia (Jakarta) as 'clever, courteous, industrious and obliging people', the Chinese of Singapore particularly impressed Victorian traveller Isabella Bird in 1879, when she described the city's 'ceaseless hum of industry' and 'the resistless, overpowering, astonishing Chinese element'.

Despite its wealth, the colony was a dissolute place, beset by crime, clan violence, appalling sanitation, opium addiction, rats, mosquitoes and tigers. Life for the majority was extremely harsh; the Chinatown Heritage Centre is probably the best place to appreciate just how harsh.

Raffles sought to cooperate with, and officially register, the various *kongsi* – clan organisations for mutual assistance, known variously as ritual brotherhoods, secret societies, triads and heaven-man-earth societies. (Many of them had their headquarters on Club St, and a couple still hold out against the area's rapid gentrification.) Labour and dialect-based *kongsi* would become increasingly important to Singapore's success in the 19th century, as overseas demand for Chinese-harvested products such as pepper, tin and rubber – all routed through Singapore from the Malay peninsula – grew enormously.

Singapore's access to *kongsi*-based economies in the region, however, depended largely on revenues from an East India Company product that came from India and was bound for China – opium.

Farquhar had established Singapore's first opium farm for domestic consumption, and by the 1830s excise and sales revenues of opium accounted for nearly half the administration's income, a situation that continued for a century after Raffles' arrival. But the British Empire produced more than Chinese opium addicts; it also fostered the Western-oriented outlook of Straits-born Chinese.

In the 19th century, women were rarely permitted to leave China; thus, Chinese men who headed for the Straits Settlements often married local women, eventually spawning a new, hybrid culture now known in Singapore as Peranakan (see p170).

Despite a massive fall in rubber prices in 1920, prosperity continued, immigration soared and millionaires were made almost overnight. In the 1930s and early '40s, politics dominated the intellectual scene. Indians looked to the subcontinent for signs of the end of colonial rule,

---

WWII Sites Open to Tourists

Fort Siloso (Sentosa Island)

Images of Singapore (Sentosa Island)

Reflections at Bukit Chandu (Southwest Singapore)

Labrador Nature Reserve (Southwest Singapore)

Memories at Old Ford Factory (Central Singapore)

Kranji War Memorial (West Singapore)

HISTORY COLONISATION & OCCUPATION

Singapore's port is still the busiest in the world in terms of shipping tonnage handled, although Shanghai's port overtook Singapore in terms of cargo tonnage.

1877	1939	1942	1942-45
Britain establishes Chinese Protectorate in each of the Straits Settlements in an effort to tackle the 'coolie trade', the exploitative labour market system run by Chinese secret societies.	Britain completes huge naval base for around $500 million, boasting world's largest dry dock, heavy defences and fuel to run the British Navy for months. Dubbed 'Fortress Singapore'.	Fortress Singapore cruelly exposed when incomplete preparation for northern invasion mean Japanese forces overrun the island. Allies surrender on 15 February.	Singapore is renamed Syonan by Japanese. Chinese massacred and brutalised, Allied prisoners incarcerated at Changi or shipped off to the Death Railway. Economy collapses.

while Kuomintang (Nationalist) and Communist Party struggles in the disintegrating Republic of China attracted passionate attention. Opposition to Japan's invasions of China in 1931 and 1937 was near universal in Singapore.

But just as political rumblings began to make the British nervous, war overtook events.

Singapore Under the Japanese

When General Yamashita Tomoyuki pushed his thinly stretched army into Singapore on 15 February 1942, so began what Singapore regards as the blackest period of its history. For the British, who had set up a naval base near the city in the 1920s, surrender was sudden and humiliating – and some historians have pinpointed the fall of Singapore as the moment when the myth of British impregnability was blown apart and the empire began its final decline.

The impact of the Japanese occupation on the collective political and social memory of Singapore cannot be underestimated, and it has partly inspired Singapore's modern preoccupation with security.

The British expected the Japanese to attack Singapore south via by the sea. Instead, they blitzed Singapore coming north from Malaysia via foot and bicycle.

Japanese rule was harsh. Yamashita had the Europeans and Allied POWs herded onto the Padang; from there they were marched away for internment. Many of them were taken to the infamous Changi Prison, while others were herded up to Siam (Thailand) to work on the horrific Death Railway.

The Japanese also launched Operation Sook Ching to eliminate Chinese opposition. Chinese Singaporeans were driven out of their homes, 'screened', then either given a 'chop' (a mark on the forehead meaning they had been cleared for release), or driven away to be imprisoned or executed (there's a memorial to one massacre at Changi Beach). Estimates of the number of Chinese killed vary – some sources put the number at 6000, others at more than 45,000.

The Japanese renamed the island 'Syonan' (Light of the South), changed signs into Japanese, put clocks forward to Tokyo time and introduced a Japanese currency (known by contemptuous locals as 'banana money').

The war ended suddenly with Japan's surrender on 14 August 1945, and Singapore was passed back into British control. While the returning British troops were welcomed, the occupation had eroded the innate trust in the empire's protective embrace. New political forces were at work and the road to independence was paved.

1945–59	1959
British resume control. Straits Settlements wound up in 1946. Until 1955 Singapore run by part-elected legislative councils, then a semiautonomous government.	First full legislative elections held. People's Action Party, led by Cambridge graduate Lee Kuan Yew, win landslide. Aggressive economic development and social programs launched.

Parliament House (Map p210)

RAFFLES THE MAN

Sir Stamford Raffles, cultural scholar, Singapore colonist, naturalist and founder of the London Zoo, died at his home in Hendon, North London, the day before his 45th birthday in 1826, probably from a brain tumour. Having fallen out with the East India Company, his death was ignored by London society, and it was eight years before a marble statue of him, commissioned by friends and family, was placed in Westminster Abbey.

The original bronze statue of Raffles in Singapore, unveiled on the Padang on 29 June 1887, now stands in front of Victoria Theatre and Concert Hall. A white stone replica on Empress Place supposedly marks the spot where he first set foot on the island.

Raffles himself was an extraordinary man, in many ways at odds with the British colonial mould. While he was a firm believer in the British Empire as a benevolent force, he also preached the virtues of making Singapore a free port and opposed slavery. Raffles was also a sympathetic student of the peoples of the region and spoke fluent Malay.

His character was probably shaped by his humble upbringing. He began his working life at 14 as a clerk for the giant East India Company, but was a tireless self-improver. In 1805, he was appointed as part of a group to cement emerging British interests in Penang. Within six years, through several promotions, he became the governor of Java, where his compassionate leadership won him enduring respect. From there he travelled to Sumatra, where he became governor of Bencoolen on the island's southern coast.

His life was marred by tragedy, however. While in Southeast Asia he lost four of his five children to disease, his massive natural history collection in a ship fire and his personal fortune in a bank collapse. The East India Company refused him a pension and after his death his parish priest, who objected to his antislavery stance, refused him a headstone.

His achievements as a statesman have often obscured his brilliance as a naturalist. He made an intricate study of the region's flora and fauna and though much of his work was lost, it is still honoured at the National University of Singapore, which maintains the Raffles Museum of Biodiversity Research.

THE LEE DYNASTY

If one person can be considered responsible for the position Singapore finds itself in today, it is Lee Kuan Yew.

Born in 1923, this third-generation Straits-born Chinese was named Harry Lee, and brought up to be, in his own words, 'the equal of any Englishman'. His education at the elite Raffles Institution and Cambridge University equipped him well to deal with both colonial power

1963	1964	1965	1971
After strong campaigning from Lee Kuan Yew, Singapore joins Sabah and Sarawak in combining with Malaya to form the single state of Malaysia.	Two outbreaks of race rioting between Malays and Chinese see 36 people killed and more than 500 injured, fuelling the already testy relations between the PAP and the Malay ruling party UMNO.	Singapore expelled from federation after unanimous vote in Malaysian Parliament in Kuala Lumpur. Lee Kuan Yew cries as he announces the news. The Republic of Singapore is born.	British forces withdraw, sparking economic crisis. PAP mounts election to win mandate for tough laws curbing unions, which succeed in luring foreign investment, mostly from the US.

and political opposition when Singapore took control of its own destiny in the 1960s.

The early years were not easy. Race riots in 1964 and ejection from the Malay Federation in 1965 made Lee's task even harder. Lee used tax incentives and strict new labour laws to attract foreign investment. This, combined with huge resources poured into developing an English-language education system that churned out a competent workforce, saw Singapore's economy rapidly industrialise.

Under Lee's rigidly paternal control, his People's Action Party (PAP) also set about eliminating any viable political opposition, banning critical publications and moulding the city into a disciplined, functional society built along Confucian ideals, which value the maintenance of hierarchy and social order above all things. The island's small size made this hothouse experiment easier to manage, enabling the effective enforcement of Singapore's famous social regulations on everything from spitting to chewing gum to littering.

Lee was successful at containing what he evidently saw as the anarchic tendencies of Singapore's citizens, inspiring ever more ambitious attempts at social engineering. For example, a (now defunct) matchmaking club was established to pair off suitable couples – one of the dating clubs was restricted to graduates.

Lee's rapid industrialisation filled government coffers and enabled the PAP to pursue massive infrastructure, defence, health, education, pension and housing schemes, giving Singaporeans a level of prosperity and security that remains the envy of many countries in the region and around the world.

Housing and urban renovation, in particular, have been the keys to the PAP's success. By the mid-1990s, Singapore had achieved the world's highest rate of home ownership.

Despite resigning as prime minister in 1990 after 31 years in the job, and handing over to the more avuncular but no less determined Goh Chok Tong, Lee still keeps an eye on proceedings and his comments on various issues frequently flag future government policy.

'Even from my sickbed,' said Lee in 1988, 'even if you are going to lower me into the grave and I feel that something is wrong, I'll get up.'

> Check out the National Museum of Singapore for accounts of life of early migrants in the formative Singapore Settlement.

> Lee Kuan Yew famously cried on national television in 1965, after Singapore separated from Malaysia. The event (separation, not the tears) marked the birth of modern Singapore.

RECENT PAST & IMPENDING FUTURE

Lee Kuan Yew's son, Lee Hsien Loong, who was deputy PM and Defence Minister under Goh Chok Tong, took over the top job unopposed in 2004. Goh took over the Senior Minister role from Lee Snr, who as-

1975	1981	1987	1989
Singapore becomes world's third-busiest port, after Rotterdam and New York, and third-largest oil refiner; also a rig- and drilling-platform manufacturer and a huge oil-storage centre.	Changi Airport opens, replacing Paya Lebar, and handles eight million passengers in its first year. By 2010 passenger traffic hits 42 million and Changi regularly named world's best airport.	The Mass Rapid Transit (MRT) train line begins operating. Today, the line is still being expanded.	Lee Kuan Yew steps down as Prime Minister, handing over reins to Goh Chok Tong. Lee becomes Senior Minister and retains oversight of government policy.

sumed the newly created title of Minister Mentor, positions both vacated in 2011.

Lee Hsien Loong faces challenges as great as those his father dealt with, principally how to continue the momentum and maintain Singapore's astonishing success. The Asian financial crisis starting in 1997, the SARS outbreak in 2003 and the global financial crisis of 2007 all had a major impact on the country's economy and its sense of vulnerability to forces beyond its control. Though economically and financially Singapore is in a strong position, the migration of its manufacturing base to cheaper competitors like Vietnam and China has forced the government to embark on a radical makeover of the country in an attempt to ensure its success extends into the future.

Majulah Singapura' (Onward Singapore), the Singapore national anthem, was composed by Zubir Said in 1958. Its lyrics are entirely in Bahasa Malay, even though English is now the national language..

2004	2008	2010	2011
Prime Minister Goh Chok Tong steps down, is replaced by Lee Kuan Yew's son, Lee Hsien Loong, who builds two casinos, reversing decades of government policy on casino gambling.	Singapore stages Formula One Grand Prix. It's the first night race.	Singapore hosts the inaugural Youth Olympics. They flop. The two casinos open and first-year profits are tipped at over $1 billion.	Watershed General Election results see the ruling PAP party face its worst result ever, winning 60.14% of the vote, down 6.46% from 2006.

Food

It's an understatement to say that Singaporeans live to eat (not eat to live). Listen in to a conversation at a hawker centre and the topic will inevitably be that of the *next* meal...even if the current one is half-finished. Self-professed food gurus wax lyrical about their search for the best <insert food dish here> and blog their way through their culinary adventures. If you want to leave with a keen understanding of being Singaporean, then it's essential to understand the lay of the (food) land.

HOW IT ALL BEGAN...

Singapore has a history of migration. As each ethnic group and subgroup came to Singapore, it brought its own cuisine along. Each type of food remains largely undiluted to this day, but as often happens when cultures are transplanted far from home, local variations and customs have crept in. Just as the people of Singapore developed their own characteristics the longer they were separated from their homelands, the character of dishes such as fish-head curry, chilli crab and *yu sheng* (raw fish salad eaten at Chinese New Year) have all evolved from traditional favourites. Singaporeans live to eat, and while you're here you might as well join them.

For Singaporeans, what's on the plate is far more important than the quality of the china (or plastic) it's served on. The smartest-dressed businessman is as comfortable sitting down on a cheap plastic chair at a plastic table and wading into a $3 plastic plate of *char kway teow* (a Hokkien dish of broad noodles, clams and eggs fried in chilli and black-bean sauce) as he is eating $80 crabs in an air-conditioned restaurant. Combine this unpretentiousness with infinite variety, high standards of hygiene and the prevalence of the English language, and you have some of the best and most accessible eating opportunities in Southeast Asia.

SPECIALITIES

Chinese

With Chinese food, the more people you can muster for a meal the better, because dishes are traditionally shared. A Chinese meal should be balanced; a yin (cooling) dish such as vegetables, fruit or clear soup, should be matched by a yang (heating) dish such as starchy foods or meat.

The best-known and most popular style of Chinese cooking is Cantonese, despite the majority of Singaporean Chinese not being of Cantonese descent. Cantonese food is usually stir-fried with just a touch of oil to ensure that the result is crisp and fresh. Typical dishes include *won ton* (dumpling filled with spiced minced pork) soup and *mee* (noodles). At the expensive end of the spectrum are shark's-fin and bird's-nest dishes.

One of the most famous Cantonese specialities is dim sum (also known as yum cha): small snack-type dishes usually eaten at lunchtime or as a Sunday brunch in large, noisy restaurants where the dishes are whisked around the tables on trolleys or carts; take what you like as they come

Must Reads

Makansutra Singapore (KF Seetoh)

The End of Char Kway Teow and Other Hawker Mysteries (Leslie Tay)

Bite: The 8 Days Eat Out Guide

Singapore Tatler: Best Restaurants Guide

by. *Xiao long bao* (pork dumplings filled with a piping hot sauce) is a must-try.

Arguably the most popular local dish is Hainanese chicken rice: a mix of steamed fowl and rice cooked in chicken stock, served with a clear soup and slices of cucumber. It's practically the national dish and the ultimate Singaporean comfort food. Eaten with dips (ginger and chilli or soy), it's light but surprisingly filling. Another popular Hainanese dish is steamboat, which features a boiling stockpot in the middle of the table, into which you dunk pieces of meat, seafood or vegetables and extract them when cooked.

Many of Singapore's Chinese are Hokkien, from southern China, infamously coarse-tongued folk whose hearty noodle dishes like *char kway teow, bak chor mee* (noodles with pork, meat balls and fried scallops) and *hokkien mee* (yellow Hokkien noodles with prawn, served either fried or in a rich prawn-based stock) are fast-food favourites.

From the area around Shàntóu in China, Teochew is a style noted for its delicacy and natural flavours (although many say it's bland). Seafood is a speciality – fish *maw* (a fish's swim bladder) crops up alarmingly often. The classic Teochew comfort food is rice porridge, served with fish, pork or frog (the latter being a Geylang favourite). Most neighbourhood *koptiam* (coffeeshops) have a *tzechar* (cooked food) stall serving a mix of all Chinese cuisines to cater to fussy local palettes.

Indian

Broadly speaking Indian cuisine can be classified into two categories: south and north. South Indian food dominates Singapore, as most Indian Singaporeans and migrant workers originate from the south, but North Indian restaurants are becoming much more widespread, thanks to the growing number of North Indian professionals and tourists in Singapore.

DIE DIE MUST TRY: HAWKER CENTRES & FOOD COURTS

Singaporean food guru KF Seetoh's tagline 'Die die must try' has become synonymous with the local obsession with food. Debates rage over where to find the definitive 'die die must try' versions of local hawker favourites. Here are some of the best hawker and food centres you 'die die must try'.

➡ **Tekka Centre** (p71) The bustling heart of Little India, where you'll find dozens of Indian and Muslim stalls, wrapped in the noise and smells from the wet market.

➡ **Golden Mile Complex** (p73) Popular with Thai workers, this is the spot to get a *tom yum* (spicy and sour soup) and a *som tam* (green papaya salad) just like they make in the Land of Smiles.

➡ **Gluttons Bay** (p46) A 'best of' Singapore hawker food selected by the guru of food himself, KF Seetoh.

➡ **Maxwell Road Hawker Centre** (p60) A throwback to the old days in the heart of Chinatown: noisy and chaotic.

➡ **Smith Street Hawker Centre** At night, Smith St in Chinatown is closed off and the road is filled with tables and diners munching seafood and drinking beer.

➡ **East Coast Lagoon Food Village** (p92) Soak up the sea breezes by the beach while wolfing down satay and seafood.

➡ **Lau Pa Sat** (p60) Dating back to 1822, it's been substantially modernised, but still pulls in the crowds, and even tour buses.

➡ **Food Republic** (p80) One of a new breed of fancy food centres, with great views of Orchard Rd below.

South Indian food tends to be hot, with the emphasis on vegetarian dishes. The typical South Indian dish is a *thali* (rice plate), often served on a large banana leaf. On this leaf is placed a large mound of rice, then various vegetable curries, *rasam* (hot, sour soup) and a dessert. South Indian food is traditionally eaten with the right hand, not utensils – though spoons are always available.

The most popular Indian dish among local Chinese is *roti prata* – a flat bread cooked with oil on a hotplate and served with a curry sauce. Prata restaurants usually list dozens of varieties, both sweet and savoury. Try a *roti telur* (prata cooked with an egg) or a *roti tissue* (ultra-thin prata cooked with margarine and sugar and served in a cone shape).

Other South Indian vegetarian dishes include *masala dosa,* a thin pancake that, rolled around spiced vegetables with some chutney and *rasam* on the side, makes a cheap light meal. An equivalent snack meal in Indian halal (Muslim) restaurants is *murtabak* – paper-thin dough filled with egg and minced mutton and lightly grilled with oil.

Another favourite Indian halal dish is *biryani,* which is different from the North Indian version. Ordering a chicken *biryani* will get you a mound of spiced, saffron-coloured rice, a piece of deep-fried chicken, a bowl of curry sauce and a small mound of salad (often with a squirt of sweet chilli sauce on top).

North Indian cuisine is more familiar to Westerners, and most commonly associated with heavier, slightly less spicy dishes, eaten with breads like *naan* (leavened bread baked inside a clay oven) and *chapati* (griddle-fried wholewheat bread). Think tandoori chicken or butter chicken.

KF SEETOH

KF Seetoh is Singapore's most famous food celebrity. He publishes *Makansutra*, a locally revered bible of hawker food, and opened the popular Gluttons Bay hawker street centre.

Malay & Indonesian

The cuisines of Malaysia and Indonesia are similar. Satay – grilled kebabs of chicken, mutton or beef dipped in a spicy peanut sauce – is ubiquitous. Other common dishes include *tahu goreng* (fried soya bean curd and bean sprouts in a peanut sauce), *ikan bilis* (anchovies fried whole), *ikan assam* (fried fish in a sour tamarind curry) and *sambal udang* (fiery curried prawns).

Both *ayam goreng* (fried chicken) and *rendang* are popular staples. *Nasi goreng* (fried rice) is widely available, but it is as much a Chinese and Indian dish as Malay, and each style has its own flavours. *Nasi lemak* is coconut rice served with *ikan bilis,* peanuts and a curry dish.

The Sumatran style of Indonesian food bends much more towards curries and chillies. *Nasi padang,* from the Minangkabau region of West Sumatra, consists of a wide variety of spicy curries and other smaller dishes served with rice. You pick and choose what you want and it's dolloped on a plate. *Mee rebus* (noodles in a thick soya-based sauce) is a Javanese dish that is also widely available in food centres.

Desserts

The lurid mini-volcanoes you'll often see at food centres are *ice kachang,* a combination of a mound of shaved ice, syrups, evaporated milk, fruit, beans and jellies. *Cendol* is similar, consisting of coconut milk with *gula melaka* (brown or palm sugar) syrup and green jelly strips topped with shaved ice. Both taste terrific – or at least a lot better than they look. Also worth trying is *ah balling,* glutinous rice balls filled with a sweet paste of peanut, black sesame or red bean and usually served in a peanut- or ginger-flavoured soup.

SINGAPORE'S TOP 10 VEGGIE DELIGHTS *SHALU ASNANI*

➡ **Rojak** A savoury fruit salad of cucumber, pineapple, mango, fried bean curd and other ingredients, tossed in a piquant dressing of tamarind, prawn paste (which can be left out for a veggie version), sugar, chilli, lime juice and a generous topping of crushed peanuts. The mix of flavours is truly tasty and incredibly fresh.

➡ **Roti prata** A light, fluffy puff-pastry pancake which is impressively flipped and twirled before being pan-fried till crispy. Being an Indian speciality, it's typically served with curry but you get exotic variations with cheese, mushrooms and even banana or chocolate! Goes great with a mug of *teh tarik* (hot, frothy milk tea).

➡ **Popiah** Fresh spring rolls made from thin wrappers stuffed with turnip, jicama, bean sprouts, shredded carrots, and other fillings depending on the individual vendor. The fillings are usually steamed, and the popiah is dressed with a sweet-spicy bean sauce and an optional chilli paste.

➡ **Mee goreng/nasi goreng** Fried noodles or fried rice. Introduced by Chinese immigrants to Singapore and to which the Malays and Indians added their own twist. What results is yellow noodles or cooked rice stir-fried with garlic, onions, chilli, vegetables, tomatoes, egg and sometimes tofu and a medley of different sauces. Usually served with a side of sliced cucumber with tomato ketchup!

➡ **Nasi padang** Originates from Indonesia and consists of a portion of steamed rice with a choice of various meat or vegetable dishes to go along with it. My favourite version is with *sayur lodeh* (vegetable coconut curry), *sambal tofu-tempeh* (spicy tofu and fermented beans) and *achar* (pickled carrot and cucumber). This dish is available at food stalls across Singapore, but go to Geylang for an authentic experience.

➡ **Gado-gado** Another outstanding salad, this one Indonesian-style. Typically made with green vegetables, fried tofu, tempeh, cucumber, steamed rice-cakes, bean sprouts and sometimes hard-boiled eggs, tossed in a spicy peanut sauce and topped with crispy tapioca crackers.

➡ **Ice kachang** Literally means 'iced beans'. It starts with layers of red beans, jelly, sweet corn and *attap chee* (palm seeds) topped with a mountain of shaved ice and dressed with different colours of syrup and sweetened condensed milk.

➡ **Dosai** Thin, crispy south Indian savoury crêpe made from rice flour, usually served with dhal (lentil curry), vegetable curry and coconut chutney. There are variations stuffed with potatoes, vegetables and spices.

➡ **Goreng pisang** Popular snack food of piping hot deep-fried banana fritters. The best goreng pisang vendors use pisang raja, which are small, sweet bananas. Nowadays, restaurants churn out fancier versions served with vanilla ice-cream or chocolate sauce, or a dusting of cinnamon and icing sugar.

➡ **Carrot cake** The most confusing Singaporean dish! Carrot cake does not contain any carrots. It's made from a combination of radish, rice flour and water which is then steamed into cakes, diced and stir-fried with eggs, pickled radish, garlic, and spring onion. You usually have a choice of 'black' (with sweet soy sauce) or 'white' (plain). Ask for some chilli for that extra kick.

This lip-smacking list was compiled by Shalu Asnani, a vegetarian chef and the proprietor of Little Green Cafe (www.littlegreencafe.com.sg). She regularly conducts vegetarian cooking classes in Singapore.

FOOD SPECIALITIES

Head to Little India to experiment with Indian sweets: *burfi, ladoo, gulab jamun, gelabi, jangiri, kesari* and *halwa,* to name a few, are made with ingredients that include condensed milk, sesame and syrups.

Nonya (Peranakan) desserts are typified by *kueh* (colourful rice cakes often flavoured with coconut and palm sugar) and sweet, sticky delicacies such as miniature pineapple tarts that are sold everywhere in small plastic tubs with red lids. The magnificent *kueh lapis,* a laborious layer cake that involves prodigious numbers of eggs, is a must-try.

One notable popular Singaporean oddity is the ice-cream sandwich, dished out by mobile ice-cream vendors and enjoyed by young and old alike. This consists of a thick slab or mini-scoops of ice cream folded into a slice of bread, though sometimes it's served between the more traditional wafer slices. There are plenty of vendors along Orchard Rd and along the northern bank of Boat Quay.

VEGETARIANS & VEGANS

The predominance of the Buddhist and Hindu religions in Singapore means finding a vegetarian restaurant, stall or cafe is usually not difficult. Little India in particular teems with vegetarian food, but food courts and hawker centres all over the island often feature a vegetarian stall, or have some vegetarian options.

One thing to be aware of is that interpretations of dishes among Chinese and Malays can be slightly different. We have encountered 'vegetable soup' that contains both chicken and prawn (the reasoning being that because it contains vegetables, it's a vegetable soup!) The solution is to be highly specific when ordering food – don't just say 'vegetarian', but stress that you eat 'no meat, no seafood' and make sure you've been understood.

Vegans are likely to find life a little more difficult, but since the consumption of dairy and other animal by-products is relatively limited, usually all you have to do is ensure there are no eggs.

HAWKER CENTRE, KOPITIAM OR FOOD COURT?

Aside from the standard Western-style restaurants and cafes, Singapore has several local species of eating venue: hawker centre, *kopitiam,* food court, food centre, canteen…all of them feature open dining areas, around which are clustered anything from a handful to a hundred stalls. The subtle distinctions between these places are often a mystery to foreigners, but Singaporeans insist they are different.

The term 'hawker' was once used to describe food vendors who moved their wares around in mobile carts, stopping and setting up their burners wherever there were customers. Of course, such itinerant behaviour was unacceptable in modern Singapore and virtually all of them are now stockaded into hawker centres.

Hawker centres are usually standalone, open-air (or at least open-sided) structures with rows of food stalls. There are usually a wide variety of different local cuisines on offer and the atmosphere is often raucous. However, the food is uniformly good. If it isn't, stalls go out of business very quickly. Some hawker centres are located along with a corresponding wet market and locals simply refer to the hawker centre as a 'market'. Confusing, no?

Food courts are indoor dining areas, often found in air-conditioned shopping malls. There's a wide variation of cuisines and prices are marginally higher. Some very swanky food courts are springing up, where the food is fancier and the prices a little higher still.

Coffeeshops, also called *kopitiam* (*tiam* is Hokkien for 'shop'), are another Singaporean institution. These are open shopfront cafes, usually with a handful of stalls inside, patrolled by an 'auntie' or 'uncle' who takes your drinks order after you've got your food.

If you have a smartphone, download the Hungrygowhere and Foursquare apps for local recommendations and reviews.

Local magazines such as *8 Days, IS,* and *Time Out* have up-to-the-minute reviews on the latest and greatest (sometimes worst) restaurants in town.

MAGAZINE REVIEWS

HAWKER CENTRE ETIQUETTE

Visitors to Singapore often say that hawker centres are among the most memorable parts of their trip. Food courts located in malls are easy, but for the first-timer the older hawker centres can be a little daunting, so it's worth brushing up on some etiquette before plunging in.

When you arrive, bag a seat first, especially if it's busy. You can either do this by placing a member of your group at a table, or do it Singaporean style and lay a packet of tissues on a seat (this behaviour has recently been viewed in the media as being rather ungracious, but hey, it works). If there's a table number, note it as the stall owner uses it as reference for food delivery. Don't worry if there are no free tables; it's quite normal to share with a complete stranger.

You're then free to wander off in search of food. Signboards list the stall's specialities, and you can buy any number of dishes from any number of stalls. Sometimes the stall will have a sign saying 'self service', which means you have to carry the food to the table yourself, not dish up your own food. Otherwise, the vendor brings your food to you (which is why you should get a table first, or they won't know where you are).

Generally, you pay when you order, but some hawkers take money when they deliver.

In most older hawker centres and *kopitiam* (coffeeshops), someone will come to your table and take your drinks order. You pay them when they deliver the drinks. In the modern food courts in malls, you have to go and order from the drinks stalls.

Some hawker centres have wandering touts who try to grab you when you arrive, sit you down and plonk menus in front of you. You are not obliged to order from them and in fact it's illegal for stalls to tout at all, which you might like to point out to any persistent pests.

Singapore's amalgam of cultures has largely made strict eating etiquette redundant. Each ethnic group still follows its own eating code for its own food, but often ignores the codes of other cuisines. You'll see Chinese eating *roti prata* (fried Indian flat bread) with a spoon and fork, Indians eating Chinese food with a spoon, Malays attacking a pizza with a knife and fork... In other words, don't feel obliged to follow any rules.

A perfect conversation ice-breaker would be to ask a Singaporean where the best 'insert dish here' can be found. You may end up being shown some great places!

FOOD HAWKER CENTRE ETIQUETTE

Peranakan Culture

What's a 'Peranakan'? It's not a word you'll see outside the former Straits Settlements. In Singapore, Peranakan (locally born) people are descendants of immigrants who married local women who were mostly of Malay origin. The result of hundreds of years of immersion and the meeting of foreign and local customs has resulted in an intriguing hybrid culture that's recently experienced a revival.

ORIGINS

The earliest records show a marriage between Hang Liu, a Ming dynasty princess, to the Malacca Sultan Mansur Shah around 1446. Larger waves of immigration in the 17th and 18th centuries formed the backbone of the Peranakan culture.

It's acknowledged that the Peranakan fall into three broad categories: the Chitty Melaka and Jawi Peranakan are descended from early migrants from India, while the Straits Chinese Peranakan are of mainland Chinese origin. No matter which group, there's a fierce sense of roots and traditions within.

In Singapore, the largest group are the Straits Chinese, a reflection of the population breakdown at large. The term 'Straits Chinese' originated within communities in the former colonial Straits Settlements of Singapore, Penang and Melaka. The focus here will be on the Straits Chinese because they're the ones with the most overt cultural influence, be it on TV, through its cuisine or via the numerous local tourist sights.

> **Must Reads**
> ....
> *A Peranakan Legacy: The Heritage of the Straits Chinese (Peter Wee)*
> ....
> *Kebaya Tales: Of Matriachs, Maidens, Mistresses and Matchmakers (Lee Su Kim)*
> ....
> *A Baba Wedding (Cheo Kim Ban)*
> ....
> *The Straits Chinese House: Domestic Life & Traditions (Peter Lee & Jennifer Chen)*

PERANAKAN CULTURE TODAY

These days, Chinese and Peranakan culture tend to overlap and it's sometimes hard to distinguish between the two. Peranakan men, called Babas, and the women, Nonya, primarily speak a patois that mixes Bahasa Malay, Hokkien dialect and English, though that's changed over time, along with the education system in Singapore. Most of the current Peranakans speak English and Mandarin. Looks-wise, Peranakan are indistinguishable from people of Han Chinese descent, but traditional families still cling on to their customs and traditions and are proud of their heritage (some say they are proud to the point of being haughty).

In 2008, the local Chinese TV station broadcast *The Little Nonya* to record numbers of viewers. The drama series focused on a Peranakan family across a 70-year period and was filmed with authentic costumes and locations that included the Baba House in Singapore and the famous Blue Mansion in Malaysia. Coincidentally, the Peranakan Museum in Singapore opened the same year. This sparked off a revival and interest in the lineage, food and traditions of the Peranakan. For visitors in particular, the food and wedding ceremonies are of interest.

WEDDINGS

A traditional Peranakan wedding puts most other weddings to shame. It's an elaborate 12-day affair that seems to go on longer! The weddings are heavily steeped in Chinese traditions from the Fujian province in China, mixed with some Malay customs. These days, such elaborate affairs are few and far between though they are making a comeback, albeit in a severely truncated one-day affair.

Traditionally, once a couple was been matchmade and a *sinseh pokwa* (astrologer) consulted to pick an auspicious date, the engagement would be sealed with gifts. Elaborate gifts of jewellery and other items were delivered to the bride's parents in a *bakul siah* (lacquered bamboo containers). Other gifts included *kuih ih* (glutinous riceballs in syrup), ham hock, wedding dresses and two pairs of red candles.

Red bunting and lanterns were traditionally hung over the door of the house. The bridal chamber, being the centrepiece of the wedding, was decorated with embroidery and beaded hangings declaring fertility and good fortune.

A whole host of rituals would have been conducted prior to the wedding. Some of the stranger ones included a young boy rolling across the bed three times in hope for a male first-born; pregnant or menstruating women being barred from entry (bad luck), or *bunga rempai* (potpourri) being placed on the bed to ward off spirits.

On the first day, the groom would dress up in Qing dynasty scholar garb and the bride in a similarly embroidered gown and hat piece, along with intricate jewellery. Rituals were performed and a tea ceremony conducted for the couple. On the second day, the couple took their first meal together, where they fed each other 12 types of food, to symbolise the 12-day process and the care they will take of one another. On the third day, they offered tea to parents and in-laws as a sign of respect.

The subsequent days would be filled with visits from friends and younger relatives, lots of feasts (whole suckling pig features heavily on the menu) before the *dua belah hari* (12th day ceremony) where the marriage was sealed and proof of the consummation confirmed with

Famous Singaporeans who are of Peranakan descent include Lee Kuan Yew, Dick Lee (singer, composer), and Goh Keng Swee (first Prime Minister of Singapore).

Perfect Peranakan souvenirs to pick up include a *kebaya* (blouse-dress, often embroidered) and *kasot manek* (beaded slippers).

BEST PERANAKAN SIGHTS AND EXPERIENCES

➡ **Peranakan Museum** The starting point to learning about all things Peranakan.

➡ **Baba House** This 'living' museum offers a beautifully restored look at a traditional Peranakan household.

➡ **Katong Antique House** Owner and fourth-generation Peranakan, Peter Wee, owns this house and museum.

➡ **Emerald Hill and Joo Chiat** These two Peranakan neighbourhoods are the best sites to visit for architecture.

➡ **Guan Hoe Soon** Located in Joo Chiat, this is the longest-running Peranakan restaurant in Singapore and a favourite of Lee Kuan Yew.

➡ **Kim Choo Kueh Chang and Rumah Bebe** Peranakan shops in Joo Chiat. You can buy Nonya *kuih* (sweets), learn to wrap *bak chang* (rice dumplings) at the former, and shop for *kebaya* (fitted embroidered tops) at the latter. You can undertake lessons to make *kasut manek* (beaded slippers). Both are housed in beautifully restored shophouses.

➡ **The Little Nonya** A successful 2008 local Chinese TV drama that explores the 70-year history of a Peranakan family. You can buy it from DVD stores in malls and at some bookstores.

TO BE PERANAKAN MEANS TO BE ACCEPTED AS A LOCAL *PETER WEE*

Peranakan culture isn't found only in Singapore. Throughout coastal Indonesia and Malaysia you'll find other pockets of Peranakan culture. To some, Peranakan culture may seem very similar to traditional Chinese culture, which makes sense, as our culture is about 80% derived from Chinese culture. However, there are subtle differences, certainly in our traditions, the way we speak and, of course, in our culinary traditions. Many of these differences come from a combination of time and the other cultures that make up the Peranakan (both local Straits inhabitants and colonial, especially British) influence.

Increasingly, there seems to be an awakening cultural awareness among members of the younger generation in Singapore. One recent event sticks out. A young couple came to my shop while planning their wedding. The bride-to-be was shopping for a *kebaya*, a beautiful hand-embroidered outfit traditionally worn by Peranakan women. This struck me as odd, and I assumed that the choice of dress had been made by the parents. So I was surprised to learn that, in fact, the parents objected. They wanted to have a more modern wedding. But it was the young people themselves who chose to get married wearing the clothing of their past.

Most Peranakan tend to be Christian because of the influence of early missionaries – French, Dutch, Portuguese, and finally English – in the area. But Peranakan culture crosses religious boundaries. There are Peranakans who are Muslims, others who maintain Buddhist traditions. The way we speak is itself unique, not quite a language in and of itself, but more like a patois, a mixture of Hokkien, Malay, English, with a tinge of Dutch, and even Portuguese. It's very unique to Malacca, Penang and Singapore, only found around here.

The Joo Chiat district derives its name from a famous Peranakan family. The main street is named after Chew Joo Chiat, who was a philanthropist in the late 19th century. Many of the original families have left, for various reasons, but some are returning. There is a lot of nostalgia for the area. We are trying to put it back together again, so that Joo Chiat can become what it once was.

Visitors to Singapore should take the time to visit the area to see the truly unique architecture that exists, especially the art deco shophouses of Koon Seng and Tembeling Rd. And of course, Joo Chiat is the place in Singapore to sample Peranakan cuisine. I always take friends out to try our *mee siam* (white thin noodles in a sourish and sweet gravy made with tamarind), laksa, and our traditional Peranakan dumplings. One Peranakan specialty is the *buah keluak*, a creamy, almost cacao like nut found in Indonesia.

There are Peranakan Indian, Peranakan Chinese, Peranakan Hokkien. Even Peranakan Eurasians. My great-great grandfather came from Melaka, but he traced his ancestry back to Xiamen (in China), and I am a Singaporean-born Peranakan. To be Peranakan means to be accepted as a local.

Peter Wee is the owner and curator of the Katong Antique House in Joo Chiat, the heart of Singapore's Peranakan cultural renaissance. His shop, which is open only by invitation, offers a unique collection of textiles, porcelain, Peranakan furniture and spices. The shop also doubles as a kind of 'living museum' of local culture.

a discreet sighting of the stain on the bride's virginity handkerchief by the bride's parents and the bridegroom's mother.

These days, Peranakan weddings tend to be compressed into a single day where all the garb, rituals, ceremonies and, of course, the feast are conducted. Thankfully, the virginity handkerchief is now banished to the history books.

FOOD

As descendants of early Chinese immigrants who married Malay women, the Straits Chinese Peranakans developed a unique cuisine that blends Chinese ingredients with Malay sauces and spices. It is commonly flavoured with shallots, chillies, *belacan* (Malay fermented prawn paste), peanuts, preserved soybeans and galangal (a ginger-like root). Thick coconut milk is used to create the sauce that flavours the prime ingredients.

In the past decade there has been a resurgence of interest in Peranakan cuisine, which was once confined to the home, and there are numerous excellent Peranakan restaurants.

Typical dishes include *otak-otak* (a delicious sausage-like blend of fish, coconut milk, chilli paste, galangal and herbs, wrapped and grilled in a banana leaf) and *ayam buah keluak* (chicken stewed with dark nuts imported from Indonesia to produce a rich sauce – the black, paste-like nut filling, eaten in small amounts with each mouthful, has an unusual, earthy flavour).

Also don't miss out on slurping the distinctive Peranakan laksa (noodles in a savoury coconut-milk gravy with fried tofu and bean sprouts).

Singapore Airlines' air stewardesses wear a modern Pierre Balmain interpretation of the traditional Nonya *kebaya*.

Languages of Singapore

The four official languages of Singapore are Malay, Tamil, Mandarin and English. Malay is the national language, adopted when Singapore was part of Malaysia, but its use is mostly restricted to the Malay community. Tamil is the main Indian language; others include Malayalam and Hindi.

Chinese dialects are still widely spoken, especially among older Chinese, with the most common being Hokkien, Teochew, Cantonese, Hainanese and Hakka. The government's long-standing campaign to promote Mandarin, the main nondialectal Chinese language, has been very successful and increasing numbers of Singaporean Chinese now speak it at home.

In 2000 the government launched a 'speak good English' campaign to improve the standard of English.

English is becoming even more widespread. After independence, the government introduced a bilingual education policy aimed at developing the vernacular languages and lessening the use of English. However, Chinese graduates found that this lessened their opportunities for higher education and presented them with greater difficulties in finding a job. English was the language of business and united the various ethnic groups, and the government eventually had to give it more priority. It officially became the first language of instruction in schools in 1987. In 2000 the government launched a 'speak good English' campaign to improve the standard of English.

All children are also taught their mother tongue at school. This helps keep the various ethnic groups in touch with their traditions, and also means that the population is effectively bilingual.

SINGLISH

You're unlikely to spend much time in Singapore without finding yourself at some point staring dumbly at someone, trying to work out what on earth they are on about. A typical sentence might – confusingly – go something like this, '*Eh*, this Sunday you going *cheong* (party) *anot*? No *ah*? Why like that? Don't be so boring *leh!*' Prepositions and pronouns are dropped, word order is flipped, phrases are clipped short and stress and cadence are unconventional, to say the least. Nominally English, the Singaporeans' unique patois contains borrowed words from Hokkien, Tamil and Malay.

There isn't a Singlish grammar as such, but there are definite characteristics, such as the long stress on the last syllable of phrases, so that the standard English 'government' becomes 'guvva-men'. Words ending in consonants are often syncopated and vowels are often distorted. A Chinese-speaking taxi driver might not immediately understand that you want to go to Perak Rd, since they know it as 'Pera Roh'.

Verb tenses tend to be nonexistent. Past, present and future are indicated instead by time indicators, so in Singlish it's 'I go tomorrow' or 'I go yesterday'.

The particle 'lah' is often tagged on to the end of sentences for emphasis, as in 'No good lah'. Requests or questions may be marked with a tag ending, since direct questioning can be rude. As a result, questions that are formed to be more polite often come across to Westerners as rude. 'Would you like a beer?' becomes 'You wan beer or not?'

You'll also hear Singaporeans addressing older people as 'uncle' and 'auntie'. They are not relatives and neither is this rude, but more a sign of respect.

For more, check out the Coxford Singlish Dictionary on the satirical website Talking Cock (www.talkingcock.com).

Slanging Like a Local

a bit the	very; as in *Wah! Your car a bit the slow one*
ah beng	every country has them: boys with spiky gelled hair, loud clothes, the latest mobile phones and a choice line in gutter phrases
ah lian	the female version of the *ah beng*: large, moussed hair, garish outfits, armed with a vicious tongue; also known as *ah huay*
aiyah!	'oh, dear!'
alamak!	exclamation of disbelief or frustration, like 'oh my God!'
ang moh	common term for Westerner (Caucasian), with derogatory undertone; literally 'red-haired monkey' in Hokkien
ayam	Malay word for chicken; adjective for something inferior or weak
blur	slow or uninformed; popular phrase is *blur like sotong*
buaya	womaniser, from the Malay for crocodile
can?	'is that OK?'
can!	'yes! That's fine.'
char bor	babe, woman
cheena	derogatory term for old-fashioned Chinese in dress or thinking
confirm	used to convey emphasis when describing something/someone, as in *He confirm blur one* (He's not very smart)
go stun	to reverse, as in *Go stun the car* (from the naval expression 'go astern')
heng	luck, good fortune (Hokkien)
hiao	vain
inggrish	English
kambing	foolish person, literally 'goat' (Malay)
kaypoh	busybody
kena	Malay word close to meaning of English word 'got', describing something that happened, as in *He kena arrested for drunk driving*
kena ketok	ripped off
kiasee	scared, literally 'afraid to die'; a coward

kiasu	literally 'afraid to lose'; selfish, pushy, always on the lookout for a bargain
kopitiam	coffeeshop
lah	generally an ending for any phrase or sentence; can translate as 'OK', but has no real meaning, added for emphasis to just about everything
lai dat	'like that'; used for emphasis, as in *I so boring lai dat* (I'm very bored)
looksee	take a look
makan	a meal; to eat
malu	embarrassed
minah	girlfriend
or not?	general suffix for questions, as in *Can or not?* (Can you or can't you?)
see first	wait and see what happens
shack	tired; often expressed as *I damn shack sial*
shiok	good, great, delicious
sotong	Malay for 'squid', used as an adjective meaning clumsy, or generally not very switched on
steady lah	well done, excellent; an expression of praise
wah!	general exclamation of surprise or distress
ya ya	boastful, as in *He always ya ya;* also expressed *He damn ya ya papaya*

Survival Guide

Transport

GETTING TO SINGAPORE

Singapore is a major air hub that services both regional and international flight routes. There are also budget airlines operating out of Singapore. Travellers will have no trouble accessing most parts of the world to and from Singapore, making it a great stopover city. You can also catch trains to Malaysia and Thailand. A slew of comfortable privately run buses also run through Malaysia up to Thailand. Book flights, tours and rail tickets online at lonelyplanet.com/bookings.

Air

Singapore's location and excellent facilities have made it a natural choice as a major Southeast Asian aviation hub, with direct services all over the world. It is also serviced by five budget airlines, which often offer extremely cheap deals if you book well in advance.

For further travel within the region, the following budget airlines operate out of Singapore. Routes change all the time, so check websites.

Air Asia (☑6307 76883; www. airasia.com)

Berjaya-Air (☑6227 3688; www.berjaya-air.com) Daily flights to Tioman and Redang islands in Malaysia.

Cebu Pacific (☑agents 6735 7155, 6737 9231, 6220 5966; www.cebupacificair.com)

Jetstar (☑800 6161 977; www.jetstar.com)

Tiger Airways (☑6808 4437; www.tigerairways.com)

Airports

Most planes will land at one of the three main terminals or the Budget Terminal at **Changi Airport** (www.changi airport.com.sg).

Regularly voted the world's best airport, Changi Airport is vast, efficient and amazingly well organised. Among its many facilities you'll find free internet, courtesy phones for local calls, foreign-exchange booths, medical centres, left luggage, hotels, showers, a gym, swimming pool and of course, plenty of shops.

For information on how to get into the city from Changi Airport, see the boxed text, p179.

Bus

Malaysia

For information on getting to Johor Bahru (JB), see p128.

If you are travelling beyond JB, the simplest option is to catch a bus straight from Singapore, though there are more options and lower fares travelling from JB.

Numerous private companies run comfortable bus services to many destinations in Malaysia including Melaka and Kuala Lumpur. The buses depart from various points in Singapore. If you're stumped, head to the **Golden Mile Complex** (off Map p204; Beach Rd) where there are many bus agencies selling tickets. You can also book online at www.busonlineticket.com.

Check latest prices and book tickets with these companies:

Aeroline (☑6358 8800; www.aeroline.com.sg; 1 Maritime Square, 02-52 Harbourfront Centre) Coaches to Kuala Lumpur and Penang departing from Harbourfront.

First Coach (☑6822 2111; www.firstcoach.com.my; 238 Thompson Rd, 02-33 Novena Square; Ⓜ Novena) Daily buses to Kuala Lumpur departing from Novena Square.

Grassland Express (☑6293 1166; www.grassland.com.sg; 5001 Beach Rd, 01-26 Golden Mile Complex) Daily buses to Kuala Lumpur, Penang, Meleka, Perak and numerous other destinations.

Transnasional Bus Service (Map p204; ☑6294 7035; www. transnasional.com.my; Lavender Street Bus Terminal, cnr Lavender St & Kallang Bahru) Daily buses to numerous destination all departing from Lavender Street Bus Terminal.

Transtar Travel (☑6299 9009; www.transtar.travel; 5001 Beach Rd, 01-15 Golden Mile Complex) Luxury coaches to Kuala Lumpur, Genting, Ipoh and Penang.

Thailand

The main terminal for buses to and from Thailand is at the **Golden Mile Complex** (off Map p204; Beach Rd). Among the travel agents there specialising in buses and tours to Thailand are **Grassland Express** (☑6293 1166; www.grassland.com.sg), with buses to Hat Yai, and **Phya Travel** (☑6294 5415; www.phyatravel.com) and **Kwang Chow Travel** (☑6293 8977), both with bus services to Hat Yai and beyond. Most buses leave around 6pm and travel overnight.

Sea

There are several main ferry terminals with services to Malaysia and Indonesia. For information about ferries to the Southern Singapore islands, see p122.

There are several main ferry terminals:

Changi Point Ferry Terminal (Map p222; ☑6546 8518; ☑2, 29, 59, 109) Located 200m north of the bus terminal.

Harbourfront Ferry Terminal (Map p218; www.singaporecruise.com; ☑6513 2200; Ⓜ HarbourFront)

Tanah Merah Ferry Terminal (Map p222; www.singaporecruise.com; ☑6513 2200; Ⓜ Tanah Merah, then ☑35)

Indonesia

Direct ferries run between Singapore and the Riau Archipelago islands of Pulau Batam and Pulau Bintan. The ferries are modern, fast and air-conditioned.

These are the main ferry operators:

BatamFast (☑6270 0311; www.batamfast.com) Ferries to Batam Centre, Sekupang, and Waterfront City depart from Har-

bourfront Ferry Terminal. Ferries to Nongsapura depart from the Tanah Merah Ferry Terminal.

Berlian Ferries (☑6546 8830) Ferries to Pulau Batam depart from Harbourfront Ferry Terminal.

Bintan Resort Ferries (☑6542 4369; www.brf.com.sg) Ferries to Bandar Bintan Telani depart from Tanah Merah Ferry Terminal.

Indo Falcon (☑6275 7393; www.indofalcon.com.sg) Ferries to Pulau Batam and Tanjung Pinang in Bintan depart from Harbourfront Ferry Terminal.

Penguin Ferries (☑6271 4866; www.penguin.com.sg) Ferries to Batam Centre, Sekupang, and Tanjung Balai depart from Harbourfront Ferry Terminal. Ferries to Tanjung Pinang depart from the Tanah Merah Ferry Terminal.

GETTING INTO TOWN FROM THE AIRPORT

Bus
Public bus 36 runs from terminals 1, 2 and 3 to Orchard Rd and the Colonial District ($1.80, one hour). Buses leave roughly every 15 minutes, the first departing at 6.09am and the last just after midnight.

Faster and more convenient are the airport shuttle buses (adult/child $9/6, 20 to 40 minutes) that leave from all main terminal arrival halls and drop passengers at any hotel, except for those on Sentosa and in Changi Village. They leave from Terminals 1 and 2 and the Budget Terminal (6.15pm to midnight, every 15 minutes; all other times every 30 minutes) and Terminal 3 (6am to 10am and 6pm to 2am, every 15 min; all other times every 30 minutes). Booking desks are in the arrival halls.

Train
The Mass Rapid Transit (MRT) is the best low-cost way to get into town. The station is located below Terminals 2 and 3, the fare to Orchard Rd is adult/child $3/$1.60 (including a $1 refundable deposit) and the journey takes around 45 minutes. You have to change trains at Tanah Merah (just cross the platform). The first train leaves at 5.30am and the last goes at 11.18pm.

Taxi
Taxi lines at Changi are fast-moving and efficient. Even at the Budget Terminal you rarely have to wait long. The fare structure is complicated, but count on spending anywhere between $18 and $35 into the city centre, depending on the time of travel. The most expensive times are between 5pm and 6am, when a whole raft of surcharges kick in. A limousine transfer service operates 24 hours a day and costs a flat $45 to anywhere on the island. Enquire at the ground transport desk at the airport.

Train

Malaysia & Thailand

Singapore is the southern terminus for the Malaysian railway system, **Keretapi Tanah Malayu** (KTM; www.ktmb.com.my). Malaysia has two main rail lines: the primary line going from Singapore to Kuala Lumpur, Butterworth, Alor Setar and then into Hat Yai, Thailand; and a second line branching off at Gemas and going right up through the centre of the country to Tumpat, near Kota Bharu on the east coast.

The crumbling art deco railway station in Singapore was closed for private redevelopment in 2011. The KTM train to Malaysia now runs out of the **Woodlands Train Checkpoint** (11 Woodlands Crossing; ☐170, Causeway Link from Queen St).

Three express trains depart every day to Kuala Lumpur (1st/2nd/3rd class $68/34/19) roughly around 8am, 1pm and 10.30pm, and take between seven and nine hours; check the website for connecting train timings. You can book tickets either at the station or via the KTM website (www.ktmb.com.my).

The luxurious **Eastern & Oriental Express** (☑6395 0678; www.orient-express.com) runs between Singapore and Bangkok, then onward to Chiang Mai and Nong Khai (for Laos). The sumptuous antique train takes 42 hours to do the 1943km journey from Singapore to Bangkok. Don your linen suit, sip a gin and tonic, and dig deep for the fare: from $3500 per person in a double compartment to $7200 in the presidential suite.

GETTING AROUND

Having invested vast sums in its public transport infrastructure, Singapore is undoubtedly the easiest city in Asia to get around. The government has built, and continues to extend, its Mass Rapid Transit (MRT) rail system and its bus network.

The *TransitLink Guide* ($2.50 from MRT ticket offices) is being updated at time of writing. It lists all bus and MRT routes and has maps showing the surrounding areas for all MRT stations. For online bus information, including a searchable bus guide and the useful IRIS service (which tells you in real time when your next bus will arrive), see www.sbstransit.com.sg. For train information, see www.smrt.com.sg. There's also a consolidated website at www.publictransport.sg.

Download the 'SBS Transit Iris' iPhone app for bus routes and trackable timings.

Mass Rapid Transit

The efficient MRT subway system is the easiest, quickest and most comfortable way to get around Singapore. The system operates from 5.30am to midnight, with trains at peak times running every three minutes, and off-peak every four to six minutes. For a map of the system, see the pull-out map at the back of this book.

In the inner city, the MRT runs underground, emerging overground out towards the suburban housing estates. It consists of four lines: North–South, North–East and East–West, and the Circle Line. More lines are set to open between now and 2020! MRT map and trip planner available online: www.smrt.com.sg.

Fares & Fare Cards

Single-trip tickets cost from $1 to $2.10 (plus a $1 refundable deposit), but if you're using the MRT a lot it can become a hassle buying and refunding tickets for every journey. A lot more convenient is the EZ-link card (see boxed text, p180). Alternatively, a **Singapore Tourist Pass** (www.thesingaporetouristpass.com) offers unlimited train and bus travel ($8 plus a $10 refundable deposit) for one day.

Bus

Singapore's extensive bus service is clean, efficient and regular, reaching every corner of the island. The two main operators are **SBS Transit** (☑1800 287 2727; www.sbstransit.com.sg) and **SMRT** (www.smrtbuses.com.sg). Both offer similar service. For information and routes, check the websites.

Bus fares range from $1 to $2.10 (less with an EZ-Link card). When you board the bus, drop the exact money

---

THE EZ-LINK AROUND TOWN

If you're staying in Singapore for longer than a week, the easiest way to pay for travel on public transport is via the EZ-Link card. You'll save up to 30% on fares by purchasing an EZ-Link card from an MRT station. This card allows you to travel by train and bus by swiping it over sensors as you enter and leave a station or bus. Cards cost $15: $10 worth of travel, and a $5 nonrefundable charge. You can top-up cards at ATM-style machines at stations. Fares using an EZ-Link card are 20% less than using cash.

The EZ-Link also gives you huge discounts on transfer trips. For example, a short bus ride proceeding an MRT journey only costs a few cents. No, that's not a typo.

CLIMATE CHANGE & TRAVEL

Every form of transport that relies on carbon-based fuel generates CO_2, the main cause of human-induced climate change. Modern travel is dependent on aeroplanes, which might use less fuel per kilometre per person than most cars but travel much greater distances. The altitude at which aircraft emit gases (including CO_2) and particles also contributes to their climate change impact. Many websites offer 'carbon calculators' that allow people to estimate the carbon emissions generated by their journey and, for those who wish to do so, to offset the impact of the greenhouse gases emitted with contributions to portfolios of climate-friendly initiatives throughout the world. Lonely Planet offsets the carbon footprint of all staff and author travel.

into the fare box (no change is given), or tap your EZ-Link card or Tourist Pass on the reader as you board, then again when you get off.

Train operator **SMRT** (www.smrtbuses.com.sg) also runs seven late-night weekend bus services between the city and various suburbs from 11.30pm to 4.30am. See the website for route details.

Tourist Buses

Singapore Airlines runs the **SIA Hop-On** (☑9457 2896; www.siahopon.com) tourist bus, traversing the main tourist arteries every 30 minutes daily, starting at Raffles Blvd at 9am, with the last bus leaving at 7.35pm and arriving back at 8.35pm. Tickets cost $12/6 per adult/child, or $6/3 with a Singapore Airlines or Silk Air boarding pass or ticket. Buy tickets from the driver.

There's also a Sentosa Hop-On bus running between Orchard Rd and Sentosa Island. The first bus leaves the Marriott Hotel for Sentosa at 9am and the last at 8pm. The service is free for SIA Hop-On ticket holders. Others pay $8/5 return/one way. Check website for timetable and pick-up locations.

Nutty and garish, the **City Hippo** (☑6228 6877; www.ducktours.com.sg) offers a confusing array of tour options round all the major sites Two-day tickets including a river cruise costs adult/child $33/17. Tours boasts live commentary and an open top deck.

Taxi

Poor old Singapore has endless problems with its taxi system. Despite an interminable cycle of debate, reform, complaint and adjustment, finding a taxi in the city at certain times (during peak hours, at night, or when it's raining) is harder than it should be. The fare system is also hugely complicated, but thankfully it's all metered, so there's no tedious haggling over fares. The basic flagfall is $2.80 to $3.20, then $0.20 for every 385m. Credit card payments incur a 10% surcharge.

You can flag down a taxi any time, but in the city centre taxis are not allowed to stop anywhere except at designated taxi stands.

If you need to ring for a taxi, these are the taxi companies:

Comfort and CityCab (☑6552 1111)

Premier Taxis (☑6363 6888)

SMRT Taxis (☑6555 8888) There are various surcharges to note:

➡ 50% of the metered fare from midnight to 6am.

➡ 35% peak-hour charges between 7am and 9am, and 5pm and 8pm.

➡ $3.50 for telephone bookings; for advance bookings you'll pay $5.20. $3 on all trips from the CBD between 5pm and midnight, Monday to Saturday. You may also have to pay another

surcharge if you take the taxi into the CBD during restricted hours (see p182).

➡ $5 surcharge from 5pm to midnight Friday to Sunday; $3 all other times for journeys from the airport.
Confused? We are too. Just follow the meter and ask for a receipt to check charges.

Bicycle

Singapore's roads are not for the faint-hearted. The roads are not only furiously hot, but also populated by fast, aggressive drivers who tend to be unsympathetic to the needs of cyclists. Fortunately there's a large network of parks and park connectors, and a few excellent dedicated mountain-biking areas at Bukit Timah Nature Reserve, Tampines and Pulau Ubin.

Other excellent places for cycling include East Coast Park, Sentosa, Pasir Ris Park and the new route linking Mt Faber Park, Telok Blangah Hill Park and Kent Ridge Park.

If you have your own bike, be aware that it's not allowed on public transport unless it's a fold-up bike. You can take fold-up bikes on trains and buses during these hours: Monday to Friday 9.30am-4pm & 8pm onwards; all-day Saturday and Sunday and public holidays. Note that only ONE fold-up bike is allowed on buses at all time, so you might as well ride if you have to.

Hire

Rent bikes at Robertson Quay from **Vanguard Designs** (☑6835 7228; www.vanguard-designs.com; 7 Rodyk St; per day $50; ☺1pm-7.30pm Mon, Wed-Fri, 10am-8pm Sat & Sun). Bikes come with a cycling map.

Bikes can also be rented at several places along East Coast Parkway, on Sentosa Island and Pulau Ubin, with prices starting from $2 on Pulau Ubin and from $5 elsewhere.

Boat

You can take a bumboat (motorised sampan) tour up the Singapore River from points everywhere from the Merlion to Boat Quay, Clarke Quay and Robertson Quay. See p51.

Visit the islands around Singapore from the Marina South Pier (see p122). There are regular ferry services from Changi Point Ferry Terminal to Pulau Ubin ($2) and Pengerang in Malaysia. To get there, take bus 2 from Tanah Merah MRT.

Trishaws

Trishaws peaked just after WWII when motorised transport was practically nonexistent and trishaw drivers could make a tidy income. Today there are only around 250 trishaws left in Singapore, mainly plying the tourist routes. Trishaws have banded together and are now managed in a queue-system by **Trishaw Uncle** (Map p204; ☑9012 1233; Queen St btwn Fu Lu Shou Complex & Albert Centre Market; rides from $39).

You can also find freelance trishaw riders outside Raffles Hotel (Map p208) and outside the Chinatown Complex (Map p201). Always

agree on the fare beforehand: we were quoted $40 for half an hour, but you can haggle a little.

Car & Motorcycle

Singaporeans drive on the left-hand side of the road and it is compulsory to wear seat belts in the front and back of the car. The *Mighty Minds Singapore Street Directory* ($12.90) is invaluable.

Driving

If you plan on driving in Singapore, bring your current home driver's licence and an international driving permit issued by a motoring association in your country.

The roads themselves are immaculate, but don't let that lull you into a false sense of security – nowhere is the infamous *kiasu* (Hokkien for 'afraid to lose') Singaporean character more evident than on the roads. Aggressive driving is common, speeding and tailgating endemic, use of signals rare, and wild lane-changing universal.

In short, we don't recommend driving in Singapore, but if you do, practise extreme defensive driving, and have your road rage under control!

As for motorcycles, they are held in very low esteem (we speak from experience here). Some drivers display almost no regard for bike safety. Be alert when riding.

Hire

If you want a car for local driving only, it's worth checking smaller operators, whose rates are often cheaper than the big global rental firms. If you're going into Malaysia, you're better off renting in Johor Bahru, where the rates are significantly lower (besides, Malaysian police are renowned for targeting Singapore licence plates).

Rates start from around $60 a day. Special deals may be available, especially for longer-term rental. There are hire booths at Singapore Changi Airport as well as in the city. These are some of the major companies:

Avis (☑6737 1668; www.avis.com.sg; 392 Havelock Rd, 01-07 Waterfront Plaza)

Express Car (☑6842 4992; www.expresscar.com.sg; 1 Sims Lane)

Hawk (☑6469 4468; www.hawkrentacar.com.sg; 32A Hillview Terrace)

Hertz Rent-a-Car (☑6734 4646; www.hertz.com; Singapore Changi Airport Terminal 2 & 3)

Restricted Zone & Car Parking

From 7.30am to 7pm weekdays, as well as from 10.15am through to 2pm Saturday, the area comprising the CBD, Chinatown and Orchard Rd is considered a restricted zone. Cars are free to enter but they must pay a toll. Vehicles are automatically tracked by sensors on overhead gantries, so cars must be fitted with an in-vehicle unit, into which drivers must insert a cashcard (available at petrol stations and 7-Elevens). The toll is extracted from the card. The same system is also in operation on certain expressways. Rental cars are subject to the same rules.

Parking in the city centre is expensive, but relatively easy to find – almost every major mall has a car park. Outdoor car parks and street parking spaces are usually operated by the government – you can buy booklets of parking coupons, which must be displayed in the window, from post offices and convenience stores.

Directory A-Z

Business Hours

Opening hours throughout the book are only listed if they differ to those listed here.

Banks Monday to Friday 9.30am to 4.30pm, some branches close at 6pm; Saturday 9.30am to 11.30am.

Government and Post Offices Monday to Friday between 8am and 9.30am to 4pm and 6pm; Saturday between 8am and 9.30am to 11.30am and 1pm.

Restaurants Top restaurants generally open between 12pm to 2pm for lunch and 6pm till 10pm for dinner. Casual restaurants and food courts are open all day.

Shops 10am to 6pm, larger shops and department stores open till 9.30pm or 10pm. Some smaller shops in Chinatown and Arab St close on Sunday. It's busiest in Little India on Sundays.

Customs Regulations

➡ You are not allowed to bring tobacco in unless you pay duty. You will be slapped with a hefty fine if you fail to declare and pay.

➡ You are permitted 1L of wine, beer or spirits duty-free (only if you've been out of Singapore for more than 48 hours and to anywhere else but Malaysia).

➡ It's illegal to bring any of these with you: chewing gum, fire crackers, obscene or seditious material, gun-shaped cigarette lighters, endangered species or their by-products, and pirated recordings and publications.

Discount Cards

If you arrived via Singapore Airlines or Silk Air, you can get discounts at shops, restaurants and attractions by presenting your boarding pass. See www.singaporeair.com/boardingpass for information.

Electricity

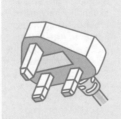

230V/50Hz

Emergency

Useful emergency numbers:
Ambulance (☎995)
Fire (☎995)
Police (☎999)

Gay & Lesbian Travellers

Sex between males is illegal in Singapore, carrying a minimum sentence of 10 years. In reality, nobody is ever likely to be prosecuted, but the ban remains as a symbol of the government's belief that the country is not ready for the open acceptance of 'alternative lifestyles'.

Despite that, there are lots of gay and lesbian bars. A good place to start looking for information is on the websites of **Utopia** (www.utopia-asia.com) or **Fridae** (www.fridae.com), both of which provide excellent coverage of venues and events across Asia.

Singaporeans are fairly conservative about public affection, though it's more common to see displays of familiarity among lesbian couples these days. A gay male couple doing the same would definitely draw negative attention.

Health

Hygiene in Singapore is strictly observed and the tap water is safe to drink. However, hepatitis A does ocassionally occur. You only need vaccinations if you come from a yellow-fever area. Singapore is not a malarial zone but dengue fever is an increasing concern.

Prickly Heat

This is an itchy rash caused by excessive perspiration trapped under the skin. It usually strikes people who have just arrived in a hot climate. Keep cool, bathe often, dry the skin and use a mild talcum or prickly heat powder, or resort to airconditioning.

Dengue Fever

Singapore has suffered a sharp rise in cases of this nasty mosquito-borne disease in recent years. There is no vaccine so avoid mosquito bites. The dengue-carrying mosquito bites day and night, so use insect-avoidance measures at all times. Symptoms inlcude high fever, severe headache and body ache. Some people develop a rash and diarrhoea. There is no specific treatment – just rest and paracetamol. Do not take aspirin. See a doctor to be diagnosed and monitored.

Internet Access

Every top hotel has internet access and will help get you set up if you bring your own laptop. The backpacker hostels all offer free internet access and wi-fi.

SingTel (www.singtel.com. sg), **StarHub** (www.starhub. com) and **M1** (www.m1.com) are local providers of broadband internet via USB modem dongles. Bring your own or buy one from them. You can get prepaid data SIM cards if you have your own dongle.

Internet cafes come and go all the time. There are various ones around the Chinatown and Little India area.

Legal Matters

Singapore's reputation for harsh laws is not undeserved: don't expect any special treatment for being a foreigner. Despite the surprisingly low-key police presence on the street, they appear pretty fast when something happens. Police have broad powers and you would be unwise to refuse any requests they make of you. If you are arrested, you will be entitled to legal counsel and contact with your embassy.

Don't even think about importing or exporting drugs. At best, you'll get long jail terms, at worse, you'll get the death penalty.

Medical Services

Singapore's medical institutions are first-rate and generally cheaper than private healthcare in the West.

WIRELESS@ SG: FREE WI-FI ACCESS

Singapore has an ever-expanding network of around 1000 wireless hotspots – and most cafes and pubs operate them. The Wireless@ SG hotspots are currently free to access till 30 March 2013. A list of hotspots can be found by following the Wireless@SG link at www.infocomm123.sg. There's a catch though: you need a local mobile phone number to sign-up for an account. Grab a SIM card from a convenience store or mobile-phone store (you will need to show your passport in order to buy one).

But needless to say, travel insurance cover is advisable. Check with insurance providers what treatments and procedures are covered before you leave home. Note that local GPs also dispense medication on premises, saving you a trip to the pharmacy.

Clinics

Your hotel or hostel should be able to direct you to a local GP: there are plenty around.

Raffles Medical Clinic (☑6311 1111; www.raffles hospital.com; 585 North Bridge Rd; ☺24hr; Ⓜ Bugis) A walk-in clinic at the Raffles Hospital.

Singapore General Hospital Accident & Emergency Department (☑6321 4311; ☺24hr; Ⓜ Outram Park) Located in Block 1 of this big compound.

Emergency Rooms

The following operate 24-hour emergency rooms:

Gleneagles Hospital (☑6735 5000; 6A Napier Rd)

Mount Elizabeth Hospital (☑6735 5000; 3 Mt Elizabeth Rd)

Raffles Hospital (☑6311 1111; 585 North Bridge Rd)

Singapore General Hospital (☑6321 4311; Level 2, Block 1, Outram Rd)

Money

The country's unit of currency is the Singapore dollar, locally referred to as the 'singdollar', which is made up of 100 cents. Singapore uses 5¢, 10¢, 20¢, 50¢ and $1 coins, while notes come in denominations of $2, $5, $10, $50, $100, $500 and $1000. The Singapore dollar is a highly stable and freely convertible currency.

ATMs

Cirrus-enabled machines widely available at all malls.

Changing Money

Banks change money, but virtually nobody uses them for currency conversion because the rates are better at the moneychangers dotted all over the city. These tiny stalls can be found in just about every shopping centre (though not necessarily in the more modern malls). Rates can be haggled a little if you're changing amounts of $500 or more.

Credit Cards

Widely accepted, except at local hawkers and food courts. Note that smaller stores might charge you an extra 2% to 3% for credit-card payments.

Post

Postal delivery in Singapore is very efficient. Call ☎1605 to find the nearest branch or check www.singpost.com.sg.

Letters addressed to Poste Restante are held at the **Singapore Post Centre** (Map p214; ☎6741 8857; 10 Eunos Rd; Ⓜ Paya Lebar). It's open on Sunday, as is the post office on **Kilinney Rd** (Map p212; ☎6734 7899; 1 Killiney Rd; Ⓜ Somerset). There's another branch on **Orchard Rd** (Map p212; B2-62 ION Orchard, 2 Orchard Turn; Ⓜ Orchard). Terminal 2 at Changi Airport has two branches.

Public Holidays

Listed are public holidays in Singapore. For those days not based on the Western calendar, the months they are likely to fall in are provided. The only holiday that has a major effect on the city is Chinese New Year, when virtually all shops shut down for two days.

New Year's Day 1 January

Chinese New Year Three days in January/February

Good Friday April

PRACTICALITIES

➡ English dailies in Singapore include the broadsheet *Straits Times* (which includes the *Sunday Times*), the *Business Times*, and the afternoon tabloid *New Paper*.

➡ Pornographic publications are strictly prohibited, but toned-down local editions of *Cosmopolitan* and lads' magazines like *FHM* and *Maxim* are allowed.

➡ Singapore uses the metric system for weights and measures. Weights are in grams and kilograms and volume in millilitres and litres.

Labour Day 1 May

Vesak Day May

National Day 9 August

Hari Raya Puasa October/ November

Deepavali October

Christmas Day 25 December

Hari Raya Haji December/ January

Taxes & Refunds

As a visitor you are entitled to claim a refund of the 7% Goods & Services Tax on your purchases, provided you meet certain conditions (see p35).

Telephone

Country code (☎65)

Directory information (☎100)

Flight information (☎1800 542 4422) Voice activated.

STB Touristline (☎1800 736 2000)

There are no area codes within Singapore; telephone numbers are eight digits unless you are calling toll-free (☎1800).

You can make local and international calls from public phone booths. Most phone booths take phonecards.

Singapore also has credit-card phones that can be used by running your card through the slot.

Calls to Malaysia (from Singapore) are considered to be STD (trunk or long-distance) calls. Dial the access code ☎020, followed by the area code of the town in Malaysia that you wish to call (minus the leading zero) and then your party's number. Thus, for a call to ☎346 7890 in Kuala Lumpur (area code ☎03) you would dial ☎02-3-346 7890. Call ☎109 for assistance with Malaysian area codes.

Mobile Phones

In Singapore, mobile phone numbers start with ☎9 or 8.

You can buy a local SIM card for around $18 (including credit) from post offices, convenience stores and local telco stores – by law you must show your passport to get one. The main local telcos are:

SingTel (www.singtel.com.sg)

StarHub (www.starhub.com)

M1 (www.m1.com)

Phonecards

Phonecards are particularly popular among Singapore's migrant workers – the domestic maids and construction workers that keep the city ticking over – so there are plenty on sale. There's a small thriving phonecard stall outside the Centrepoint shopping centre on Orchard Rd, and plenty of retailers around Little India, but check which countries they service before you buy.

Time

Singapore is eight hours ahead of GMT/UTC (London), two hours behind Australian Eastern Standard Time (Sydney and Melbourne), 13 hours ahead of American Eastern Standard Time (New York) and 16 hours ahead of American Pacific Standard Time (San Francisco and Los Angeles). So, when it is noon in Singapore, it is 8pm in Los Angeles and 11pm in New York the previous day, 4am in London and 2pm in Sydney.

Tourist Information

Before your trip, a good place to check for information is the website of the **Singapore Tourism Board** (www.visitsingapore.com).

In Singapore, there are several tourism centres offering a wide range of services, including tour bookings and event ticketing, plus a couple of electronic information kiosks.

Singapore Visitors@Orchard Information Centre (Map p212; ☑1800 736 2000; cnr Orchard & Cairnhill Rds; ⊗9.30am-10.30pm; MSomerset)

Singapore Visitors@ION Orchard (Map p212; Lvl 1 ION Orchard, 2 Orchard Turn; ⊗10am-10pm; MOrchard)

InnCrowd (Map 204; ☑6296 4280; 73 Dunlop St; ⊗10am-10pm; MLittle India) Very helpful staff at this backpackers' hostel, even if you don't stay there.

Travellers with Disabilities

Facilities for wheelchairs used to be nonexistent in Singapore, but in recent years a large government campaign has seen ramps, lifts and other facilities progressively installed around the island. The pavements in the city are nearly all immaculate, MRT stations all have lifts and there some buses and taxis equipped with wheelchair-friendly equipment.

The **Disabled Persons Association of Singapore** (www.dpa.org.sg) has information on accessibility in Singapore.

Visas

Citizens of most countries are granted 30-day entry on arrival by air or overland (though the latter may get 14-day entry), though it's not uncommon to be granted up to a 90-day entry. Citizens of India, Myanmar, China, the Commonwealth of Independent States and most Middle Eastern countries must obtain a visa before arriving in Singapore. Visa extensions can be applied for at the **Immigration & Checkpoints Authority** (☑6391 6100; www.ica.gov.sg; 10 Kallang Rd; MLavender).

Menu Decoder

Chinese

ah balling – glutinous rice balls filled with a sweet paste of peanut, black sesame or red bean and usually served in a peanut- or ginger-flavoured soup

bak chang – local rice dumpling filled with savoury or sweet meat and wrapped in leaves

bak chor mee – noodles with pork, meatballs and fried scallops

bak choy – variety of Chinese cabbage that grows like celery, with long white stalks and dark-green leaves

bak kutteh – local pork rib soup with hints of garlic and Chinese five spice

char kway teow – Hokkien dish of broad noodles, clams and eggs fried in chilli and black-bean sauce

char siew – sweet roast-pork fillet

cheng ting – dessert consisting of a bowl of sugar syrup with pieces of herbal jelly, barley and dates

choi sum – popular Chinese green vegetable, served steamed with oyster sauce

congee – Chinese porridge

Hainanese chicken rice – chicken dish served with spring onions and ginger dressing accompanied by soup, rice and chilli sauce; a local speciality

hoisin sauce – thick seasoning sauce made from soya beans, red beans, sugar, vinegar, salt, garlic, sesame, chillies and spices; sweet-spicy and tangy in flavour

kang kong – water convolvulus, a thick-stemmed type of spinach

kway chap – pig intestines cooked in soy sauce; served with flat rice noodles

kway teow – broad rice noodles

lor mee – local dish of noodles served with slices of meat, eggs and a dash of vinegar in a dark-brown sauce

mee pok – flat noodles made with egg and wheat

spring roll – vegetables, peanuts, egg and bean sprouts rolled up inside a thin pancake and fried

won ton – dumpling filled with spiced minced pork

won ton mee – soup dish with shredded chicken or braised beef

yu char kueh – deep-fried dough; eaten with congee

yu tiao – deep-fried pastry eaten for breakfast or as a dessert

yusheng – salad of raw fish, grated vegetables, candied melon and lime, pickled ginger, sesame seeds, jellyfish and peanuts tossed in sweet dressing; eaten at Chinese New Year

Indian

achar – vegetable pickle

fish-head curry – red snapper head in curry sauce; a famous Singapore-Indian dish

gulab jamun – fried milk balls in sugar syrup

idli – steamed rice cake served with thin chutneys

keema – spicy minced meat

kofta – minced meat or vegetable ball

korma – mild curry with yoghurt sauce

lassi – yoghurt-based drink, either sweet or salted

mulligatawny – spicy beef soup

pakora – vegetable fritter

paratha – flat bread made with ghee and cooked on a hotplate; also called *roti prata*

pilau – rice fried in ghee and mixed with nuts, then cooked in stock

raita – side dish of cucumber, yoghurt and mint, used to cool the palate

rasam – spicy soup

roti john – fried roti with chilli

saag – spicy chopped-spinach side dish

sambar – fiery mixture of vegetables, lentils and split peas

samosa – fried pastry triangle stuffed with spiced vegetables or meat

soup tulang – meaty bones in a rich, spicy, blood-red tomato gravy

tikka – small pieces of meat and fish served off the bone and marinated in yoghurt before baking

vadai – fried, spicy lentil patty, served with a savoury lentil sauce or yoghurt

Malay & Indonesian

ais kacang – similar to *cendol* but made with evaporated milk instead of coconut milk; it is also spelt 'ice kacang'

attap – sweet gelatinous fruit of the attap palm

belacan – fermented prawn paste used as a condiment

belacan kang kong – green vegetables stir-fried in prawn paste

cendol – local dessert made from a cone of ice shavings filled with red beans, *attap* and jelly, then topped with coloured syrups, brown-sugar syrup and coconut milk

gado gado – cold dish of bean sprouts, potatoes, long beans, *tempeh*, bean curd, rice cakes and prawn crackers, topped with a spicy peanut sauce

itek manis – duck simmered in ginger and black-bean sauce

itek tim – a classic soup of simmered duck, tomatoes, green peppers, salted vegetables and preserved sour plums

kari ayam – curried chicken

kaya – jam made from coconut and egg, served on toast

kecap – soy sauce, pronounced 'ketchup' (we got the word from them)

kepala ikan – fish head, usually in a curry or grilled

kueh mueh – Malay cakes

lontong – rice cakes in a spicy coconut-milk gravy topped with grated coconut and sometimes bean curd and egg

mee siam – white thin noodles in a sourish and sweet gravy made with tamarind

mee soto – noodle soup with shredded chicken

nasi biryani – saffron rice flavoured with spices and garnished with cashew nuts, almonds and raisins

nasi minyak – spicy rice

pulut kuning – sticky saffron rice

o-chien – oyster omelette

rojak – salad made from cucumber, pineapple, yam bean, star fruit, green mango and guava, with a dressing of shrimp paste, chillies, palm sugar and fresh lime juice

sambal – sauce of fried chilli, onions and prawn paste

soto ayam – spicy chicken soup with vegetables, including potatoes

tempeh – preserved soya beans, deep-fried

Peranakan

ayam buah keluak – chicken in a rich, spicy sauce served with buah keluak (a unusually flavoured black paste-like nut)

carrot cake – omelette-like dish made from radishes, egg, garlic and chilli; also known as *chye tow kway*

kueh pie ti – deep-fried flour cup filled with prawn, chilli sauce and steamed turnip

otak – spicy fish paste cooked in banana leaves; a classic Peranakan snack, also called *otak-otak*

papaya titek – type of curry stew

popiah – similar to a spring roll, but not fried

satay bee hoon – peanut sauce-flavoured noodles

shui kueh – steamed radish cakes with fried preserved-radish topping

Behind the Scenes

SEND US YOUR FEEDBACK

We love to hear from travellers – your comments keep us on our toes and help make our books better. Our well-travelled team reads every word on what you loved or loathed about this book. Although we cannot reply individually to postal submissions, we always guarantee that your feedback goes straight to the appropriate authors, in time for the next edition. Each person who sends us information is thanked in the next edition – and the most useful submissions are rewarded with a free book.

Visit **lonelyplanet.com/contact** to submit your updates and suggestions or to ask for help. Our award-winning website also features inspirational travel stories, news and discussions.

Note: We may edit, reproduce and incorporate your comments in Lonely Planet products such as guidebooks, websites and digital products, so let us know if you don't want your comments reproduced or your name acknowledged. For a copy of our privacy policy visit lonelyplanet.com/privacy.

OUR READERS

Many thanks to the travellers who used the last edition and wrote to us with helpful hints, useful advice and interesting anecdotes:

Bazga Ali, Samuel Bilbie, Elaine Bleiberg, Nikki Buran, Ashley Cooper, Matt Evans, Sabrina Giambartolomei, Eva Hofmann, Frank Khoo, Etienne Le Jeune, Bronya Monro-Stevens, Nathan Pan, Haus Patterson, Karen Ramsay, Stephan Schaller, Bertram Schneider, Ann Shield, Bob Simon, Vicky Smith, Juri Strante, Chris Tandy, Lim Teng Aun, Jörg Tredup, Mark Worsnop

AUTHOR THANKS

Shawn Low

As always thanks to the Commissioning Editors who worked on this: Ilaria for believing that I'm the best person for the book and Stephanie for briefing. Thanks to the Lonely Planet crew who are working on this: editors, cartographers, Managing Editors, Layout Designers etc. I've been behind the scenes and know how hard you all work. Big props and cheers to co-author Daniel. It was good hanging out. To everyone else I might have forgotten: apologies in advance. Will buy you a round of Tiger if you remind me next time our paths cross. This book will always bear bittersweet memories...

Daniel McCrohan

Huge thanks to my friends in Singapore – Char-Maine Tan, Mick Lee, Adi Thayi, Sean Collins and Ma Huaqing – for great company and superb tips. Special thanks to Kenny Png for his music expertise, to Shalu Asnani for revealing Singapore's culinary delights and to Michelle Tan for being a fab travel buddy. A raised glass of Tiger to my colleague and friend Shawn Low; cheers, mate. And to Taotao, Dudu and Yoyo, and all my family in Europe, thank you for your patience and love.

ACKNOWLEDGMENTS

Climate map data adapted from Peel MC, Finlayson BL & McMahon TA (2007) 'Updated World Map of the Köppen-Geiger Climate Classification', *Hydrology and Earth System Sciences*, 11, 163344

Cover photograph: Merlion fountain, at the Merlion Park, Ausili Tommaso/4Corners.

Many of the images in this guide are available for licensing from Lonely Planet Images: www.lonelyplanetimages.com.

THIS BOOK

This 9th edition of *Singapore* was researched and written by Shawn Low and Daniel McCrohan. The 8th edition was researched and written by Mat Oakley and Joshua Samuel Brown. The 7th edition was written by Mat Oakley. This book was commissioned in Lonely Planet's Melbourne office, and produced by the following:
Commissioning Editors Stefanie Di Trocchio, Ilaria Walker and Kalya Ryan

Coordinating Editors Holly Alexander, Jessica Crouch
Coordinating Cartographer Alex Leung
Coordinating Layout Designer Virginia Moreno
Managing Editor Bruce Evans
Senior Editors Susan Paterson, Angela Tinson
Managing Cartographers David Connolly, Adrian Persoglia
Managing Layout Designer Jane Hart
Assisting Editor Rebecca Chau

Assisting Cartographer Katalin Dadi-Racz
Cover Research Naomi Parker
Internal Image Research Aude Vauconsant
Thanks to Janine Eberle, Ryan Evans, Liz Heynes, Laura Jane, David Kemp, Piers Pickard, Trent Paton, Averil Robertson, Lachlan Ross, Michael Ruff, Julie Sheridan, Laura Stansfeld, John Taufa, Gerard Walker, Clifton Wilkinson, Jessica Rose, Paul Iacono

Index

See also separate subindexes for:

✗ EATING P196

● DRINKING & NIGHTLIFE P197

☆ ENTERTAINMENT P197

🔒 SHOPPING P197

🏃 ACTIVITIES P198

🛏 SLEEPING P198

🍷 DRINKING & NIGHTLIFE

☆ ENTERTAINMENT

🛍 SHOPPING

Sights p000
Map Pages **p000**
Photo Pages **p000**

🤸 ACTIVITIES

🛏 SLEEPING

Singapore Maps

Map Legend

Sights
- Beach
- Buddhist
- Castle
- Christian
- Hindu
- Islamic
- Jewish
- Monument
- Museum/Gallery
- Ruin
- Winery/Vineyard
- Zoo
- Other Sight

Eating
- Eating

Drinking & Nightlife
- Drinking & Nightlife
- Cafe

Entertainment
- Entertainment

Shopping
- Shopping

Sleeping
- Sleeping
- Camping

Sports & Activities
- Diving/Snorkelling
- Canoeing/Kayaking
- Skiing
- Surfing
- Swimming/Pool
- Walking
- Windsurfing
- Other Sports & Activities

Information
- Post Office
- Tourist Information

Transport
- Airport
- Border Crossing
- Bus
- Cable Car/Funicular
- Cycling
- Ferry
- Metro
- Monorail
- Parking
- S-Bahn
- Taxi
- Train/Railway
- Tram
- Tube Station
- U-Bahn
- Other Transport

Routes
- Tollway
- Freeway
- Primary
- Secondary
- Tertiary
- Lane
- Unsealed Road
- Plaza/Mall
- Steps
- Tunnel
- Pedestrian Overpass
- Walking Tour
- Walking Tour Detour
- Path

Boundaries
- International
- State/Province
- Disputed
- Regional/Suburb
- Marine Park
- Cliff
- Wall

Geographic
- Hut/Shelter
- Lighthouse
- Lookout
- Mountain/Volcano
- Oasis
- Park
- Pass
- Picnic Area
- Waterfall

Hydrography
- River/Creek
- Intermittent River
- Swamp/Mangrove
- Reef
- Canal
- Water
- Dry/Salt/Intermittent Lake
- Glacier

Areas
- Beach/Desert
- Cemetery (Christian)
- Cemetery (Other)
- Park/Forest
- Sportsground
- Sight (Building)
- Top Sight (Building)

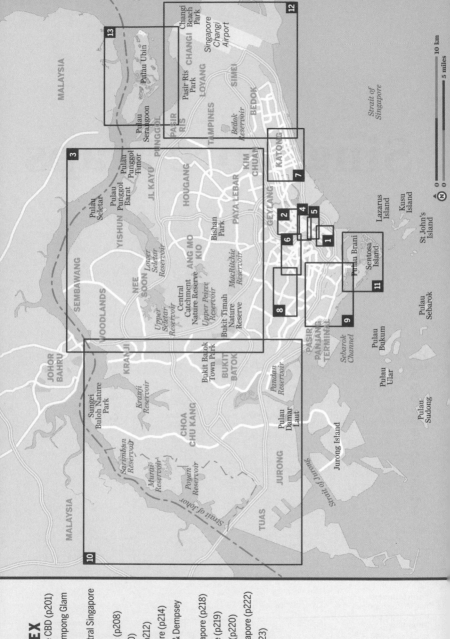

MAP INDEX

CHINATOWN & THE CBD *Map on p202*

Key on p201

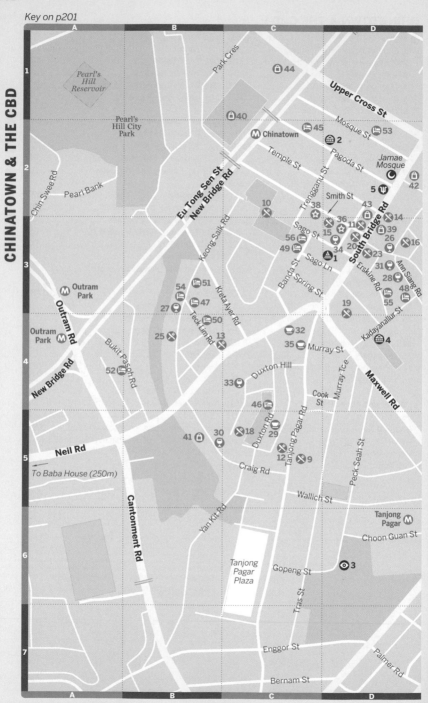

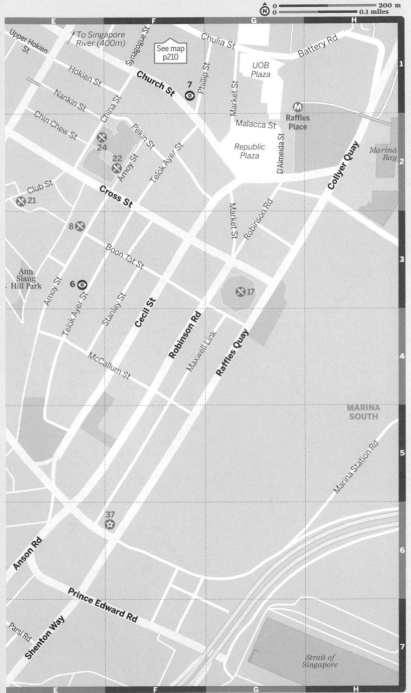

LITTLE INDIA & KAMPONG GLAM

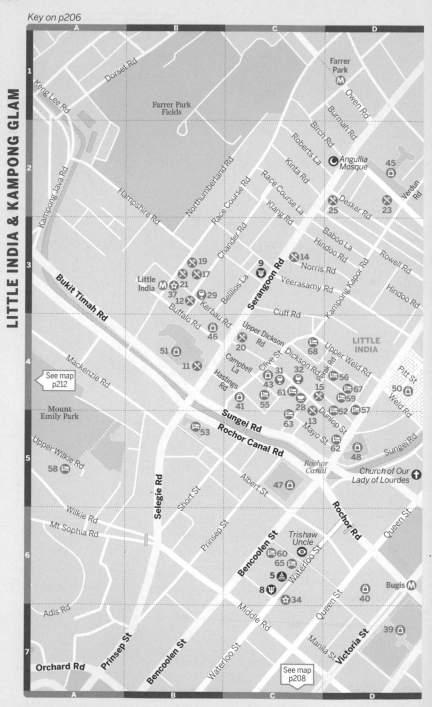

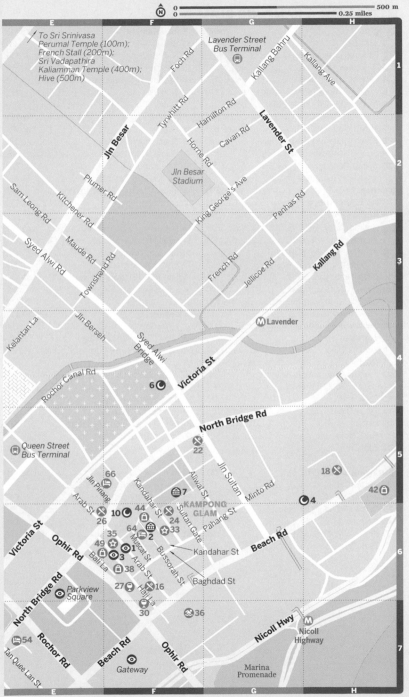

LITTLE INDIA & KAMPONG GLAM

0   500 m
0   0.25 miles

To Sri Srinivasa
Perumal Temple (100m);
French Stall (200m);
Sri Vadapathira
Kaliamman Temple (400m);
Hive (500m)

Lavender Street
Bus Terminal

Foch Rd
Tyrwhitt Rd
Hamilton Rd
Cavan Rd
Horne Rd
Kallang Bahru
Kallang Ave
Lavender St
Jln Besar
Plumer Rd
Kitchener Rd
Sam Leong Rd
Maude Rd
Townshend Rd
Syed Alwi Rd
King George's Ave
Penhas Rd
French Rd
Jellicoe Rd
Kallang Rd
Jln Besar
Stadium

Kelantan La
Jln Berseh
Syed Alwi
Bridge
Rochor Canal Rd
Victoria St
6
Lavender

North Bridge Rd

Queen Street
Bus Terminal
22

Jln Pinang
66
Kandahar St
Aliwal St
Jln Sultan
Minto Rd
18
42

7
KAMPONG
GLAM
4
Arab St
10
44
26
24
Sultan Gate
Pahang St
Beach Rd
35
64
2
33
Muscat St
49
3
Arab St
Bussorah St
Kandahar St
38
Bali La
Baghdad St
27
16
Hajj La
Parkview
Square
30
36
Victoria St
Ophir Rd
North Bridge Rd
Rochor Rd
54
Tan Quee Lan St
Beach Rd
Ophir Rd
Gateway
Nicoll Hwy
Nicoll
Highway
Marina
Promenade

LITTLE INDIA & KAMPONG GLAM *Map on p204*

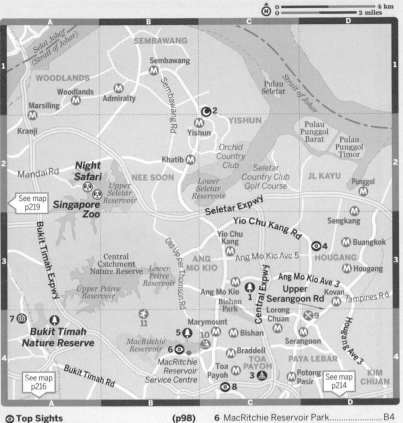

COLONIAL DISTRICT

Key on p209

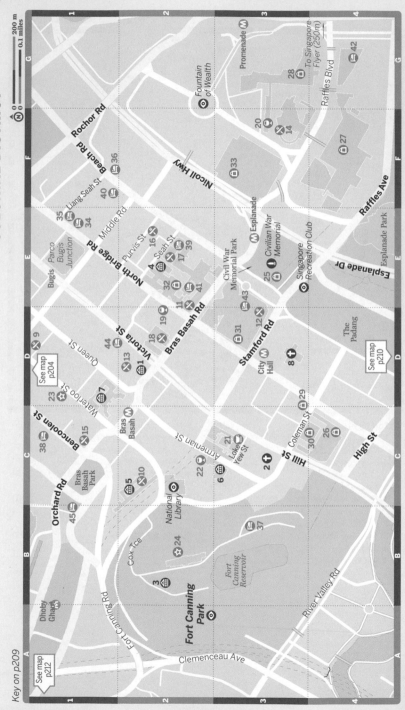

N

0   200 m
0   0.1 miles

Rochor Rd

Beach Rd

Fountain
of Wealth

Promenade

To Singapore
Flyer (250m)

Raffles Blvd

42

28

27

Raffles Ave

20
14

33

Nicoll Hwy

Esplanade

Liang Seah St

36

40

Middle Rd

35

34

North Bridge Rd

Purvis St

16

Seah St

17   39

Parco
Bugis
Junction

Bugis

4

32

41

Esplanade Park

Esplanade Dr

Civil War
Memorial Park

Civilian War
Memorial

Singapore
Recreation Club

Raffles Ave

Bras Basah Rd

19

11

18

Victoria St

44

13

Queen St

9

Stamford Rd

31

43

12

25

See map
p204

Waterloo St

7

23

Bras
Basah

Bencoolen St

38

15

Armenian St

City
Hall

8

The
Padang

See map
p210

Orchard Rd

45

Bras
Basah
Park

5
10

National
Library

22

Loke
Yew St

21

6

2

Hill St

Coleman St

29

30

26

High St

Cox Tce

24

37

Fort
Canning
Reservoir

River Valley Rd

3

Fort Canning
Park

Dhoby
Ghaut

Fort Canning Rd

Clemenceau Ave

See map
p212

THE QUAYS

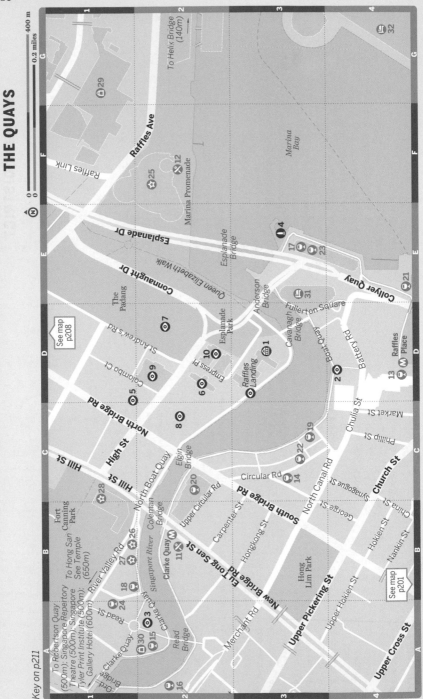

Key on p211

See map p208

See map p201

THE QUAYS *Map on p210*

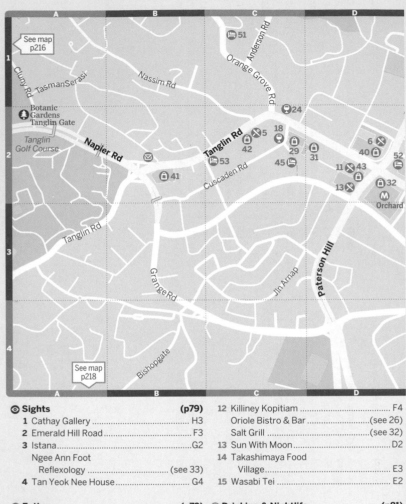

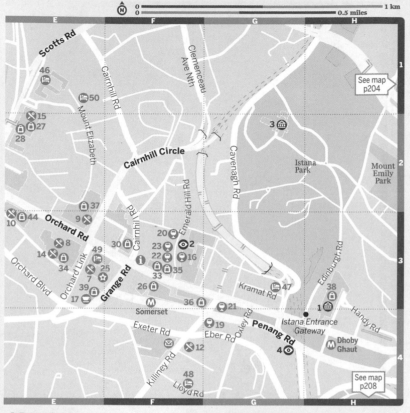

EASTERN SINGAPORE

See map p222

See map p207

Strait of Singapore

East Coast Park Service Rd

East Coast Park

Katong Park

Meyer Rd

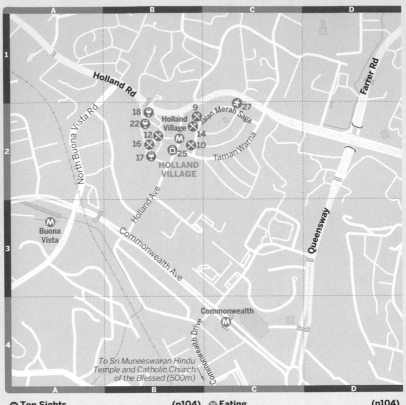

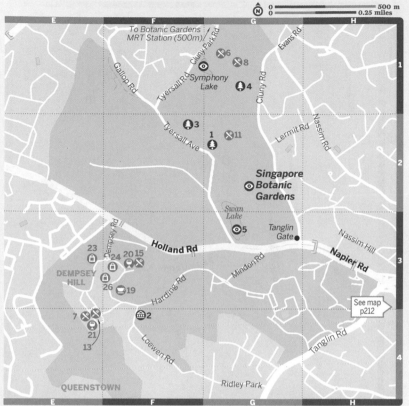

SOUTHWEST SINGAPORE

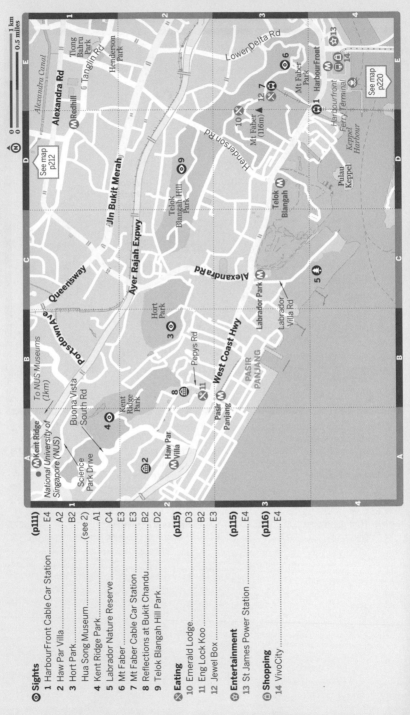

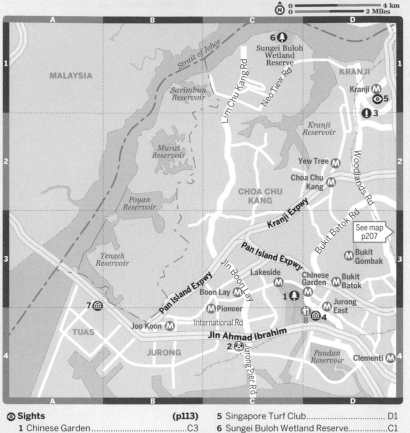

SENTOSA ISLAND

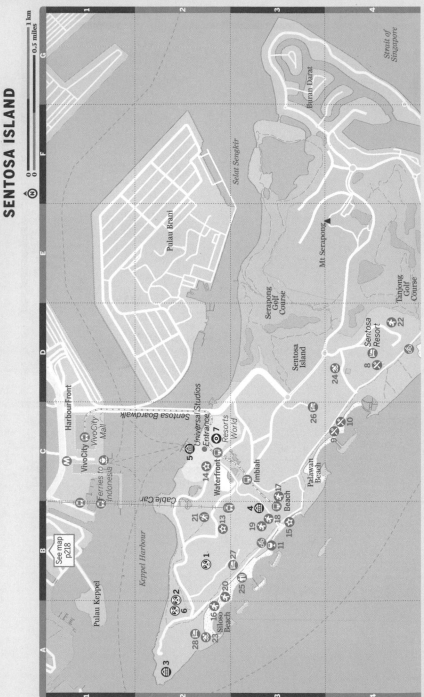

SENTOSA ISLAND

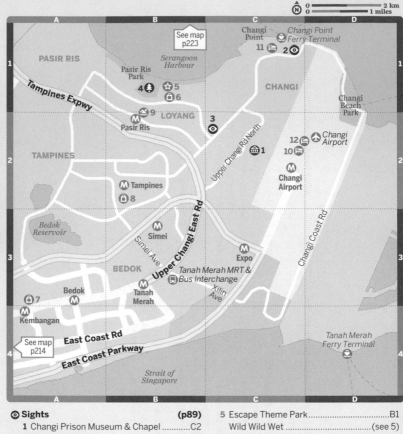